Advance Praise for
Building Moral Intelligence

"Michele Borba is an inspiring educator, an experienced parent, and a terrific writer. She has identified the core issues for parenting moral kids and presented them with passion, wit, and enormous practicality. Her new book gives us solid empirical research but also specific day-to-day activities that will really make a difference in our children's lives."
— Michael Gurian, author, *Boys and Girls Learn Differently, The Wonder of Boys, The Good Son,* and *A Fine Young Man*

"While many people in public life decry the lack of character and moral development among our kids, few take this concern further, into the realm of practical steps to address the issue in the lives of real children and youth. Michele Borba has done so in her book *Building Moral Intelligence.* As one whose work takes him into prisons to interview kids who kill, I can testify to the need for adults to cultivate moral intelligence—and the consequences when we don't. This book is a tool for parents to use in the struggle."
— James Garbarino, author, *Lost Boys: Why Our Sons Turn Violent and How We Can Save Them*

"This smart and helpful book integrates much of what we know about raising moral children. I especially like the book's constructive way of pulling together a wide range of theoretical approaches and coming up with a wealth of sensible child-rearing tips."
— William Damon, professor and director, Stanford University Center on Adolescence

"An important book, beautifully researched and highly readable—one that will surely help parents raise a generation of more peaceful, ethical children. I give this book my highest recommendation."
— Naomi Drew, author, *Peaceful Parents, Peaceful Kids*

Building Moral Intelligence

Building Moral Intelligence

The Seven Essential Virtues That Teach Kids to Do the Right Thing

Michele Borba, Ed.D.

Author of *Parents* Do *Make a Difference*

JOSSEY-BASS
A Wiley Company
San Francisco

Published by

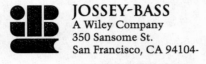

JOSSEY-BASS
A Wiley Company
350 Sansome St.
San Francisco, CA 94104-

www.josseybass.com

Jossey-Bass books and products are available through most bookstores. To contact Jossey-Bass directly, call (888) 378-2537, fax to (800) 605-2665, or visit our website at www.josseybass.com.

Substantial discounts on bulk quantities of Jossey-Bass books are available to corporations, professional associations, and other organizations. For details and discount information, contact the special sales department at Jossey-Bass.

We at Jossey-Bass strive to use the most environmentally sensitive paper stocks available to us. Our publications are printed on acid-free recycled stock whenever possible, and our paper always meets or exceeds minimum GPO and EPA requirements.

Library of Congress Cataloging-in-Publication Data
Borba, Michele.
    Building moral intelligence : the seven essential virtues that teach kids to do the right thing /
      Michele Borba.— 1st ed.
        p. cm.
      Includes bibliographical references and index.
      ISBN 0-7879-5357-1 (alk. paper)
        1. Moral development. 2. Virtues—Study and teaching. 3. Moral education. 4. Child rearing.
    I. Title.
    BF723.M54 B67 2001
    649'.7—dc21   2001000060

FIRST EDITION
HB Printing   10 9 8 7 6 5 4 3 2 1

Contents

To Craig,
My husband, best friend, and finest model of moral intelligence I know

Foreword

As Aristotle taught, people do not naturally become morally excellent or practically wise. They become so, if at all, only as the result of life-long personal and community effort.

JON MOLINE

Character is destiny.

HERACLITUS

In 1988, researchers Samuel and Pearl Oliner published *The Altruistic Personality,* the most extensive study ever conducted of individuals who rescued Jews from the Holocaust. In interview after interview, rescuers referred to the way they were raised.

Said one man: "My parents taught me discipline, tolerance, and serving other people. If somebody was ill or in need, my parents would always help." Said another: "My father taught me to love God and my neighbor, regardless of race or religion. At my grandfather's house, when they read the Bible, he invited everybody in. Jews and Catholics were received in our place like everybody else."

Rescuers didn't consider themselves moral heroes. Again and again, they spoke of simply doing "what had to be done." Most of them hardly deliberated before acting.

Aristotle described character as a "settled disposition" to behave in a morally good way. Why is character important? The character of the rescuers saved Jews from the Nazis. Without a good character, we can't lead a fulfilling life. The psychiatrist Frank Pittman observes: "The stability of our lives depends upon our character. It is character, not passion, that keeps marriages together long enough to do their work of raising children into mature, responsible, productive citizens. In this imperfect world, it is character that enables people to survive, to endure, and to transcend their misfortunes."

How can we develop good character in our children? In *Building Moral Intelligence,* Michele Borba shows us how. She defines character—what she calls "moral intelligence"—in terms of seven core virtues: empathy, conscience, self-control, respect, kindness, tolerance, and fairness. Virtues such as these are objectively good human qualities, necessary for all human beings everywhere.

A renewed concern for character is one of the most important ethical developments of our times. Scholarly discussion, media attention, and everyday conversation have focused attention on the character of our elected leaders, our fellow citizens, and our children. The national character education movement is bringing the language of virtue back into the classroom. But if we are to succeed in renewing our moral culture, we must begin in the home. The family, as Michele Borba reminds us, is the first school of virtue.

In *Building Moral Intelligence,* Michele Borba shows us why each of the core virtues is vital, how to assess its development in a child, and, most important, how to nurture its growth. No parenting book I know of offers so many practical insights, workable strategies, and inspiring stories, books, videos, and other family-friendly resources for intentionally teaching these crucial character strengths.

In her earlier book, *Parents* Do *Make a Difference* (another excellent resource for both parents and teachers), Michele Borba affirmed a truth that undergirds this book as well: Even in our increasingly toxic culture, parents are powerful people. We can still have the inside track in our children's development because we can have the closest relationship. For an example of how to do that, listen to Christian Barnard, originator of the heart transplant, describing his relationship with his father:

> Whenever we were ill, my father got up at night to doctor us. I suffered from festering toenails that pained so much I would cry in bed. My father used to draw out the fester with a poultice made of milk and bread crumbs, or Sunlight soap and sugar. And when I had a cold, he would rub my chest with Vicks and cover it with a red flannel cloth. Sunday afternoons, we walked together to the top of the hill by the dam. Once there, we would sit on a rock and look down at the town below us. Then I would tell my problems to my father, and he would speak of his to me.

Morality builds on love. When we build a bond of love with our children, we will have a channel of influence. And then, in a world that surrounds them with bad examples, our example is likely to have the deepest and most enduring impact.

When I interview people and ask them how their parents influenced their lives and character, they speak most of their parents' example. Mary, a young mother of four, recalls her father:

> Dad always closes his letters with, "Work hard and pray a lot." This never sounds phony because it's what he does. He has worked hard all his life. He built the two homes we lived in and did all the repairs. And he prays throughout the day. My most powerful image of my father is of catching him kneeling at the foot of his bed, late at night before he retired, saying his personal prayers.

A caution: Even parents who do all the right things—form a close relationship, set a good example, and apply the advice and tools of a book like *Building Moral Intelligence*—will still find raising children the hardest job on earth. Kids will still make mistakes, just as all of us did. Judith Martin, author of the Miss Manners column, once quipped: "Raising a civilized child takes 20 years of constant teaching and another 10 of review."

Transmitting values is hard work—the work of sustaining a civilization. As we enter the new millennium, we do well to remember that the most important measure of a nation is not its gross national product, its technological genius, or its military might. It is the character of its people. And we influence that one child at a time. Raising a moral child will always be a challenging task but an easier one because of the wonderful book you hold in your hand.

— Thomas Lickona
Author, *Raising Good Children*
Director, Center for the 4th and 5th Rs
(Respect and Responsibility)

Acknowledgments

There's a wonderful Chinese proverb that says, *"A child's life is like a piece of paper on which every passerby leaves a mark."* I've been enormously blessed because I've had so many people leave such significant marks on my own life. And each has helped shape my writing and the scope of my work. I express my heartfelt thanks:

To the hundreds of teachers and parents who have attended my seminars throughout the years. I am grateful to each and every one of them for so honestly sharing their concerns and successes with me. This book would not have come to fruition without their practical wisdom on how best to teach children these virtues.

To the dozens of teachers and administrators who allowed me the privilege of conducting research at their school sites to analyze the effectiveness of implementing these ideas with their students. In particular I thank Gary LeCount and the staff of Jefferson Elementary School in Hays, Kansas; Dan Wilson and the staff of Crew View Elementary School in Brooklyn Park, Minnesota; and Ron Sveinson and the staff of William F. Davidson

Elementary School in Surrey, British Columbia. One of the greatest honors of my life has been to work with such extraordinarily dedicated teachers.

To my family, who have left the largest and most enduring mark in my life: they are my "rock." To my husband and best friend, Craig, for his unending support, encouragement, and love through every phase of this book and my life; to my parents, Dan and Treva Ungaro, for epitomizing that miraculous concept, "unconditional love"; to my mother-in-law, Lorayne Borba, for her continual encouragement and optimism; and finally to the joys of my life: my sons, Jason, Adam, and Zach, for keeping me so centered and grounded in reality and for the constant love and fun they have brought to my life.

To a few friends who have been my personal cheering squad throughout this project: Annie Leedom, for being the perpetually optimistic, talented, and loyal friend, Internet publicist, and all-around cheerleader— even on those most discouraging days; Steve Leedom, for having such a gift of putting my vision onto paper, for creating a gorgeous website for me on his Now Imagine, and for tutoring me so *patiently* through some extremely stressful computer crashes; Jane Brewer, for being such a fabulous source of educational materials; Jane Bluestein, for being the best sounding board as this model slowly evolved; and to Barbara Keane and Judy Baggott, for their humor, fabulous friendship, and gentle ribbings ("Aren't you done yet?").

To my publicists, Dottie DeHart and Celia Rocks, at Rocks-DeHart Public Relations, for being the kind of marketing team that authors usually only dream about; these ladies made my dream become a reality. They not only are intelligent, creative, and tenacious but also have become great friends who give me unending encouragement.

To the staff at Jossey-Bass—especially Adrienne Biggs, Katie Crouch, Bruce Emmer, Michele Jones, Amy Scott, Lasell Whipple, Jennifer Whitney, and Alison Wong—whose professionalism and dedication to producing only the best is a marvel. Working with them is truly a privilege. Special thanks to Alan Rinzler, my editor at Jossey-Bass, for so many things: his idea for this book and then his wholehearted belief and commitment to it; his uncanny—and sometimes unnerving—ability to pinpoint where a change was needed; his suggestion of the title, format, and "grittier" tone; his patience as I went through my "creative phases"; his superb insights, research suggestions, and guidance through every possible step.

And finally, to the numerous people whose work has contributed enormously to my thinking about the development of moral intelligence over the years. These include Robert Coles, William Damon, Daniel Goleman, Nancy Eisenberg, James Garbarino, Lawrence Kohlberg, Bruce Perry, and Peter Scharf. Special thanks goes to Thomas Lickona, not only for serving as a powerful mentor but also for reading through the manuscript with so much tenacity and offering such valuable suggestions. Your work has been a godsend to children: I only hope I've done it justice.

Building Moral Intelligence

NOTE TO THE READER

All the stories in this book are based on cases of children and their families and teachers whom I have known and worked with over the last twenty years. A few stories are composite cases of children I have treated, and their actual names as well as their parents' names have been changed to protect their privacy. All examples from schools are gathered from my actual observations. The exceptions are children interviewed for newspapers or written about in books as examples of children displaying these seven essential virtues of moral intelligence.

Introduction

Sow a thought and you reap an act; sow an act and you reap a habit; sow a habit and you reap a character; sow a character and you reap a destiny.

CHARLES READE

There is a clear and pressing crisis in today's society, one that involves our most cherished possession: our children. Everyone agrees there is a problem; lawmakers, doctors, clergy, businesspeople, educators, parents, and the general public alike have voiced their concerns. And concerned we all should be. Each day's news adds to a growing litany of shocking tragedies and statistics about American kids, and they've left us shaken, deeply worried, and in search of answers.

By far our biggest worry is youth violence, and that alone should warrant a national declaration of emergency. Although the hard data on youth crime and violence show a recent decline, there is little cause for comfort: the American Academy of Pediatrics reports that the United States has the highest youth homicide and suicide rates among the twenty-six wealthiest nations in the world. In fact, our kids are *ten times* more likely to commit murder than comparably aged youths in Canada. Perhaps most disturbing is that our killers are getting younger and younger. As I write, this week a six-year-old intentionally suffocated her three-year-old brother with the help of her five-year-old friend. Just months earlier, a six-year-old boy settled a schoolyard score by killing his first-grade classmate with a .32 semiautomatic. Each incident is unthinkable, yet others equally horrifying follow.

There are other signs that stir our national conscience as well. Peer cruelty is steadily increasing: an estimated 160,000 children each day miss school for fear of being picked on by their peers, and, considering the accessibility of weapons, the potential for physical injury is high. Other disturbing indicators include substance abuse among younger kids; the growing disrespect for parents, teachers, and other legitimate authority figures; the rise of incivility; the increase of vulgarity; and widespread cheating and commonplace dishonesty. A recent national survey of 10,000 high school students revealed that nearly half admit they stole something from a store in the previous year; one in four said they would lie to get a job; and seven in ten admitted to cheating on an exam within the previous twelve months. Heavy alcohol and drug use is increasing among our younger kids: recent studies found 22 percent of fifth graders have been drunk at least once, and the *average* age at which a child first uses marijuana is twelve. In two decades, the number of diagnoses of hyperactivity and attention deficits has risen 700 percent. In the last four decades, adolescent suicide in our country has increased 300 percent, and depression has risen 1,000 percent. These statistics are especially frightening when you consider that in one survey, over one-half of American teenagers reported they can get a gun in an hour and one in four high school students say they took a weapon to school at least once in the past year. Our kids are troubled and our crises continues.

These episodes and statistics distress us, of course, and as a nation we are reacting in alarm: school officials have installed metal detectors and sophisticated cameras to heighten security; moms marched on Washington for stricter gun control; the president of the United States called for emergency summit meetings of congressional leaders; some parents have started charter schools, while others have opted for home schooling; lawmakers passed laws to prosecute juveniles as adults, and the courts sentenced them as such. We've tried an endless variety of educational strategies as well: teachers have taught self-esteem and conflict resolution skills, and counselors have addressed social skills and anger management. Individual states have implemented retention policies, lowered class sizes, and boosted academic standards. Psychologists have even developed complete new theories: Howard Gardner revolutionized our understanding of children's cognitive capacities with his view of multiple intelligences, as Daniel Goleman did in transforming our awareness of emotional intelligence.

Despite our frantic efforts, however, the crisis remains, and we know so because our children are still hurting. That's because we have missed one critical piece: the moral side of our children's lives. It is moral strength that kids need most to keep their ethical bearings in this often morally toxic world. Moral issues haven't been completely overlooked: the work of Jean Piaget and Lawrence Kohlberg has helped us understand the stages of children's moral reasoning; William Bennett provided literature anthologies to cultivate kids' moral imaginations; William Kilpatrick's book *Why Johnny Can't Tell Right from Wrong,* offered ways to engage our youth in moral reflection. But in these troubling times, parents need far more if they are to succeed in helping their kids not only *think* morally but also *act* morally, and unless children know how to act right, their moral development is defective. After all, we've always known that the true measure of character rests in our actions—not in mere thoughts.

Enhancing our children's moral intelligence is our best hope for getting our kids on the right course so that they do act as well as think right. It's also our best hope for their developing the traits of solid character. In his book *The Moral Intelligence of Children,* Robert Coles wrote of the urgent need to address this crucial aptitude in our children. Developing this miraculous moral capacity in your child is the best way to protect his moral life now and forever, and *Building Moral Intelligence* will teach you how.

MORAL INTELLIGENCE: THE BEST HOPE FOR SAVING OUR KIDS' MORAL LIVES

Moral intelligence is the capacity to understand right from wrong; it means to have strong ethical convictions and to act on them so that one behaves in the right and honorable way. This wonderful aptitude encompasses such essential life characteristics as the ability to recognize someone's pain and to stop oneself from acting on cruel intentions; to control one's impulses and delay gratification; to listen openly to all sides before judging; to accept and appreciate differences; to decipher unethical choices; to empathize; to stand up against injustice; and to treat others with compassion and respect. These are the core traits that will help your child become a decent, good human being; they are the bedrock of solid character and strong citizenship, and they are ones we want most for our kids.

It's increasingly apparent that a number of kids are in serious trouble because they've never acquired moral intelligence. With only flimsy consciences, poor impulse control, underdeveloped moral sensitivity, and misguided beliefs, they are greatly handicapped. Although the causes of moral decline are complex, one fact is undeniable: the moral atmosphere in which today's kids are being raised is toxic to moral intelligence, for two major reasons. First, a number of critical social factors that nurture moral character are slowly disintegrating: adult supervision, models of moral behavior, spiritual or religious training, meaningful adult relationships, personalized schools, clear national values, community support, stability, and adequate parenting. Second, our kids are being steadily bombarded with outside messages that go against the very values we are trying to instill. Both factors are contributing greatly to our kids' moral demise as well as to their loss of innocence.

Our challenge is even tougher because those incessant toxic messages come from a variety of sources to which our kids have extremely easy access. Television, movies, video games, popular music, and advertising are certainly among the worst moral offenders because they flaunt cynicism, disrespect, materialism, casual sex, vulgarity, and the glorification of violence. The amount of bad stuff in cyberspace is staggering: pornography, stalkers, satanism, pedophiles, and so many new hate sites even the best filters can't screen them all. Of course the popular media aren't the only toxic influences; anyone or anything that counters your family's moral convictions is a potential threat, so add peers, other adults, and even the evening news to your list.

The truth is that toxic influences are so entrenched in our culture that shielding your child from them is almost impossible. Even if you've blocked their accessibility and prohibit them in your home, once your child steps outside they lurk at every corner. That's why it's crucial that you build his moral intelligence so he has a deeply developed inner sense of right and wrong and can use it to stand up against those outside influences. Moral intelligence will be the muscle he needs to counter those negative pressures and will give him the power to act right with or without your guidance.

The best news is that *moral intelligence is learned,* and you can start building it when your kids are toddlers. Although at that age they certainly don't have the cognitive capacities to handle complex moral reasoning, that's when the rudiments of moral habits—such as exercising self-control, being fair, showing respect, sharing, and empathizing—are first acquired. In fact, the latest research on moral development finds that babies six months of age are already responding to others' distress and acquiring the foundation for empathy. The mistake parents often make is waiting until their kids are six or seven—the so-called Age of Reason—to cultivate their moral capabilities. Parents' delaying in this way only increases children's potential for learning destructive negative habits that erode moral growth and make it so much harder for them to change.

Although moral intelligence can be learned, achieving it is far from guaranteed. It must be consciously modeled and nurtured, and because you are your child's first and most important moral instructor, there is no one better than you to inspire these essential moral virtues. The sooner you begin purposefully cultivating your child's capacity for moral intelligence, the better her chances of acquiring the foundation she'll need to develop solid character and of growing to think, believe, and act morally.

THE SEVEN ESSENTIAL VIRTUES OF MORAL INTELLIGENCE

Moral intelligence consists of seven essential virtues—*empathy, conscience, self-control, respect, kindness, tolerance,* and *fairness*—that help your child navigate through the ethical challenges and pressures she will inevitably face throughout life. These core virtues are what give her the moral bearings by which to stay on the path of goodness and to help her behave morally. Or, as a seven-year-old told me, "They're the things in me that help me be good." *And all can be taught, modeled, inspired, and reinforced so that your child can achieve them.* Here are the seven essential virtues that will nurture a lifelong sense of decency in your child:

1. *Empathy* is the core moral emotion that allows your child to understand how other people feel. This is the virtue that helps him become more sensitive to the needs and feelings of others, be more likely to help those who are hurt or troubled, and treat others more compassionately. It is also the powerful moral emotion that urges your child to do what is right because he can recognize the impact of emotional pain on others, stopping him from acting cruelly.

2. *Conscience* is a strong inner voice that helps your child decide right from wrong and stay on the moral path, zapping her with a dose of guilt whenever she strays. This virtue fortifies your child against forces coun-

tering goodness and enables her to act right even in the face of temptation. It is the cornerstone for the development of the crucial virtues of honesty, responsibility, and integrity.

3. *Self-control* helps your child restrain his impulses and think before he acts so that he behaves right and is less likely to make rash choices with potentially dangerous outcomes. This is the virtue that helps your child become self-reliant because he knows he can control his actions. It is also the virtue that motivates generosity and kindness because it helps your child put aside what would give him immediate gratification and stirs his conscience to do something for someone else instead.

4. *Respect* encourages your child to treat others with consideration because she regards them as worthy. This is the virtue that leads your child to treat others the way she would like to be treated, and so lays the foundation to preventing violence, injustice, and hatred. When your child makes respect a part of her daily living, she will be more likely to care about the rights and feelings of others; as a result, she will show greater respect for herself, too.

5. *Kindness* helps your child show his concern about the welfare and feelings of others. By developing this virtue, your child will become less selfish and more compassionate, and he will understand that treating others kindly is simply the right thing to do. When your child achieves kindness, he will think more about the needs of others, show concern, offer to help those in need, and stick up for those who are hurt or troubled.

6. *Tolerance* helps your child appreciate different qualities in others, stay open to new perspectives and beliefs, and respect others regardless of differences in race, gender, appearance, culture, beliefs, abilities, or sexual orientation. This is the virtue that influences your child to treat others with kindness and understanding, to stand up against hatred, violence, and bigotry, and to respect people primarily on the basis of their character.

7. *Fairness* leads your child to treat others in a righteous, impartial, and just way so that she will be more likely to play by the rules, take turns

and share, and listen openly to all sides before judging. Because this virtue increases your child's moral sensitivity, she will have the courage to stick up for those treated unfairly and demand that all people—regardless of race, culture, economic status, ability, or creed—be regarded equally.

MORAL INTELLIGENCE BUILDER
The Seven Essential Virtues of
Moral Intelligence and Solid Character

The seven essential virtues that follow comprise the complete plan for building your child's moral intelligence provided in this book. These seven traits are what your child needs most to do what's right and resist any pressures that may defy the habits of solid character and good ethical living.

Virtue	Definition
Empathy	Identifying with and feeling other people's concerns
Conscience	Knowing the right and decent way to act and acting that way
Self-control	Regulating your thoughts and actions so that you stop any pressures from within or without and act the way you know and feel is right
Respect	Showing you value others by treating them in a courteous and considerate way
Kindness	Demonstrating concern about the welfare and feelings of others
Tolerance	Respecting the dignity and rights of all persons, even those whose beliefs and behaviors differ from our own
Fairness	Choosing to be open minded and to act in a just and fair way

BUILDING MORAL INTELLIGENCE STEP BY STEP

Building Moral Intelligence provides a step by step blueprint for enhancing your child's moral capacity based on the ethical principles of these seven essential virtues. This book provides you with the tools to teach these critical principles to your child. Each time your child achieves another virtue, she expands her moral intelligence capacities even further, and she climbs another rung on the moral development ladder.

Three virtues form the foundation of your child's moral intelligence: *empathy, conscience,* and *self-control.* In truth, they are so critical to moral intelligence that I call them the *moral core.* When any one of the three is underdeveloped, the child is left morally defenseless against toxic influences coming his way; when all three of the core elements are weak, the child becomes a time bomb waiting to explode. A solid core is crucial to developing children's moral intelligence because it gives kids the power to counter outside and inside vices so that they do what's right.

Once the foundation to moral growth is solidly laid, the next two virtues of moral intelligence can be added: *respect,* a deep valuing of all life; and *kindness,* which is a sense of human decency and compassion in relationships. The final virtues, *tolerance* and *fairness,* are the cornerstones to integrity, justice, and citizenship. Together, these seven virtues become your child's moral compass, guiding her toward responsible living and ethical conduct. They are the tools she will use to chart her moral fate.

Once your child achieves these essential seven virtues, her moral education is by no means complete. Moral growth is an ongoing process that continues throughout your child's lifetime, and along the way she'll be adding dozens more virtues to her moral repertoire; in fact, morality experts have identified more than four hundred virtues. As her moral intelligence capacities expand and if the right conditions for moral growth are present, she'll have the potential to attain even higher moral virtues, such as self-discipline, humility, courage, temperance, integrity, mercy, and altruism. But the origin of her moral I.Q. will always consist of the seven essential virtues that you helped her achieve. She will use these virtues as a template for creating her character and defining her humanity, and she'll refer to them the rest of her life.

HOW TO USE THIS BOOK

What you have in your hands is a guide to teaching the traits of moral intelligence most needed by children and teens in today's troubled world. I've purposely ordered the seven essential virtues into a logical teaching sequence. Because the virtues of empathy, conscience, and self-control lay the foundation for the later virtues—respect, kindness, tolerance, and fairness—I urge you to focus first on building these three core virtues. This approach gives your child the best foundation for solid moral growth.

To help you build these seven essential virtues, each chapter offers a wealth of research-based practical strategies for enhancing moral intelligence. The goal of these activities is to teach your child new moral habits she'll need to lead a good and moral life, so choose the ones you feel are best suited to her unique temperament and learning style. Although the content of this book is quite serious, the activities are designed to be *fun, relaxing, and enjoyable.* I hope this is the tone with which you and your child will work together. Here's what you'll find in each chapter to help you expand your child's moral intelligence:

• *A self-test to evaluate your child's virtue strength.* You can use this tool to help you assess how well your child is presently achieving the virtue and to pinpoint any areas that may be hindering her moral growth.

• *Practical ways to enhance the virtue.* Literally dozens of practical suggestions and activities are provided to teach the virtue and model the behaviors associated with it. Throughout each chapter you'll also find Moral Intelligence Builders—easily distinguishable in their bordered boxes—that discuss other simple, research-based ways to boost the virtue.

• *A real story about a child who illustrates the virtue.* You'll find a story to tell your child about a real child who demonstrated the virtue and made a positive difference in the world. It will help your child recognize the virtue's power and think of ways he too might make a difference in the world.

• *Discussion questions about the virtue.* Also included are questions to pose to your child to help her think about the importance of using the virtue in her life. These can be springboards for you to use in talking together about real dilemmas your child has faced or may face in the future, important moral issues in the world, and how to make moral choices that are wise and ethical.

• *Further resources to enhance the virtue.* At the back of the book is a Resources section, organized by chapter, that lists wonderful children's literature selections, videos, websites, and organizations to share with your child. You can use these resources to expand her understanding of the virtue, encouraging her to incorporate it into her life.

SHAPING OUR CHILDREN'S MORAL DESTINIES

Teaching any new habit—especially those as important as the behaviors associated with these seven essential virtues—takes time, commitment, and patience. Of course, the optimum goal is for our kids to become less and less dependent on our moral guidance by incorporating these moral principles into their daily lives and making them their own. That can happen only if you emphasize the importance of the virtues over and over and your child repeatedly practices these moral behaviors. After all, that's how people learn habits and internalize principles, as Aristotle pointed out hundreds of years ago when he said, "We are what we repeatedly do." Consistent, repeated, short lessons about these virtues are precisely what your child needs to achieve them.

Also keep in mind that *telling* your child about the virtue is never as powerful as *showing* what the quality looks like by demonstrating it in your own life. Try to make your life a living example of these seven virtues for your child to see. Doing so is the surest way to help your child "catch" them and want to use them in his own life both now and later.

As parents and teachers, we can no longer sit back and hope our kids become caring and decent human beings. Too many societal influences are endangering our children's moral growth. There is an answer to our fears, and it lies in what all the research tells us: *we can make a difference in our children's lives because the seven essential virtues that build moral intelligence are learned—and we can teach them.* Deliberately teaching these virtues at home, at school, and in our communities is the best assurance we have that our kids will lead decent, moral lives.

Building our children's moral intelligence capacities will be perhaps our greatest legacy. It can affect *every* aspect of their lives now as well as the quality of their future relationships, professions, productivity, parenting skills, citizenship—even their contributions to art, commerce, and literature and to their local community and society as a whole. These virtues are timeless: they will remain vital long after our children leave home, begin their adult lives, and use the virtues to raise their own children. Because the moral foundation we provide for our children now is what ultimately will define their reputations as human beings, building that foundation may well be our most crucial and challenging task as parents. And we haven't a moment to lose, for the moral destinies of our sons and daughters are at stake. Are you up for the challenge?

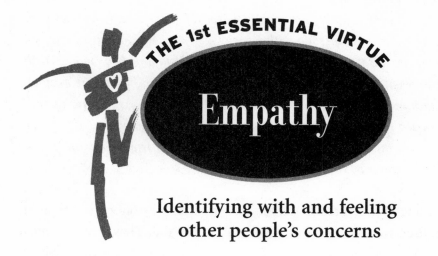

THE 1st ESSENTIAL VIRTUE

Empathy

Identifying with and feeling other people's concerns

In 1997, eleven-year-old Nathaniel Abraham from Pontiac, Michigan, told his friend that he was going to shoot somebody. He allegedly stole a gun and practiced his aim on stationary targets. Then he walked to a convenience store, pointed his gun at a stranger, and shot Ronnie Greene Jr. in the head. The eighteen-year-old youth died hours later. The next day the sixth grader bragged about the killing to his friends. At his trial, Nathaniel turned and looked at his mother and other relatives and showed no emotion as he was convicted. The sixty-five-pound youth became one of nation's youngest children charged with first-degree murder.

On February 1993, two-year-old James Bulger was separated from his mother in a shopping center in Liverpool, England. A security camera showed two ten-year-olds, Jon Venables and Robert Thompson, leading the toddler away. The boys threw more than twenty bricks at the two-year-old, kicked him, tore off his lower lip, stripped him, and possibly molested him. They then left James's body on the tracks to appear as though the murder were accidental, and went into a video store to watch cartoons on television.

On a school snow day in northeast Pennsylvania, nine-year-old Cameron Kocher was playing Nintendo with Jessica Carr, age seven. A parent stopped the game because the kids had made a mess and the two had argued; Cameron went home angry. He then took a rifle from his family gun cabinet, went back and shot Jessica, and hid the spent cartridge. As Jessica's mother futilely tried to save her daughter, Cameron went back to playing Nintendo. Later he told the other kids who were crying over their friend's death, "If you don't think about it, you won't be sad."

Shocking as these stories are, they are true. Each involved grade school children who knew it was wrong to kill but did. They were all cold-hearted kids without an ounce of empathy—the one virtue that experts say could possibly have stopped them from committing their horrific acts. The good news is that empathy can be fostered in kids, and we can begin when they are very young. Doing so may be the best hope for preventing yet another tragic story.

THE CRISIS IN THE DEVELOPMENT OF EMPATHY

Empathy, the first essential virtue of moral intelligence, is the ability to understand and feel for another person's concerns. It's the powerful emotion that halts violent and cruel behavior and urges us to treat others kindly. Because empathy emerges naturally and quite early, our children are born with a huge built-in advantage for their moral growth. But whether our kids will develop this marvelous capacity to feel for others is far from guaranteed. Although children are born with the capacity for empathy, it must be properly nurtured, or it will remain dormant. And therein lies the crisis: over the past years, many environmental factors that research has found to be critical to the enhancement of empathy are disappearing, replaced by more negative ones. Although there certainly are other conditions that hinder kids' capacities to feel for others, the following five factors are especially lethal in squelching empathy, and point to a crisis in its development.

Emotional Unavailability of Parents

Studies find that when it comes to enhancing kids' empathy, not just any parent will do. Milestone studies by John Gottman of the University of Washington found that the parents who are best at developing empathy in their children are those who are both actively involved in their kids' lives and emotionally available. That's why it's especially troubling that total one-on-one time between parents and their kids has dwindled dramatically over the past few decades. A university study found that today's mothers who work outside the home spend an average of eleven minutes a day in exclusive quality interaction time with their children on weekdays and about thirty minutes on weekends. The data for fathers were only eight and fourteen minutes, respectively. Nonworking mothers didn't fare much better, devoting an average of thirteen minutes per day. A recent poll taken of children as young as nine years old revealed that only 40 percent of boys and 50 percent of girls spent almost all weekend with their parents, and 25 percent of the young boys reported spending no hours with their families. The emotional availability of parents is diminishing for a number of reasons, including parental illness, death, work, fatigue, and divorce. Whatever the cause, critical empathy-building moments for kids are being lost as well.

Absence of Supportive Fathers

Research confirms what many have known all along: involved dads can make a major contribution to raising empathic kids. A long-term study begun in the 1950s, for instance, found that children whose fathers were positively involved in their care when they were age five were found thirty years later to be more empathic adults than those whose fathers were absent. Another study involving first-grade boys in intact families revealed that children whose fathers took more responsibility for their sons' discipline and schoolwork and were more involved in their children's personal problems had significantly higher levels of empathy. And this was true regardless of the father's own level of empathy.

Aside from the many fathers who don't take an active parenting role, there are the troubling numbers who have chosen to be completely absent from their kids' lives. A recent White House report found that fewer than 25 percent of young boys and girls experience an average of at least one hour a day of relatively individualized contact with their fathers. The figures are particularly staggering for African American children: in 1994, 60 percent of black children lived in one-parent homes. So another critical nurturer of empathy—good old dad—is not at home to teach the lessons of compassion and right and wrong.

Barrage of Cruel Media Images

Over the past decade, our kids have been bombarded with television, movies, music, video and arcade games, and Internet content that emphasize violence, nastiness, and cruelty. It is affecting our kids. Here's why: behavior is generally learned by imitating observed experiences, so the more examples of caring our kids witness, the greater the chance that those will be the kinds of behaviors they copy. A number of studies have found that watching television programs with prosocial messages increases cooperation, sensitivity, and caring among children and that the children will tend to imitate those kind behaviors. Research also shows that those prosocial behaviors are substantially enhanced when parents watch with their children and discuss or role-play those kind behaviors.

Of course, the reverse is also true: the continual barrage of cruel images teaches our kids cruel behaviors that stifle their capacity for empathy. As Madeline Levins states in her book *See No Evil,* "There is a large body of research focusing on the effects of media violence on preschool children. Almost without exception, the research has found that viewing violence makes children more aggressive, more restless, more fearful, less creative, and less intuitive." The American Academy of Pediatrics points out that well over one thousand studies overwhelmingly conclude that viewing violent entertainment can increase aggressive values and behavior in children. They further state that viewing violence can desensitize kids to empathy because it can decrease the likelihood that they will take action on behalf of victims when violence occurs.

Raising Boys to Mask Their Feelings

Studies find that when it comes to emotions, parents raise sons very differently than they do daughters. Parents discuss feelings more and use a greater array of words for emotions with their daughters than they do with their sons. They also encourage their daughters to share their feelings, whereas boys are typically told to mask their emotional pain. Considering that a major determinant of whether a child develops the ability to feel for others is how well he understands and can express his own feelings, it is easy to see that parents' attitudes toward their son's emotional expression can hinder a boy's empathy development.

William Pollack, author of *Real Boys,* explains, "Research shows that boys begin their lives with a natural sense of empathy, which is antithetical to violence. By second grade boys seem far less attuned to feelings of hurt and pain in others and begin to lose their capacity to express their own emotions and concerns in words." In fact, boys learn that the only emotion that it is socially acceptable for them to express is anger; other feelings must be stifled. And as their anger slowly intensifies, their potential for empathy is diminished. The result, Pollack notes, can be lethal: "This is the process that pushes boys to wear a mask of bravado. And this, in large part, is what makes them violent."

Abuse in the Cradle

Fascinating new research by Bruce Perry of Baylor College of Medicine finds that the first three years of a child's life are pivotal in building the capacity for empathy or planting the seeds of violence. A large determinant as to which way a child's moral development goes is how she is treated by her primary caregivers. Perry states that empathy can be greatly impaired in those first thirty-six months as a result of repeated stress—abuse, neglect, and trauma. Mark Barnett of Kansas State University explains that if young kids "have not had their emotional needs satisfied, they may not realize that they need to be concerned about or sensitive toward others' emotional needs." Considering the staggering numbers of child abuse cases, we are forced to conclude that many of America's youngest citizens may have dismal moral futures.

The U.S. Department of Health and Human Services estimates that nearly three million children were reported to child-protection service agencies for abuse and neglect in 1997; *one in three victims of physical abuse was a baby less than twelve months old.* Child Protective Services reports that three-quarters of child fatalities involve children under three years of age. Although reported cases of child abuse and neglect vary per agency, they appear to be declining. But that's certainly no cause to celebrate: any report of child abuse is one case too many. Although your child may not be affected by these issues, chances are she will be associating with other kids who are. Because peers are moral influences, in the end all our kids are affected.

Many environmental factors identified as critical for the growth of empathy are dwindling. Although no one factor by itself predisposes a child to cruelty, researchers stress that the interaction of factors may be enough to trigger antisocial behavior. Therefore it's vital that we do everything we can to counteract these negative influences by nurturing the core moral emotion of empathy. As long as we allow these negative influences to continue, many children's capacity to feel for others will be extinguished, and their emotional lives will be empty.

WHAT IS EMPATHY?

Empathy—the ability to identify with and feel another person's concerns—is the foundation of moral intelligence. This first moral virtue is what sensitizes our kids to different points of view and increases their awareness of others' ideas and opinions. Empathy is what enhances humanness, civility, and morality. Empathy is the emotion that alerts a child to another person's plight and stirs his conscience. It is what moves children to be tolerant and compassionate, to understand other people's needs, to care enough to help those who are hurt or troubled. A child who learns empathy will be much more understanding and caring, and will usually be more adept at handling anger.

Our children are often exposed to an unsettling world of violence, drugs, cruelty, and incivility; empathy may be the best antidote. By learning to show empathy to others, our kids can help create a more tolerant, peaceful world. This chapter shows you proven ways to build empathy in your child so that she will develop the virtue that lays the critical foundation for nonviolence and for doing what is right because she feels it in her heart.

MORAL INTELLIGENCE BUILDER
Signs of Strong Empathy to Share with Kids

There are many ways people display empathy toward others, and the more aware that kids are of what those actions look and sound like, the more likely they are to incorporate those behaviors into their daily lives. Here are a few examples of empathy to discuss and role-play with your child:

What People with Empathy Say

"You look upset."

"I understand how you feel."

"I'm sad that you got hurt."

"That happened to me too once. It makes me feel sad for you."

"My heart is racing. I feel like I won, too."

"I'm happy for you."

"I bet it hurts a lot. It happened to me."

What People with Empathy Do

Notice when people are hurting, and feel for them.

Tear up when they see someone crying.

Walk up to console others in pain.

Comfort another because they understand the person's hurt.

Feel excited for others when they win.

Wince when they see the hero hurt at the movies.

Talk soothingly to those in pain.

Mirror the facial expressions of the distressed person.

HOW EMPATHIC IS YOUR CHILD?

The statements that follow describe behaviors usually displayed by children with strong empathy toward others. To evaluate your child's strengths in this first virtue, write the number you think best represents your child's current level on the line following each statement and then add all the scores to get her total score. If your child scores 40 to 50, she's in great shape with this aspect of moral intelligence. If she scores 30 to 40, she could benefit from virtue enhancement. A score of 20 to 30 shows signs of potential problems. A score of 10 to 20 reveals potential danger; consider getting help to increase this essential virtue.

5 = Always 4 = Frequently 3 = Sometimes 2 = Rarely 1 = Never

A Child with Healthy Empathy	My Child
Is socially sensitive; has a lot of feeling for others.	_____
Shows sensitivity toward the needs and feelings of others.	_____
Correctly reads others' nonverbal cues: gestures, body language, facial expressions, tone of voice.	_____
Readily picks up others' facial expressions and reacts appropriately.	_____
Recognizes when someone is distressed and responds appropriately.	_____
Shows she understands another person's feelings.	_____
Tears up or looks upset when someone else is distressed.	_____
Acts concerned when someone is treated unfairly or unkindly.	_____
Shows a willingness to understand someone else's point of view.	_____
Can verbally identify someone else's feelings.	_____
Total Score	_____

THREE STEPS TO BUILDING EMPATHY

Empathy, the key emotion for supporting a sense of right and wrong, is a trait that emerges early in kids. Whether it blossoms or lies dormant largely depends on whether it is nurtured. There are three steps to building this critical aspect of moral intelligence. Because the foundation for empathy is the understanding of emotions, the first teaching step helps your child develop an awareness of emotions and develop a feeling vocabulary. He'll need this skill to successfully identify a wide variety of emotions so that he can tune in to the feelings of others. The second step provides ways to enhance your child's sensitivity to other people's feelings so that he'll become more aware of their needs and concerns. The last step helps expand your child's awareness of perspectives other than his own. Only then will he really be able to step into other people's shoes and feel with them. These three steps increase the empathic capabilities that your child will need to face a world that too often stresses apathy, cruelty, coldness, and self-centeredness.

Here again are the three teachable steps you can use to nurture this essential first virtue in your child and build her moral intelligence:

Step 1: Foster Awareness and an Emotional Vocabulary
Step 2: Enhance Sensitivity to the Feelings of Others
Step 3: Develop Empathy for Another Person's Point of View

STEP 1: FOSTER AWARENESS AND AN EMOTIONAL VOCABULARY

I was in an office with James and Jeremy, third graders at a school in Minnesota where I was consulting. Their teacher explained that although the boys seemed to have good hearts, they were forever making fun of classmates and didn't seem to grasp the hurt they caused. Their teacher warned them to stop, yet today they teased a boy to tears, so she wanted me to talk to them about it. I began by trying to understand their concept of teasing. "Is it ever OK to make fun of someone?" I asked.

"Sure," James said. "I make fun of Jeremy all the time, and we're still friends."

Jeremy agreed, "He makes fun of my hair all the time, but it's no big deal."

I said, "Some things we're teased about don't bother us much. What did you tease your classmate about today? It must have bugged him, because you made him cry."

"We just told Seth that he talks weird," James said. "You can't understand most of what he's saying. So it's not like it's not true."

"Seth probably has a speech problem," I explained. "He must get teased a lot about it, and it bothers him. How do you think he feels being teased about his speech?"

The boys couldn't answer. "How would you feel if you were teased about something you really cared about?" I asked. And again I was met with silence. "You saw Seth. How do you think he felt about being teased?" Now both boys looked clearly puzzled. Then it dawned on me: it wasn't that these boys didn't understand that teasing was hurtful. The problem was that they couldn't identify how Seth felt about it, so it was almost impossible for them to empathize with his hurt. These boys simply didn't have a strong enough emotional education to identify either how they might feel or how the other boy felt. They didn't have a clue about how to imagine their victim's discomfort.

Of course we want our kids to be compassionate and sensitive to other people's feelings. The problem is that many kids' empathy potential is greatly handicapped because they don't have the ability to identify and express emotions. They have tremendous difficulty feeling for the other person simply because they may not recognize the other person's hurt, elation, discomfort, anxiety, pride, happiness, or anger. What these kids need is an education that provides stronger emotional intelligence: an adequate vocabulary of feelings and then the encouragement to use it. Once they are more emotionally literate and can understand their own feelings, their empathy will grow, because they will be far more capable of understanding and feeling other people's concerns and needs. This first step will show you how to develop your child's emotional literacy.

How to Listen to Your Child with Empathy

Last month I was in a long line at a ticket counter in the Scranton Airport with a number of other passengers eager to get home. One three-year-old boy was clearly agitated with the wait. As his mom finally reached the front of the line, he began pulling his blanket from a bag, mumbling "I need Blankey." His mother sternly told him to act like a big boy, and stuffed the blanket back in the suitcase. This just upset the boy more, and, wailing louder, he struggled to pull it out again. The tension escalated, and the embarrassed mom looked ready to spank her distraught child. At that moment, a boy about thirteen years old kneeled in front of the boy and softly said, "Are you scared your blanket's going to get lost? Your mom's going to carry that bag on the plane, so don't you worry."

The little boy immediately stopped crying and looked up at his mom, who confirmed that the bag holding his blanket would not be checked. The child's relief was instantaneous. The mom thanked the older boy, then asked him how he knew what was bothering her son. He smiled and explained, "Whenever I traveled as a kid I used to worry my blanket would get lost, so I knew how he must feel." I had just witnessed the power of empathy.

John Gottman, a professor of psychology at the University of Washington and the author of *The Heart of Parenting,* conducted two ten-year studies of 120 families. He found that kids whose parents acted as "emotion coaches" learned to acknowledge and master their emotions better; they were more self-confident and physically healthier. They also scored higher in math and reading, had better social skills, got along better with friends, and had lower levels of stress. Experts find that most parents generally don't use the emotion coaching method, which is unfortunate, because it is found to greatly benefit kids' emotional literacy as well as their empathy. There are four parts to the technique. To help you remember the parts, just think of the word *TALK;* each part begins with a letter of the word:

> *T—Tune in* to your child's feelings and listen with empathy.
> *A—Acknowledge* what is causing the emotion.
> *L—Label* how the child is feeling.
> *K—Kindle* a resolution for the child's need.

Here are the four parts to listening with empathy and how you might use them with your child:

Tune In to Your Child's Feelings and Listen with Empathy   The first part is often the toughest for parents: listening calmly to your child with your ears, eyes, and heart. Tune in to her body language: it often tells so much more than her words. For instance, is she stressed or elated or angry or frustrated? Your job is to gather information to find out what is bothering her. Experts say the surest way to stop your child from sharing is to discount her feelings: "That's nothing to be angry about," or "You're too old to get so upset." So be supportive and don't judge or discount her emotions. Because they convey your interest, sometimes the briefest of words, such as "Really," "Oh?" or "Gosh," are best at encouraging kids to continue talking.

Acknowledge What Is Causing the Emotion   The second part is to acknowledge what situation is causing your child to feel the way she does.

Sometimes you can easily figure out what is contributing to the emotion, and sometimes you'll have to ask a few questions to be sure you understand. Once you discover the issue, identify it: "When you find out you have soccer practice . . . ," or "When you have to wait for Matt to call you to find out if he is coming over . . . "

Label How the Child Is Feeling　The third part is to label the emotion you think your child is feeling and say it back to her. This step sounds so simple, but it is powerful because it validates that you understand how she's feeling. For many kids, just knowing you understand can be very healing. It also helps your child develop a stronger emotional vocabulary. Here are a few examples: "You seem nervous," "Do you feel irritated?" "Are you feeling frustrated?"

Kindle a Resolution for the Child's Need　The final part is to help your child resolve her emotional need. It often is helpful to add a response that shows you empathize with her plight: "I can understand why you might feel that way," or "I'd feel the same way if that happened to me." Sometimes your child may want you to help her think of a solution to her problem, and other times she just wants to hear that you understand her need or desire. You can always ask, "Would you like some ideas on solving it?"

You don't always to have to do the four parts in order. Include them in whatever way seems most natural in your conversation. Here are examples of how putting the four parts together might sound:

Child's Concern	Parent's Empathic Response
"I don't want to go to soccer practice."	"Do you notice that whenever you know you have soccer practice you feel a bit uptight because you don't think you can kick as well as the other kids? Would you like me to help you think of how to improve your kicking?"

Child's Concern	*Parent's Empathic Response*
"I don't ever want Matt coming to this house again."	"It seems that whenever you invite Matt to come over, you get irritable. Is it because he takes so long to call you back, and you're stuck waiting? I can understand why you might be upset."
"I hate going to the doctor."	"Whenever you have a doctor's appointment, you are afraid he's going to give you a shot. This time you won't have to have a shot."
"That camp is stupid."	"Staying away from home seems to make you feel a little anxious because you don't know the other kids. Let's see if someone you know is going to be at the same camp this year. Would that help?"

Four Ideas to Help Kids Develop a Stronger Emotional Vocabulary

Of course, no child is comforting and caring all the time, but some kids are definitely more compassionate, and for years psychologists have pondered why. Recent studies offer a helpful hint: kids who are more empathic are generally more emotionally literate. In other words, these kids understand how to recognize and express their emotional states and those of others. How well kids can identify feelings depends in part on whether they have an accurate emotional vocabulary. These next activities are designed to help kids develop a stronger emotional vocabulary so that they have the skills to recognize feelings in others.

1. Use feeling questions. To enhance your child's emotional vocabulary, use words and questions that help your child tune in to feelings; for example, "You seem [tense, anxious, worried] about something. What's the matter?" or "Your friend seems really [unhappy, angry, upset]. What

MORAL INTELLIGENCE BUILDER
An ABC Emotional Vocabulary

In order for kids to read the feelings of others, they must have an adequate emotional vocabulary. To enhance your child's emotional intelligence, teach him the feeling words in the list that follows. Consider using a different feeling word each day or a new word each week.

A

afraid
agitated
alarmed
angry
antsy
anxious
apprehensive
ashamed
awful
awkward

B

bashful
bewildered
bitter
bored
brave

C

calm
caring
cautious
cheerful
comfortable
concerned
confident

confused
content
critical
cross
curious
cynical

D

depressed
delighted
disappointed
discouraged
disgusted
distressed
disturbed
down

E

eager
edgy
embarrassed
encouraged
enraged
enthused
exasperated
excited
exhausted

F

fatigued
fearful
fidgety
frightened
frustrated
funny
furious

G

glad
gloomy
greedy
grouchy
guilty

H

happy
hassled
hateful
helpless
hesitant
hopeful
horrible
hostile
hurt
hysterical

I

impatient
indifferent
inferior
insecure
intense
irate
irked
irritated

J

jealous
jittery
joyous

L

lazy
leery
lonely
loved
loving

M

mad
mean
mischievous
miserable
moody

N

nervous
nice
numb

O

overwhelmed

P

panicky
patient
pessimistic
pleased
proud
puzzled

Q

queasy

R

rejected
reluctant
resentful
restless
ridiculous
riled
rushed

S

sad
safe
scared
secure
sensitive
shaky
shocked
shy
silly
sleepy
sorry

stressed
surprised
suspicious
sympathetic

T

terrified
tired
troubled

U

uncomfortable
unsafe
unsettled
upset

V

vicious
victorious

W

warm
weary
wonderful
worried

X

excited
exhausted

Y

yucky

Z

zany

do you think is bothering her?" Once your child develops an emotional vocabulary, ask often, "How do you feel?" or "How do you think he feels?"

2. Say your feeling ABCs. Each night with her two preschoolers, Jane Brewer, an educational administrator and mom, plays a fun game called Feeling ABCs. "We say the alphabet together," explains Brewer, "but for each letter we also try to include a feeling word. So it goes something like this: *A, angry; B, brave; C, calm;* and so on. We usually don't get beyond *G,* but the point is we're having fun together, and my kids are also learning a feeling vocabulary." You might want to try this idea with your kids.

3. Have feelings with dinner. This activity helps family members tune in to each other's conversations and at the same time learn to express their feelings. One night or more a week, have a dinner conversation that includes discussing the feelings each member had during the day. You might begin by picking a feeling—such as proud—and asking, "What was the proudest moment you had this week?" Then everyone can take turns sharing his or her experiences, starting with the stem, "I felt proud this week when . . . " Some families even like to vote on who had the most interesting (or unusual, exciting, different) experience.

4. Create feeling cards. Gather a set of three-by-five index cards, scissors, glue, a pen, and old magazines. On each card, write the names of some of the most common emotion words, starting with just a few and then adding more as older ones are learned. For very young children, include only the six basic emotions: happiness, sadness, anger, surprise, fear, and disgust. Then help your child find pictures from magazines or computer programs to depict each emotion; glue them onto the corresponding card. Now use them like flash cards. Show your child the picture and ask him to guess the feeling. Later you can tell your child the emotion word and have him act it out with his face and body or discuss a time when he experienced the emotion.

Older kids can use a much more extended list of emotion words. Each week, make a few cards (depending on your child's age and learning aptitude) containing new feeling words from the preceding Moral Intelligence Builder, "An ABC Emotional Vocabulary." Use the cards throughout the week to help expand his emotional vocabulary by playing games with the words. Here are a few games you can play with your child for any feeling word. These examples use the emotion of anger: think of synonyms [furious, incensed, irate]; name antonyms [calm, peaceful, serene]; identify times you felt angry; name body signs that tell you you're angry [flushed cheeks, rapid heartbeat, clenched fists]; and describe a time you've seen another person experience anger.

STEP 2: ENHANCE SENSITIVITY TO THE FEELINGS OF OTHERS

It was Colby's sixth birthday, and his mom, Mary, was cutting pieces of his birthday cake to serve his friends. The children lined up, plates in hand, waiting to be served. Ronnie, Colby's best friend, was next, and Mary noticed that he had a plate in each hand. "Extra hungry, Ronnie?" she laughed.

The six-year-old smiled. "No, I just thought I'd bring a piece to Daiwana."

"How nice, Ronnie," Mary answered. "Did she ask you to bring her one?"

"No," Ronnie whispered. "She just looks like she might like one. She's been sitting by herself and seems kind of sad. This might make her feel better."

Mary turned and saw the little girl sitting rather forlornly by herself and recognized that she did seem sad. She marveled at Ronnie's sensitivity; while everyone else had overlooked the little girl, Ronnie hadn't missed it. In fact, Ronnie always seemed to pick up on other people's feelings, and Mary wondered how she could help her own son be more sensitive like Ronnie.

Ronnie exemplified what it means to be emotionally sensitive: he recognized the emotional cues of his friend, interpreted them as sadness, then acted on them. One of the biggest reasons some kids are more sensitive is that they can correctly interpret people's emotional cues: their tone of voice, posture, and facial expressions. Without that understanding, a child is greatly limited in his ability to react to another person's needs.

Six Simple Ways to Nurture Kids' Sensitivity

Here are six ideas you can use almost anytime to tune up your child's awareness of the feelings of others.

1. Praise sensitive, kind actions. One of the simplest and most effective ways of enhancing any behavior is by reinforcing the action as soon as it happens. So whenever you notice your child acting in a sensitive and caring manner, let her know how pleased it makes you feel: "Karen, I love how gentle you are with your baby sister. You pat her so softly, and it makes me so happy knowing how caring you are."

2. Show the effect of sensitivity. Sensitive, kind acts—even small ones—can make a big difference in people's lives, so point them out to help your child see the impact his actions made. "Derrick, your grandmother was so pleased when you called to thank her for the present." "Suraya, did you see the smile on Ryan's face when you shared your toys?"

3. Draw attention to nonverbal feeling cues. Pointing out the facial expressions, posture, and mannerisms of people in different emotional states sensitizes your child to other people's feelings. As occasions arise, explain your concern and share what clues helped you make your feeling assessment: "Did you notice Grandma's face when you were talking with her today? I thought she looked puzzled. Maybe she is having trouble hearing. Why not talk a little louder when you speak with her?" "Did you see the expression on Meghan's face when you were playing today? She looked worried about something because she had a scowl on her face. Maybe you should ask her if everything is OK."

4. Ask often, "How does he feel?" One of the easiest ways to nurture your child's sensitivity is to ask her to ponder how another person feels. As opportunities arise, pose the question often, using situations in books, TV, and movies as well as real life. "How do you think the mommy feels, knowing that her little girl just won the prize?" "The tornado destroyed most of the town in Georgia; see it here on the map? How do you think the people feel?" "How do you think Daddy feels hearing that his mom is so sick?" Each question forces your child to stop and think about other people's concerns, and nurtures sensitivity to their needs.

5. Use the formula "feels + needs." Michael Schulman and Eva Mekler, authors of *Bringing Up a Moral Child*, reviewed studies and found that an effective way to increase sensitivity is to ask children questions to help them discover people's needs and feelings. Such questions were found to expand children's awareness of what people might be experiencing. As a result, the children became more sensitive to how they might be able to help. To use the idea with your child, look for occasions to draw attention to people's feelings and then ask her to guess what the person might need in order to remedy the feeling. Here is how a parent might use the method:

Parent: Look at that little girl crying in the sandbox. How do you suppose she feels?

Child: I think she is sad.

Parent: What do you think she needs to make her feel better?

Child: Maybe she could use someone to hug her because she hurt her knee.

6. Share why you feel the way you do. One of the best ways to help kids become sensitive to others' feelings is to share your own. Use situations as they arise to describe how you feel about them and why: "I'm so excited! My new computer is being delivered to me today." "I am frustrated; yesterday the auto body shop told me that fixing the car would cost five hundred dollars, and now they say it's going to cost a lot more." "I'm so tired. The barking dogs kept me up all night."

Five Fun Ways to Help Kids Read Nonverbal Emotions

Drs. Stephen Nowicki and Marshall Duke, child psychologists at Emory University in Atlanta, conducted tests with more than one thousand children and found that one out of ten children, despite normal and even superior intelligence, has significant problems with nonverbal communication. The psychologists said that this disability prevents kids from recognizing particular emotional signals that are so important in getting along with others as well as interpreting the feelings of their peers. The researchers' recommendation: enhance your child's skills in reading nonverbal messages! Doing so will not only boost her interpersonal skills but

MORAL INTELLIGENCE BUILDER
Nine Factors That Favor the Development of Empathy

Suzanne Denham, author of *Emotional Development in Young Children,* identified nine factors that researchers say generally increase the chances that a child will display more empathy (although there are certainly no guarantees):

1. *Age.* The ability to take the perspective of others increases with age, so older children are generally more empathic than younger kids.
2. *Gender.* Younger children are more likely to empathize with a peer of the same sex because they feel a greater sense of commonality.
3. *Intelligence.* Smarter kids are more likely to comfort others because they are better able to discern other people's needs and devise ways to assist them.
4. *Emotional understanding.* Children who freely express their emotions are usually more empathic because they are more capable of correctly identifying other people's feelings.
5. *Empathic parents.* Kids whose parents are empathic are likely to become empathic themselves because the parents model those behaviors, which in turn are copied by their children.
6. *Emotional security.* More assertive and well-adjusted kids are more likely to assist others.
7. *Temperament.* Kids who are by nature happier and more social are more likely to empathize with a distressed child.
8. *Similarity.* Kids are more likely to empathize with those who they feel are similar to them in some way or with whom they have shared a similar experience.
9. *Attachment.* Kids are more likely to empathize with their friends than with those to whom they feel less closely attached.

also nurture the development of empathy. The following are five good ideas for getting started.

1. Play "Guess the Feeling." Brainstorm as many different feeling words as you can and write each of them on an index card. Turn all the words face down or put them in a box or basket. Tell family members they are to take turns drawing the cards one at a time. Each person then acts out the emotion using only his or her body. No words are allowed. Everyone else tries to guess the emotion that is being acted out.

2. Make comic mood characters. Cut out with your child an assortment of pictures from newspapers and magazines showing people depicting a wide array of different emotions. Glue them onto paper. Guess together how each person feels based on how his or her body looks; help your child draw balloons over each person's head and together write inside what you think he or she may be saying. Tell your child she has just designed comic mood characters.

3. Read with feeling! This activity helps children recognize that our tone of voice conveys moods. Start by reading any children's literature selection. Reading the same short passage each time, give your voice a different emotional tone [bored, excited, tired, sad, angry] and challenge your child to identify the tone. Take turns reading or role-playing the same passage or different ones with your child.

4. Watch TV silently. Turn off the sound on your television and watch the show together. Make a game out of trying to guess how the actors feel, just from what you see. Point out the kinds of nonverbal behaviors people do to express their feelings. (A person exhibiting tension behaviors might rapidly blink her eyes, twirl her hair, grind her teeth, clench her fists, and tighten her jaw. A person showing uninterested behaviors might roll his eyes, look away, walk away, or turn away from the speaker. A person expressing interest might nod, lean into the speaker, smile, raise her eyebrows, or stand or sit close to the speaker.)

5. Hold a feeling watch. With your child, watch other people's faces and body language at the shopping mall, grocery store, park, or playground. Try together to guess their emotional state without hearing their conversation: "How does her body look now?" "How do you think he feels?" "Look at the expression on her face. What do you think she's feeling right now?" "Listen to the sound of that man's voice. How do you think he feels?" "Look how that girl is standing with her fists so

MORAL INTELLIGENCE BUILDER
A Story to Tell Kids About Empathy

Michael Crisler, a first grader in Denver, Colorado, was born with a rare birth defect that left him with severe facial deformities. By the age of seven, he had already experienced several painful surgeries. So when he read about the tragedy of the Oklahoma bombing, Michael identified with the victims' pain and was particularly moved by the plight of the children at the America's Kids Day Care Center in the ill-fated Alfred P. Murrah Federal Building. "I know what it feels like," he explained, "because I've been in a hospital, too." So Michael decided to do something to aid the smallest victims of the bombing by organizing a local bowl-a-thon. Its success surpassed his wildest dreams. He raised one of the largest single cash donations: $27,077. The check, which he proudly presented to then Oklahoma governor Frank Keating, was set aside as a relief fund for survivors and families of victims of the Oklahoma City bombing. Michael explained, "I wanted to do this to help little kids." The first grader's remarkable sensitivity toward the Oklahoma victims and his desire to do something to comfort them because he understood their pain clearly showed he is a child with empathy.

Michael found out about the Oklahoma bombing victims by reading about it in the newspapers and seeing it on television. Even though he never personally met any of the victims, he felt their distress. That's what empathy is: you understand and feel other people's concerns and needs so well that you want to do something to make their situation better. There are many people each day who could use comforting and support. They might live next door to you or across the ocean in a different country. So keep your eyes and ears open for opportunities to make a difference in people's lives. Showing empathy is one way you can make the world a more caring place. What could you do?

tight. See the scowl on her face? What do you think she's saying to the other girl?"

STEP 3: DEVELOP EMPATHY FOR ANOTHER PERSON'S POINT OF VIEW

Recently I was visiting a first-grade classroom in Dayton, Ohio, and the teacher had just asked her students to join her on the rug to hear a story. While the children eagerly gathered to sit in a circle around her, one boy sat by himself with his head in his hands a few feet back from his classmates. I wasn't the only one to notice the isolated child: Joey, another six-year-old, was trying to figure out the situation. He quietly began inching his way back until he was seated next to the boy. Then he leaned over and whispered something in the boy's ear. The other child nodded shyly and smiled back. Joey patted him on the back, then both boys turned to listen to the story.

As soon as the teacher dismissed the students to their seats, my curiosity got the best of me, and I pulled Joey aside and asked what he had said that had such an effect on the other child. "Dashon just looked lonely," Joey explained. "He just moved here and doesn't know many kids, so I asked if I could sit with him. I just knew how he felt: Dashon needed a friend."

I had just witnessed a six-year-old with remarkable empathy: Joey recognized his classmate's loneliness and identified with his distress. And because he could imagine how it feels to be alone, he extended kindness to the dejected boy. Even at a young age, Joey already was capable of taking the view of the other person so that he was able to extend empathy.

Dr. Ezra Stotland from the University of Washington was one of the first researchers whose work demonstrated the development of empathy. The subjects in Stotland's study were asked to watch as a person reacted to heat being applied to his hand. The subjects didn't know that the victim was actually Stotland's assistant, who had been taught to act as if he was feeling pain: the "heat" didn't really exist. When the subjects were told just to focus on the assistant's movements, they reported very little empa-

MORAL INTELLIGENCE BUILDER
The Stages of Empathic Development

Martin Hoffman, a renowned authority on moral development, believes children slowly develop empathy in a series of stages, in which they gradually move from an egocentric, self-centered, "always thinking about me" perspective to one in which they not only care about the other person but also can feel and understand the other person's point of view. The more you understand these stages and your child's current empathy level, the better you will be at helping her reach the next stage. Keep in mind that because kids vary enormously in their experiences and abilities, the listed ages should serve only as a guide. The following stages are adapted from Dr. Hoffman's acclaimed work.

Stage 1: Global empathy   **The first year of life**

The child cannot clearly distinguish between himself and his world, so he is unclear as to who is experiencing the distress and interprets it as his own. *The six-month-old baby heard another baby cry and began to cry too.*

Stage 2: Egocentric empathy   **Beginning around age 1**

The child's reactions to others in distress begin to slowly change. She now understands that another person's discomfort is not her own. *The two-year-old saw her mommy crying, so she sat next to her and softly patted her arm.*

Stage 3: Emotional empathy   **Early preschool years**

Around the age of two or three, the child begins to develop role-taking capabilities. He recognizes that someone's feelings may be different from his, is better able to decipher the source of another person's distress, and finds simple ways to offer comfort or show support. *"You look sad. Your car broke. You can use this one."*

Stage 4: Cognitive empathy   **Elementary school years, beginning around age 6**

The child can now see things from another person's perspective, so there is a noticeable increase in her efforts to support and comfort those in need. The ability to use language to comfort others also substantially increases. *"That older woman looks like she needs help getting into the elevator," Kelly thought; she held the elevator door open so the woman could walk in safely.*

Stage 5: Abstract empathy   **Late childhood: ages 10 to 12**

The child can now extend empathy beyond those he personally knows or can directly observe to include groups of people he may have never met. *"The people in India look so hungry. If I sent some of my allowance each week, it might make them feel better."*

thy for his "pain." But when the researchers told the subjects either to imagine having the heat placed on their own hands or to suppose how the victim felt, the subjects reported noticeably more empathy.

Stotland's research found that encouraging a child to imagine how the other person feels or to put herself in that person's place is a powerful way to nurture empathy. This third step shows some of the most effective ways to help a child imagine another person's feelings and thoughts so that she can really step into another person's shoes and feel with him.

Three Simple Ways to Increase Children's Role-Taking Abilities

Years ago at a conference in Santa Clara, I had the good fortune of watching Virginia Satir, a renowned therapist and the author of *Peoplemaking* and many other classic books, conduct a marriage-therapy session. Satir began by asking a couple to sit in chairs across from one another on the stage. She explained that once in their chairs they were to assume the role of the other person by acting, thinking, and feeling only as his or her spouse would react. Then, before a packed room, under Satir's guidance the couple began to role-play their marital problems totally from the other person's view. At the conclusion of the session, both admitted they'd never seen the other person's perspective before; they left the stage elated that they had finally been able to resolve a marital problem that had almost caused a divorce. The rest of the audience was spellbound. We had witnessed not only an enormously gifted therapist but also the power that perspective-taking has in increasing empathy. These next three ideas show ways to help your child imagine the thoughts and feelings of other people and see beyond herself.

1. **Switch roles to feel the other side.** The next time there's a conflict between siblings, between your child and a friend, or even between you and your child, ask each participant to stop and think how the other person would feel if the roles were reversed. Then ask each person to talk about the problem as if she were the other person: "What would the other

person say and do?" The method can be a valuable way of helping each person gain a different perspective on a troublesome situation. It's often helpful to use puppets with younger children so that each puppet represents a person in the conflict. The child can then act out the problem with the puppets.

You don't have to use role switching only with conflicts: use it in any situation to help your child understand the point of view of the other people involved. "Why do you think Matt always insults everyone?" [He probably doesn't feel really good about himself. Maybe bringing the other person down makes him feel he's better.] "Why do you think Kelly is always following you?" [Maybe she's lonely and doesn't know how to make friends.] "Why did Dad yell at you?" [Because he's trying to get the taxes done and feels really stressed right now.] Taking the other person's perspective tends to enhance your child's empathy, so use it often.

2. Walk in my shoes. Here's a great tip that Jill, a mom of one of my ex-students, shared with me to help your kids understand your point of view. Jill explained that her twelve-year-old daughter, Kaysa, couldn't understand why she was so upset when Kaysa forgot to tell Jill where she was. One day Jill said, "Step into my shoes and pretend you're me. I don't know where you are, and it's getting dark. What am I saying and feeling?" Kaysa literally put on Jill's shoes, pretending to be her and role-playing what she would say and feel about the predicament. Jill said Kaysa immediately apologized, explained she had just never realized Jill would be so concerned, and promised she would never forget to call home again.

You may want to try the technique with your child. Choose a real situation that concerns you, and have your child step into your shoes, imagining what it would be like to experience the event from your perspective.

3. Imagine how the person feels. To help your child identify with the feelings of others is to have him imagine how the other person feels about a specific circumstance. Suppose your child just sent a thank-you card to his aunt for the birthday present he received. Use it as an opportunity to help your child recognize his aunt's feelings when she receives the card by.

having him pretend to be the aunt. "Pretend you're Aunt Jen right now. You open up your mailbox and find this card. How will you feel when you read what it says?" You later can expand the imagining technique to include individuals your child has not personally met: "Pretend you're a new neighbor, and you're moving into this town and don't know anyone. How will you feel?" Asking often, "How would you feel?" helps children grasp the needs and feelings of other people.

Discipline That Builds Empathy

Steve watched his nine-year-old son, Lucas, play baseball at the park with the neighborhood kids. Lucas was playing first base, and his team was ahead by three runs. Aaron, a seven-year-old, was batting next, and as soon as he

---

MORAL INTELLIGENCE BUILDER
Talking About Empathy with Kids

Here are some questions to discuss with kids to help them think about the importance of empathy in their lives.

- Have you ever seen a movie where you got teary-eyed because something sad happened to someone and you felt that character's sadness? What was the movie? What made you so sad?
- What does empathy mean? Have you ever had a time when you felt the feelings of someone else? What does it mean when we try to put ourselves in someone else's shoes?
- Do you know anyone with a disability? What kind do they have? Try to imagine what it feels like to have that disability. What would be the hardest part of having that disability? How do you suppose other people would treat you sometimes? How would you feel?
- What are some ways to let someone who is hurt or sad know how you feel? How do you think it makes the other person feel, knowing you understand how she feels?

---

stepped up to the plate, Steve got nervous. Aaron was not only younger than the other kids but also less coordinated. He hoped the other players would show a little compassion for Aaron, never expecting the response from Lucas's teammates. "Easy out!" yelled the third baseman. Another shouted, "Hey, everybody, move in!" Then he heard his son yell, "Don't worry, guys. He couldn't hit a basketball." Steve was furious, and wondered how Lucas could be so insensitive. How was his son going to develop empathy when he was hanging around with a group of kids who obviously didn't care one bit about people's feelings?

Sensitizing children to how someone else feels is a significant and serious enterprise. Research by Dr. Martin Hoffman and a number of others has shown that parents who consistently react to their children's misbehavior by focusing on the feelings of the person they harmed tend to have children who are more empathic. The four parts in the lesson that follows help turn children's insensitive moments into teaching tools that sensitize them to the feelings and needs of others and nurture the seeds of empathy. The four parts can be remembered with the acronym *CARE:*

C—*Call attention* to the insensitive, uncaring behavior.
A—*Ask*, "How would you feel?"
R—*Recognize* the consequences of the behavior.
E—*Express* and *explain* your disapproval of the insensitive action.

Call Attention to the Insensitive Behavior   Use this first part of the CARE lesson any time your child acts unkindly. It's an opportunity to sensitize her to the feelings of other people and to the disastrous effect unkind actions have on others; it's a critical step to developing empathy. As soon as you see an uncaring behavior, call attention to it. We're always more successful in helping kids change their behavior when we "nip it in the bud" before it has a chance to escalate and become a habit. Here are some examples of how to call attention to uncaring behaviors: "Making fun of Aaron by yelling out that he couldn't hit a basketball was very cruel." "Telling Bert to leave because you wanted to play with Sally was inconsiderate." "Not turning down your stereo when Grandpa asked you to was rude."

Ask, "How Would You Feel?"   Now that you have pointed out the uncaring behavior, help your child understand why the action was unacceptable. Ideally, we want our children to think about how their behavior affected the other person, but empathy does not always come naturally. A good place to start is by asking questions that help your child think about how she would feel if someone had done the same behavior to her. You might ask, "Lucas, how would you feel if Aaron yelled out in front of everybody that you can't hit?" "If someone said that to you, how would you feel right now?" "Would you want to be treated like that?"

Recognize the Consequences of the Behavior   The third part is to help children put themselves in someone else's shoes and think how it feels to be the recipient of uncaring actions. Feeling from another person's perspective is often difficult for children, but by using insightful questions we can gently guide them in considering the other person's feelings—the foundation of empathy. Here are a few examples of questions that help children realize the impact of their uncaring actions: "Switch places and pretend you're Aaron. How do you feel right now?" "Put yourself in her shoes. Tell me what you think she's thinking." "What do you think he would like to say to you?"

Express and Explain Your Disapproval of the Uncaring Behavior   Finally, explain why you consider the child's behavior to be unacceptable and insensitive. In plain language, explain what concerns you about the behavior and how you feel about uncaring actions. This is the moment for you to make sure your child clearly understands what is wrong about the behavior and why you disapprove. It will help your child shift her focus from herself and consider how her actions can affect other people. "I'm very concerned when I hear you treating people badly without considering their feelings. I expect you to treat your friends the same way you would want to be treated." "I am upset when you talk in that tone to me. It is disrespectful and uncaring, and I expect you to treat people with respect."

The true parenting challenge is to use those unplanned moments when a child's behavior is unacceptable as learning tools to help your child develop

---

MORAL INTELLIGENCE BUILDER
Finding Real Ways for Kids to Gain a New Point of View

Many children lack empathy because their experiences have never allowed them to think about perspectives other than their own. Here's a learning assignment that enhances children's ability to feel from another point of view. It starts by asking your child to imagine having a disadvantage, such as living in a homeless shelter, having a learning disability, or being blind, deaf, or motor impaired. Any predicament that your child has not experienced will do. The goal is to stretch your child's thinking about the situation so that he sees it from a different view. Then have him write, talk, or draw his view of what it might feel like if he had to live with the situation himself.

Next, invite him to actually experience the situation: visit a homeless shelter, juvenile hall, a prison, a nursing home, or a soup kitchen. Many teachers ask students to experience a disability by wearing a blindfold, sitting in a wheelchair, or not communicating using their voice for a period of time. When you return, have the child write about it again or talk about it, asking, "Is your perspective the same or different?"

Finally, go back and volunteer at the same place you thought about and then visited. Help the child really get to know the people, and then ask, "What happened to your feelings about the people now?"

Too often we rob children of really experiencing a situation from another point of view so that they never truly empathize with the individuals. There is no substitute for experiencing the real thing—especially when it comes to developing empathy. Look for opportunities for your child to experience different perspectives so that he can really understand what it feels like to walk in someone else's shoes.

empathy. These are always the best lessons; they help the child discover for herself why she should be kind, and allow her to see that her uncaring actions may affect others.

WHAT TO DO ABOUT THE CRISIS IN THE DEVELOPMENT OF EMPATHY

- To teach kids empathy, you must show kids empathy. The best moments to teach empathy are usually not planned—they just happen. Capitalize on those moments to help your child understand the power that "feeling with others" can have.

- Expand your child's emotional intelligence by asking often, "How do you feel?" Children must be able to identify different emotional states in themselves before they can become sensitive to the feelings of others.

- Know what your kids are watching and listening to; protect them from cruel, degrading, desensitizing images that can corrupt their empathic development.

- Children are likely to be more empathic if they understand why empathy is important and how it affects others. So point out the positive impact empathy can have on others.

- If you want your child to feel for others, expect and *demand* that your child feel for others.

- Tune up your empathic behaviors so your child regularly sees you show concern for other people's "hurts and needs." Then act on your concerns to comfort others so that your child can copy your actions.

- Provide opportunities for your child to experience different perspectives and views in your community—for example, by visiting nursing homes, homeless shelters, centers for the blind, pediatric wards, soup kitchens, veterans' hospitals, and political campaign headquarters. The more your child experiences different perspectives, the more likely she will be able to empathize with others whose needs and views differ from hers.

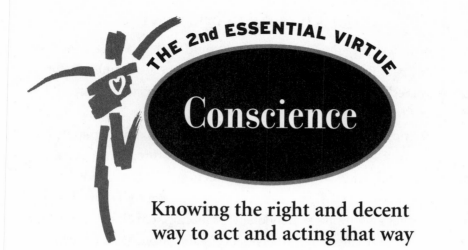

THE 2nd ESSENTIAL VIRTUE

Conscience

Knowing the right and decent way to act and acting that way

"Last night my twelve-year-old son showed me the A on his math test," the father told me following my parent workshop in Michigan. "I was really proud of him, figuring he had studied so hard," he explained. "Then I noticed that he'd printed half the answers on his hand. When I confronted him, he said that everybody else was doing the same thing and that it's no big deal, so I shouldn't get so worked up about it. Well, I happen to think it is a big deal—he cheated! It felt to me as if my own son didn't have a conscience!"

The man paused, then added, "I have five kids—my oldest is almost thirty now—but I really think it was so much easier being a parent back in those days. Everyone used to have the same values, and we all supported each other. We never had to worry about what our kids watched or listened to because the message was too violent or vulgar. Sometimes I feel more like a vigilante than a father. It seems everything in our culture these days counters the kinds of morals and conscience I want my son to have." Then he said what I've heard so many other parents say lately: "I just wonder if parents these days really can make much of a difference in creating a strong sense of conscience in our kids."

THE CRISIS OF CONSCIENCE

The close of America's twentieth century could well have been called the Decade of Moral Erosion. Scandals involving top government officials led headlines; accusations of perjury, adultery, plagiarism, and illegal drug use (among others) were rampant. The Internet became scarier: new sites included hate groups, satanism, terrorism, pornography, gun sales, and bomb-making instructions. Television featured more casual sex, materialism, vulgarity, cynicism, and dysfunctional behavior; video games became even cruder; music lyrics or rock groups were ruder; movies were often steamier and always more violent. Troubling statistics strongly hint that the steady onslaught of morally questionable messages is taking a toll on the development of conscience in our children. Let us look at six disturbing signs of the crisis of conscience in our youth.

Rise of Youth Violence

There is no doubt that youth violence is a major concern of Americans, and so it should be. Rates of violence among adolescents are considerably higher in the United States than in other countries. The American Academy of Pediatrics reports that the United States has the highest youth homicide and suicide rates among the twenty-six wealthiest nations in the world. What is especially alarming is that so many young offenders seem *to show little remorse, nor do they see anything wrong in their actions.* Those are clear signs of a crisis of conscience that must be taken seriously.

Here are the facts: since World War II, serious assault by juveniles in the United States has seen a sevenfold increase, and although recent data reveal that the level of violent crime is dropping in some parts of the United States, it's too soon to celebrate. As James Garbarino, author of *Lost Boys,* points out, "While the overall youth homicide rate dropped in 1997, the rate among small town and rural youth increased by 38 percent." This statistic indicates that whereas youth crime once concerned mainly large urban areas (which, tragically, we largely ignored), the problem is now everywhere. So every child—yours and mine included—stands the chance of being affected.

Additional data add to an already troubling portrait of youth that seem morally adrift. The National School Safety Center estimates that 525,000 "attacks, shakedowns and robberies occur in an average month in public secondary schools. The Centers for Disease Control and Prevention estimate that 22 percent of students have been victims of a disturbing new epidemic haunting American high schools, known as *teen dating violence*— noninjurious physical aggression involving insults, raised fists, shoving, face slapping, and outright battering. But violent crime isn't only about "big kids": some of the most alarming reports list the offenders as youths ten to fourteen years of age.

Certainly a multitude of factors cause youth violence, but one reoccurring theme is so prevalent that it cannot be overlooked: many young people today have underdeveloped consciences, which greatly increases their tendency to act on their aggressive, antisocial urges. Research by Barbara Stilwell and her colleagues on the development of conscience offers insight into the seeds of violence. They found that the average fifteen-year-old still exhibits a "confused conscience," which limits his ability to engage in reality-based moral thinking and to appreciate the consequences of his behavior. Stilwell explains that what kids need most at this stage for moral growth is what she calls "external conscience": essential conditions such as limits, love, supervision, rules, and strong moral examples that foster a strong conscience. Tragically, those are the very conditions that many of our more violence-prone kids don't get. With underdeveloped consciences and limited external supports, they are vulnerable to aggressive urges, and violence too often is the result. Left alone to make sense of their flimsy moral beliefs and with only weak consciences at their disposal, it's all too easy for them to conclude that revenge (by any means) is acceptable—and then to act.

Increase in Peer Cruelty

One of the most troubling signs of a crisis of conscience is the epidemic of peer cruelty: the National Education Association estimates that 160,000 children miss school *every day* due to fear of attack or intimidation by other students. It was noted at a recent meeting of the National Association of School Psychologists that one in seven children is a bully or the target of a bully. What bullies subject their victims to is plain viciousness: ridiculing, threatening, pushing, shoving, slapping, kicking. In most incidents, the bully terrifies his prey with little feeling of shame or remorse. In fact, conscience rarely enters the picture: studies show that if the bully feels that he's caused any anguish—particularly if his victim cries or appears upset—he is much more likely to strike again (and again and again). With each strike, his capacity to feel for his victim and his shame for his cruelty go down another notch, and the crisis of conscience becomes ever more acute.

Rise in Youth Stealing

Visiting most high school libraries reveals another sign of our moral decline: many have had to install security systems to detect book theft because it so rampant. A high school librarian in the Los Angeles Unified School District told me, "Some years the students take more books than we can buy: it's as though they've rationalized that it's OK to steal." But it's not just libraries that need more security. A national survey of over one hundred thousand young people found that half had shoplifted at least once; most admitted they would do it again. And another recent nation-wide survey conducted by the Josephson Institute of Ethics of more than twenty thousand middle and high school students revealed that 47 percent of the respondents admitted to stealing something from a store in the past twelve months and more than a quarter of high schoolers saying they had committed store theft at least twice. FBI figures show that in the past ten years juvenile theft has increased 22 percent.

A local storeowner told me shoplifting is so common that he and other local businesses have had to install security cameras and hire guards to watch customers—and youths are always his biggest offenders. He commented, "They don't think anything about taking people's property, and if caught, they never think it's any big deal." He then added, "It's as though a lot of these kids never developed consciences." A recent survey of middle school students validates his hypothesis: 37 percent of those polled say they feel pressure to steal something from a store. "Thou shall not steal" certainly seems to be tenet long forgotten.

Escalation of Youth Cheating

One of the most prevalent and distressing trends among students in the past decade is widespread cheating. Since 1969, the percentage of high school students who admitted to cheating on a test increased from 34 percent to 68 percent. A national survey found that of more than six thousand college freshmen and sophomores, 76 percent admitted to cheating in high school. The Center for Academic Integrity at Duke University found that three-quarters of college students confessed to cheating at least once. In fact, plagiarism among college students has become so rampant that many professors have to rely on a specially designed website to scan their students' papers to validate originality.

Teachers say that cheating is prevalent even in the early grades. A fourth-grade teacher in Atlanta told me, "I have to carefully monitor my students' test taking because they're constantly copying answers from each other. The really sad thing is, the first-grade teacher said she's having to do the same thing!"

Even more troubling is the large numbers of students who feel that cheating is *not only acceptable but even necessary for school success.* A survey conducted by *Who's Who Among American High School Students* found that 80 percent of high-achieving high school students admitted to having cheated at least once, and half said they did not believe cheating was wrong. A recent *U.S. News & World Report* poll found that 84 percent of college students believe they need to cheat to get ahead in the world today.

The facts confirm that deception, lying, and cheating are on the rise among today's youth, but perhaps our biggest concern should be that *many kids seem to feel no remorse about their lack of integrity.* It's just another sign that morality has run amok and that the consciences of many of today's youth are weak.

Increase in Sexual Promiscuity

Another indication of flimsy conscience is sexual promiscuity: far too many young people are jumping into bed with no thought to possible outcomes, such as pregnancy, sexually transmitted diseases, and other illnesses, as well as a whole range of emotional consequences (lowered self-esteem, feelings of being used, shaken trust, and depression, to name just a few). Data strongly suggest that we should be concerned. The level of sexual activity among today's teenagers, although declining from its recent historic peak, is still nothing to celebrate: 55 percent of teens are no longer virgins by their eighteenth birthday, one in six have had four or more partners, and 8 percent had sex before they turned thirteen. The consequences can be severe: three million teenagers—about one in four of those sexually active—acquire a sexually transmitted disease *every year.*

Findings also show that more than one million adolescents become pregnant each year in the United States—about *three thousand girls a day*—and 78 percent of those pregnancies were unplanned. Teen pregnancy rates are much higher in the United States than in other developed countries—twice the level in England and Canada and *nine times as high* as in the Netherlands and Japan. Although recent data show a decrease in promiscuity, we still have a long way to go. One obstetrician told me that the majority of pregnant unwed girls she sees "never stopped to think that a baby might be the possible outcome of their promiscuity, and then they're shattered." In other words: *no moral reflection occurred.*

Too many recent news stories address tragic stories about scared young people who deliver babies in school bathrooms, motel rooms, or parking lots and then leave them there to die. A strong conscience would have helped them say no to their urges and guide them to reflect about possible consequences of their actions. Lacking that inner voice, they chose the easier path of quick sexual satisfaction, not realizing that they may well suffer from their choice the rest of their lives.

Rise in Substance Abuse

Current statistics tell us that the rate of substance abuse among our youth, although declining, is still quite high: using their consciences to "Just say no" is not on these kids' agenda. A recent nationwide survey revealed that nearly one in six high school students admitted that they had attended school drunk at least once during the past year. A national survey conducted in 1995 by the University of Michigan's Institute for Social Research found that 50 percent of all twelfth graders and 40 percent of tenth graders have used some illicit drug, including LSD, inhalants, stimulants, cocaine, crack, and barbiturates. Especially alarming is that the average age at which a child first uses marijuana is twelve. A study conducted in January 2000 revealed that eighth graders living in rural America are now 104 percent more likely to have used amphetamines, including methamphetamine, than those living in urban areas; 34 percent more likely to have smoked marijuana; and 83 percent more likely to have used cocaine. Michael Scacco, a gang prevention officer in Cathedral City, California, told me, "The fact that they are breaking the law by using drugs never seems to enter these kids' minds: they're shocked when we tell them the potential consequences."

The signs of moral decline are troubling; they point to a clear crisis of conscience among our youth. Our ignoring these signs would be perhaps the most immoral act, because the impact on our children's futures as well as on *their* children's futures could well be horrific. There are positive actions we can take to help our kids develop a strong conscience and an internal compass that tells them right from wrong: this chapter will show you what you can do. The real test of conscience is whether we will act before the damage to our children's moral development is irreparable. We don't have a minute to waste.

WHAT IS CONSCIENCE?

A strong conscience—that magnificent inner voice that helps us know right from wrong—is what lays the foundation for decent living, solid citizenship, and ethical behavior. It's what morality is all about; together with empathy and self-control, it's one of the three cornerstones of moral intelligence. And it's what every parent wants his child to possess. Helping our kids achieve this second essential virtue is critical. The question is, are we consciously teaching morality nearly enough to our kids?

The general public seems not to think so, considering these two recent polls: a 1995 *Newsweek* poll found that almost half of the American people believe that we have grown lax about enforcing moral standards; another national survey revealed that 93 percent of responding adults believe parents have failed to teach children honesty, respect, and responsibility. Those results are especially alarming because kids receive so many conflicting moral messages outside their family, often opposing their parents' standards. In 2000, the Nickelodeon channel and *Time* magazine conducted a survey of 991 kids ages nine to fourteen; it revealed that those pressures are greater than ever: 50 percent of the middle schoolers admitted knowing someone who smokes marijuana, and 36 percent feel pressure from their peers to smoke it. Nearly half know someone who has had sex; 40 percent feel pressure to do so. Thirty-seven percent of the kids surveyed say they feel pressure to steal something from a store. And four out of ten sixth graders say there is pressure from other students to drink. If we're not careful, our kids will be raised by these negative moral influences instead of by us.

The good news is that the path to morality starts right at home. Research says that parents *do* play a significant role in nurturing goodness in their kids, because morality is learned. "The conscience does not descend upon us from on high," explains Robert Coles of Harvard University. "We learn a convincing sense of right and wrong from parents who are themselves convinced as to what ought to be said and done and under what circumstances, as to what is intolerable, not at all permissible—parents who are ready to impart to their children through words and daily example what they hope to hand on to them." Without such parents, stresses Coles, "a conscience is not likely to grow up strong and certain."

This chapter shows you how to inspire this essential second virtue in your kids. You'll learn how to help them learn right from wrong, develop strong

MORAL INTELLIGENCE BUILDER
Signs of a Strong Conscience to Share with Kids

There are many ways people display strong moral actions, and the more aware that kids are of the kinds of things people with healthy consciences say and do, the more likely they are to incorporate them into their own behavior. Here are a few examples of conscience to discuss and role-play with your child:

What People with a Conscience Say	What People with a Conscience Do
"I know how to act right."	Act the way they know is right.
"You should put that back. It isn't yours."	Do not steal, cheat, or lie, because they know it's wrong.
"I only watch TV shows that my parents permit."	Obey their parents even when the parents are not watching.
"Let's do something else. This isn't right."	Are not swayed by others, and do what they know is right.
"You can count on me."	Can be trusted to do what they are told.
"I'm sorry. It was my fault."	Admit when they are wrong.
"You should tell the truth."	Obey the rules because it's the right thing to do.
"I do my own work, because copying is cheating."	

consciences to fortify them against forces countering goodness, and act right even in the face of temptation. Only then will they really be able to do what Jiminy Cricket advises Pinocchio: "Always let your conscience be your guide."

HOW STRONG IS YOUR CHILD'S CONSCIENCE?

The statements that follow describe behaviors usually displayed by children who have well-developed consciences. To evaluate your child's strengths in this second virtue, write the number you think best represents your child's current level on the line following each statement and then add all the scores to get his total score. If your child scores 40 to 50, he's in great shape with this aspect of moral intelligence. If he scores 30 to 40, he could benefit from virtue enhancement. A score of 20 to 30 shows signs of potential problems. A score of 10 to 20 reveals potential danger; consider getting help to increase this essential virtue.

5 = Always 4 = Frequently 3 = Sometimes 2 = Rarely 1 = Never

A Child with a Healthy Conscience	My Child
Admits mistakes and says he's sorry.	_____
Can identify his wrong behavior and describe why it was wrong.	_____
Is honest and can be counted on to keep his word.	_____
Rarely needs admonitions or reminders from authority figures as to how to act right.	_____
Recognizes the consequences of his improper behavior.	_____
When wrong, accepts blame and doesn't try to attribute the problem to others.	_____
Feels shame or guilt about his wrong or improper actions.	_____
Knows the right way to act and does it even when pressured by others not to.	_____
Tries to make amends if he causes physical or emotional injury.	_____
Knows how to turn a wrong action into a right one.	_____
Total Score	_____

THREE STEPS TO BUILDING A STRONG CONSCIENCE

The conscience is that powerful inner voice that helps keep our kids on the moral path of doing right and zaps them with a dose of guilt whenever they stray. Because you are your child's primary moral teacher, there's much you can do to build goodness in your child and influence her moral development.

There are three main steps to nurturing a strong conscience in your child. When it comes to bringing up moral kids, research tells us that some parenting practices and conditions are clearly more effective than others. The first step shows you how to create the context for developing a strong conscience in your child, which may well be one of your most important parenting tasks. You'll learn six of the best parenting practices to enhance your child's moral growth from a young age. Once you lay the groundwork for helping your child know right from wrong, the second step is to instill strong virtues that will guide her to make right choices and behave morally. These virtues will serve as the moral compass that she'll need in every stage of her moral growth. The third step shows you how to use the most effective kind of discipline that not only helps your child learn right from wrong but also expands her moral reasoning to higher levels. These three steps help your child develop the second essential virtue of moral intelligence—a strong conscience—to help her behave morally and live ethically.

Here again are the three teachable steps you can use to build your child's conscience and to boost her moral intelligence:

Step 1: Create the Context for Moral Growth
Step 2: Teach Virtues to Strengthen the Conscience and Guide Behavior
Step 3: Use Moral Discipline to Help Your Child Learn Right from Wrong

STEP 1: CREATE THE CONTEXT FOR MORAL GROWTH

Every parent's first concern is the same: "Is my baby healthy?" This question is one that doctors usually can answer. Another big question is far more difficult: "Will my child become a good and decent human being?" Most doctors would have to admit that they just don't know, and parents are often left wondering if they really do make any difference in how their kids turn out. Lately child development experts have asked the same question, and a barrage of research on children's moral development has resulted.

The findings are conclusive: the parent's style as a moral instructor does play a significant part in whether his kids lead ethical lives, and certain parenting practices clearly are better than others in guiding children's conscience development. This first step shows you the most effective parenting behaviors for enhancing moral growth.

Six Parenting Practices That Promote Development of a Strong Conscience

Why do some kids turn out good and moral, while others stray from the ethical path? Research says there are some parenting practices that clearly *do* make a difference in helping kids learn right from wrong. Here are the six parenting practices that are significant in raising kids with strong, healthy consciences.

1. Be a strong moral example. You are your child's first and most important moral teacher. By watching your choices and reactions and hearing your casual comments, your kids learn moral standards. So what you do in those little ordinary moments of life may be powerful moral lessons. How you treat your family, friends, neighbors, and strangers; what movies you watch and the kinds of books and television shows you choose; how you react to everyday moral conflicts: your child cheating, his friend lying, the neighbor littering—all are decisions and characteristics kids watch closely. Robert Coles explains: "It's those everyday, minute-by-minute cues that the little ones pick up on." So make sure the behaviors your kids are picking up on are ones that you want your kids to copy. One of the greatest questions to ask yourself at the end of each day is, If I were the only example my child has from whom to learn right from wrong, what would she have learned today?

2. Develop a close, mutually respectful relationship. Studies find that kids are most influenced by those persons toward whom they feel the strongest attachment and deepest respect. They are more likely to copy these individuals' moral beliefs. One of the surest ways to nurture your child's morality is by developing a close, loving relationship with him. Experts say that the key is to make sure the relationship is mutually respectful: you treat your child with love and respect, and he treats you the same way in return. Of course, building that kind of relationship clearly takes one-to-one personal, uninterrupted time, but doing so is the best way to ensure that your child's primary moral instructor is you.

3. Share your moral beliefs. Speaking frequently to your child about values and beliefs is called direct moral teaching, and studies find that parents who raise ethical kids do it a lot. Look for moral issues and talk about them as they come up. Use every source you can, from TV shows and news events to situations at school, at home, and with friends; tell your kids how you feel about these issues and why. Judy Baggott, a mom who lives in Palm Springs and has three teenagers, found that one of the best sources for her moral discussions were columns from "Dear Abby." She would look for letters addressing such issues as cheating, shoplifting, teenage drinking, and sexual promiscuity and save them for relaxed family times to share her beliefs and hear her children's moral reasoning. For example, she might say, "This is what I would have said and why," or "If you were Abby, what would you have said? Do you think the writer's actions were right or wrong?"

4. Expect and demand moral behaviors. Experts find that parents who raise moral kids expect their kids to act morally—and even demand that they do. Chances are that the kids will, simply because their parents require that they do. Dr. Marvin Berkowitz, chairman of the Center for Character Development, emphasizes that the best moral expectations are those that are high yet reachable and that are clearly communicated to kids. Once those expectations are set, parents must stick to them *and not back down*. Here are a few examples of moral expectations that other families count on all members to follow:

Honesty:	"Everyone in our family is always expected to be honest with one another."
Kindness:	"In this home, we will always treat one another kindly and act just as we would like to be treated by others."
Peacefulness:	"In this family, we talk calmly to one another and listen respectfully. We try to solve our conflicts peacefully and honestly."
Respect:	"We talk to one another respectfully with words that build each other up and don't put each other down. We also honor and respect each other's privacy and property."
Responsibility:	"Each of us shares a responsibility to make our home run smoothly. We all agree to do our chores to the best of our ability, and we finish our work before we play."
Effort:	"Everyone is expected to always do his or her personal best."
Perseverance:	"In this family, we don't give up."

5. Use moral reasoning and questioning. Thomas Lickona believes that questioning is an important parenting tool for enhancing children's consciences. He says that the right kind of questions can help kids expand their ability to take another person's perspective and understand the consequences of their behavior, gradually teaching children to ask themselves, "Is this the right thing to do?" and "What will happen if I do this?" Here are a few questions a parent can ask that enhance her child's moral reasoning:

"Why do you think I'm concerned?"
"How would you feel if someone treated you that way?"
"If everybody in the class always cheated, what would happen?"
"If you don't follow through on your word, what do you think will happen to my trust in you?"

6. Explain your parenting behavior. I vividly remember overhearing one mother tell another about the "baffling" behavior of one of her eleven-year-old daughter's guests at her slumber party. Apparently the girls had decided to watch a video, and the mom was quite surprised when her daughter's friend joined her in the kitchen instead of watching the movie with the rest of the group. When she asked the child why she wasn't with the other girls, she told her they were watching a PG-13 movie that she wasn't allowed to watch. Then she explained quite matter-of-factly that her parents didn't feel the content was suitable. What amazed me most was both mothers' shock over the girl's response and how neither could imagine their daughter doing the same thing.

The girl's response probably would not come as a surprise to most experts, though. Studies find that because the parents clearly explained the reasons for the rule, their daughter understood their view and abided by their standards. Many researchers contend that parents often don't "plainly explain" the reasoning behind their standards strongly enough, so their children's commitment to them is often weak. Kids need to know not only that we want them to do the right thing but also *why* we want them to act that way. Clearly describing why you set a standard helps enhance your children's moral growth.

Are You Walking Your (Moral) Talk?

Experts tell us that what we do may be far more powerful moral lessons than what we say. To convey that point at a workshop in Indianapolis, I asked the parents to brainstorm kinds of adult behaviors that might send confusing moral lessons to kids. And the list they generated shocked many into admitting they might be far more guilty than they ever realized. One parent expressed the feelings of many that night: "I just never stopped to think how my behavior affects my child's moral growth. I guess I better make sure my own behavior is intact before I go accusing anybody else of immoral conduct." Here are a few behaviors that more than a fair share of

A Story to Tell Kids About Conscience

Sometimes it takes courage to do what you know is right, and that's just what ten-year-old Juan Cordova did. Things weren't always easy at Juan's school. It's in a tough neighborhood where the crime rate is high, and gangs are everywhere. Juan saw how often the gang members would threaten, harass, and even hurt the other students. Most of his classmates were afraid of the gangs, but they were even more afraid to tell the teachers about their threats. That wasn't so surprising: even the adults in the neighborhood feared reporting the gang members' activities, because the delinquents always managed to get back at anyone who turned them in.

Juan knew that what they were doing was not right and that they shouldn't be allowed to get away with their actions. So the fifth grader decided that if no one else would report them, he would tell the police, even though the gang threatened to beat him up if he told. Because Juan followed his conscience, other members of the community decided to support him and try to get the hoodlums off the streets and put in jail. In the end, many of the gang members were convicted of robbery and other crimes, all because of Juan Cordova, a ten-year-old who followed his conscience, even though it was a difficult choice. Juan made a difference.

It isn't always easy to make the right choices. Can you think of a time when doing the right thing was hard for you? Your conscience is the voice inside your head that reminds you to do the right thing. Why do you think some people, like Juan Cordova, have such strong consciences? Do you think there's anything kids can do to build stronger consciences, so that they make good decisions?

the parents that night admitted to doing occasionally. As you read them, you might want to reflect on your own actions. How well are you walking the moral talk for your kids?

- Your boss phones, and you tell your child to say you're not there.
- Your child misses school because she oversleeps, and you write a note excusing her tardiness by claiming she was ill.

- You drive faster than the speed limit with your child as a passenger.
- You eat a small "sample" from the grocery store's candy bin without paying.
- You watch a movie and then sneak into another theater to see a second movie without paying.
- You do the majority of your child's work on a school project but had him sign his name.
- You take a small "souvenir" from a restaurant or hotel (an ashtray, soap dish, small towel, or the like) that was not meant to be taken.
- You buy a ticket for a "child under twelve" even though your child is older.

Think of the incidents in your day-to-day life that might be sending mixed moral lessons about honesty and integrity to your kids. Be careful: kids watch us much more than we sometimes realize, and what they see is often not what we want them to see. A quick way to check whether you are walking your talk with your kids is to ask yourself, How would my child describe my moral behavior to someone else? Is it how I would like to be described?

STEP 2: TEACH VIRTUES TO STRENGTHEN THE CONSCIENCE AND GUIDE BEHAVIOR

Last fall I was observing a school in Rochester, New York, that had recently implemented a character education program. I was hired to evaluate their efforts. As I walked the corridors, it was obvious that conscience was the character trait being targeted that month. Posters, banners, signs, and quotations about conscience, honesty, and integrity hung on the halls, in the office, on outside walls, and in the cafeteria. I was impressed with the staff's efforts to accentuate the trait to their students.

I walked into a fifth-grade room and saw that conscience was also being reinforced inside classrooms: the teacher had covered her bulletin boards with posters reminding kids, "Be honest. Follow your conscience and act right." The students were busily studying in teams for a science test they were to have the next day, and I stayed to watch. One group quickly caught my eye: two of the team members were noticeably upset, so I asked if they needed some help.

"We're supposed to try filling out the answers together without looking," one boy whispered, "but Teisha keeps copying them from the book." He explained, "We're going to be tested tomorrow as a team; if she doesn't learn them, we're going to get a bad grade."

There sat Teisha, busily copying answers from her science book onto a small sheet of paper while glancing at the teacher to make sure she wasn't watching. I figured this was a great time for a "teachable moment" to discuss the virtue of conscience.

"Sounds like you have a big test tomorrow, Teisha. Wouldn't now be a good time to study so that your team can get a better grade tomorrow?"

Her answer wasn't quite what I expected. She looked to make sure the teacher couldn't hear, then quietly said, "It's no big deal. I'll just copy the answers from this paper like I always do. I don't know what he's so worried about—we'll get a good grade."

"That would be cheating," I answered. "Can you think of a way to learn the answers honestly?" But the reaction from one team member wasn't quite what I expected: he laughed! "What's funny?" I asked.

"It's just that everybody's always talking about that word," he explained as he pointed to a few signs in the room about honesty. "But most of the kids in here cheat. I don't know what the big deal is; they want us to get good grades." Two of the other members nodded in agreement while Teisha continued copying the words on her "cheat sheet."

Here was a school that had spent hours designing posters about a critical moral virtue, but it had overlooked the most important step: teaching kids to believe in the value of the virtue. And without that conviction as to the importance of honesty and a strong conscience, the students would never adopt the virtue in their own lives. It's a mistake in the teaching of morality that I fear teachers and parents make far too frequently.

Of course we want our kids to do what's right and act in virtuous ways, but have we really taken time to teach them what morality is and why it is important? Often we may *assume* that our kids know the meaning and value of some of the most essential virtues of moral growth and a strong conscience—truth, fairness, honesty, integrity—but our misjudgments can be costly. Our children's understanding and belief in the virtues is what helps them adopt a code of ethical behaviors. Most important, virtues are what help guide our children's consciences and give them solid knowledge of the good and right way to behave. So if our instructions about virtues haven't been clear enough or we haven't taught those virtues well enough, our kids can be left vulnerable to immoral temptations from within and without and may make bad choices. This second step shows you how to teach the virtues of moral intelligence so that your child will not only know right from wrong but also develop a strong belief in the virtues so that she will *consciously choose* to act right.

Six Ways to Teach Virtues That Promote the Development of a Strong Conscience

There is one question I always like to ask parents at my workshops: "What kind of person do you want your child to become?" On the top of most parents' lists are clearly significant characteristics: respectful, kind, responsible, fair, just, peaceful, honest, and persevering. Then I ask one more question: "When was the last time you talked about that virtue with your child and told him or her how strongly you believe in it or acknowledged your child for practicing the virtue?" The reaction to this question is almost always one of silence, which says so much.

Parents often shortchange one of the most critical ways to raise moral kids: deliberately teaching the virtues of ethical living. In fact, our children's whole character is defined by which virtues they determine are important to their life. It is those same virtues that will help guide their conscience and their moral choices. So it is critical that we commit to teaching our kids the virtues we want them to acquire most, and there are dozens children need if they are to live good lives. No matter what virtue you choose, there are six ways to teach it:

1. Identify the virtues you want most to develop in your child. The first step is to choose the specific virtues you want your child to acquire most. The clearer you are in knowing what traits you deem most significant, the greater the likelihood that your child will learn them, simply because you will be more committed to teaching them. To help you in your selection, refer to "Virtues That Enhance Strong Moral Intelligence," the Moral Intelligence Builder that appears later in this section; choose the four to eight virtues you feel are most important. Or you can work on the seven virtues described in each chapter of this book. Finally, number your choices in the order you want to teach them; write them in your calendar or daily planner. Doing so will remind you to include addressing them in your daily family life just as you would your other plans.

2. Accentuate a virtue each month. Research says it takes at least three weeks to learn a new behavior or skill, and the same premise applies to cementing good virtues. I suggest you select a virtue each month and commit a few minutes each day to helping your child learn it. Then write the virtue in huge letters across the top of a monthly calendar to remind all family members of your selection. You might also help your child make a poster describing the virtue of the month. For example: "Conscience: It means knowing the right and decent way to act and doing it." "Honesty: It means having the inner strength to be truthful to yourself and others." "Responsibility: It means I'm doing what is right to myself and others and that I can be counted on." I know a family who makes a cloth banner about the virtue of the month using colored markers and felt letters, and hangs the banner in the kitchen. Lansing School District puts the name of the virtue on its screen saver; when someone uses a computer, the first thing he sees is the screen saver message accentuating the virtue: "It's perseverance month. Remember to work your hardest and not give up!"

3. Describe the value and meaning of the virtue. The third way to teach a virtue is to help your child know exactly what the virtue means and why it is important to learn. The trick is to be sure to explain the virtue in a way that is in keeping with your child's level of understanding and *never to assume he understands your meaning.* Here are three ways teachers and parents describe the meaning of virtues:

- *Hold virtue talks.* Deliberately set aside time to talk with your child about the chosen virtue. Many families hold special family meetings to introduce the virtue of the month, describe why it's important, and even show a family video addressing the trait (*Pinocchio* for conscience, *Rudy* for perseverance, *The Diary of Anne Frank* for courage, *Charlotte's Web* for caring). Some schools introduce a moral virtue each month at a schoolwide assembly, where the teachers describe its value and sometimes even present a short skit about it.

- *Hold family read-alouds.* Choose a children's literature selection that embodies the virtue—such as *On My Honor* for honesty, *The Rainbow Fish* for fairness, *The Velveteen Rabbit* for love, or *Molly's Pilgrim* for tolerance—and use it as a springboard for describing why the virtue is so valuable. As you read, ask your child, "How did the characters display the virtue? How did the other characters feel when the character acted honestly [fairly, generously, and so on]?"

- *Find articles featuring the virtue.* Make it a point to look through the newspaper or watch the nightly news deliberately searching for examples of real people demonstrating the virtue. Some families cut out news articles and share them during dinner. Crestview Elementary in Minneapolis has students collect current news articles about the virtue and pin them to a bulletin board.

4. Teach what the virtue looks and sounds like. There is no perfect way to teach a virtue, but research says that telling children about the trait is never as powerful as showing them what it looks like. One of the easiest ways to demonstrate a virtue is by using your own behavior as a living example. The important point is to make sure the child knows exact ways she can display the virtue. Here are a few ideas that teach kids what a virtue looks and sounds like:

- *List the virtue's characteristics.* Help your child create a list describing the kinds of things people do to display the virtue. Here are a few behaviors for truthfulness: giving back extra change, keeping a promise, telling the truth, admitting a mistake, and not copying someone's work. Younger kids can make a collage showing examples of the virtue using magazine pictures and drawings.

- *Teach the words of the virtue.* Help your child tune in to the language of individuals who actively practice the virtue so that he can learn to use the terms in his life. If you are targeting conscience, for example, you might ask, "What are the kinds of things you hear people who have a strong conscience say?" Write a list of phrases, such as, "I know how to act right," "You should tell the truth," "I'm sorry," "It was my fault," and "You should put that back. It isn't yours." If you are targeting perseverance, your list might read, "I can do it!" "I'll try again," "I won't give up!" and "I do the best I can." Make the word list into a poster to hang up; encourage family members to say at least one phrase a day.

- *Role-play the virtue.* Some teachers find it helpful to use another student or colleague to role-play what the virtue looks like. To show your child the virtue of conscience, you might play-act such behaviors as putting things back that don't belong to you, coming home at the agreed-on curfew time, doing work without copying, or admitting when you are wrong. To show your child the virtue of caring, you might play-act such behaviors as patting someone on the back, putting your arm around a person and looking concerned, offering a tissue to wipe away tears, or saying "I'm sorry," "Can I help?" or "What do you need?"

5. Reinforce the virtue in daily life. The best teaching moments aren't ones that are planned—they happen unexpectedly. Look for those moments and use them to reinforce the virtue. Use everything from family squabbles ("Don't forget, this month we're really working on following our conscience and doing what we know is the right thing to do"; "Remember, we're trying to be more peaceful this month. How can you say what's bugging you without making your sister mad?") to trips to the mall ("Let's be on the lookout for people who do kind things for others") to car pooling ("Wasn't that driver considerate to let us into the lane?"). Most important, reinforce the virtue in your own child's behavior: "That was being honest. I know it's hard to admit mistakes, but you did. I'm proud of you." "That was being peaceful. You used your words and not your fists." Your goal is to help your child see why it is important to incorporate the virtue into her life.

6. Find opportunities for your child to practice the virtue. We can spend hours talking to kids about the virtue, but unless they practice using the virtue, it rarely becomes a learned behavior. So the critical last step is to find ways for your child to incorporate the trait in her daily living. Some families take a few minutes each night at the dinner table to share how they experienced the virtue during their day. You might start a session about kindness by asking, "What kind things did you do for someone today?" or "Did someone do a kind deed for you today?" "How do you think it made that person feel?" Teachers often ask students to keep an ongoing log of their virtue progress by writing each day what one thing they did that day to demonstrate the trait. You can have your child record her virtue efforts and results in a notebook. Younger children might use a large monthly calendar to mark a happy face on the dates they practiced the behavior.

MORAL INTELLIGENCE BUILDER

Virtues That Enhance Moral Intelligence

altruism
assertiveness
calmness
caring
charitableness
chastity
citizenship
compassion
compatibility
consideration
cooperation
courage
courtesy
dependability
determination
discipline
empathy
excellence
fairness
faithfulness
fidelity
flexibility
forgivingness
friendliness
frugality
generosity

gentleness
genuineness
graciousness
gratitude
helpfulness
honesty
honor
humility
idealism
industriousness
initiative
insightfulness
integrity
joyfulness
justness
kindness
love
loyalty
mercy
moderation
modesty
obedience
optimism
patience
peacefulness
perseverance

politeness
prudence
purposefulness
reliability
resourcefulness
respect
responsibility
reverence
self-control
self-discipline
self-motivation
sensitivity
serenity
simplicity
sincerity
steadfastness
tactfulness
temperance
tenacity
thankfulness
tolerance
trustworthiness
truthfulness
understanding
unselfishness

Building Moral Intelligence

Three Fun Ways to Cultivate Children's Virtue Development

"Samantha is so wonderful!" her mom began telling me. "She's kind and reliable and fair. The problem is, she doesn't see herself as a good person. She has a very short attention span and has a difficult time concentrating, so she's reminded a lot in school to 'get busy.' All those reminders, though, are really getting in the way of what I think matters most: that she knows she's a compassionate kid with a good conscience. How do I help her recognize her assets?"

One of the greatest gifts you can instill in any child is a deep-seated belief that says, "I am a good and moral person." Here's are three ideas I shared with Samantha's mom to help enhance her daughter's self-beliefs and see the good qualities about herself. All are fun and easy to do, and they help your child recognize his virtuous traits.

1. Make a virtue mobile. Construct a mobile from an old clothes hanger and yarn. Your child can draw pictures of his deserved virtuous characteristics—honest, considerate, kind, fair—on paper shapes at least six inches in size. Then cut them out and attach them from the hanger with yarn lengths. One mom told me she cut out cloud shapes from white cardboard and helped her daughter glue magazine pictures and words that described her strongest virtuous traits—such as caring, patient, positive, and courteous—to each shape. They even glued a few pieces of cotton along the edges to give it a real "cloudy" feel. She hung the finished mobile over her child's bed so that every morning and night she would be reminded of her virtues.

2. Create a virtue scrapbook. Caran told me that her six-year-old foster son, Tyler, seemed to always be in trouble and was developing a low opinion of himself. Every time she praised a "good" behavior, he would discount it and call himself a "bad boy." Caran decided that if he wouldn't "hear" his good qualities, she would *show* them to him. Using a small photo album, photographs, magazine cutouts, and marking pens, she created a virtue scrapbook of Tyler's "goodnesses": his kindness toward animals, loyalty to his family, determination in soccer, assertiveness in saying his point of view, and prayerfulness in church. She presented the scrapbook to him and told him of all his virtuous qualities as she pointed to the pictures in the book. Caran told me that the boy kept it under his pillow for weeks, and whenever he had a hard day he plopped himself on the bed and "read" his book about the "Good Tyler."

3. Develop a virtue self-portrait. This activity helps your child recognize her ongoing moral growth. Start by drawing an outline of your child on butcher paper; hang it up. Over the next weeks, gradually begin to fill in the outline with pictures—from newspapers, magazines, photographs, drawings, or computer-generated graphics—that depict your child's newly acquired virtues. Here are some examples: a photograph showing

---

MORAL INTELLIGENCE BUILDER
How to Effectively Reinforce Your Child's Conscience and Virtuous Behavior

One of the most effective ways to enhance your child's conscience and virtuous behavior is to reinforce it whenever your child displays it. Just *name the virtue*, then *specifically describe exactly what he did right*. That way your child will be more likely to repeat the behavior. Here are a few examples of how to reinforce a child's moral growth and virtuous behaviors:

Honesty: "I know it took courage to tell Grandpa that you broke his pipe. That was being very honest, and I admire you for it."

Responsibility: "I noticed how you set your alarm so you could wake up earlier and study more for your test before the bus came. That was being very responsible."

Trustworthiness: "You had several chores, and you finished them before you went out to play. That means you're trustworthy—I can count on you to do what you say you will do."

---

her studying to represent her responsibility, a drawing showing her arm around someone to depict kindness, cutout letters of the words *peaceful*, *self-disciplined*, and *respectful* to represent those virtues. Hang it up so your child sees a cumulative portrait of her moral self. Continue to add images to the portrait as new virtues develop in your child.

STEP 3: USE MORAL DISCIPLINE TO HELP YOUR CHILD LEARN RIGHT FROM WRONG

We all want our kids to act right and make good moral choices, but obviously no child behaves perfectly. In fact, a big part of childhood is learning how to turn wrongs around and make them right. Researchers tell us that how we react to our children's unethical behaviors can be a critical determinant of whether they learn from their mistakes and expand in their moral understanding. A. Lynn Scoresby, author of *Bringing Up Moral Children in an Immoral World,* tells us a key reason why we need to respond correctly: "Moral decision making is learned and therefore it is up to us to teach our children to do it well." This last step helps you use the best kind of discipline for helping kids learn right from wrong and develop solid moral reasoning so that they do make good moral choices and develop strong consciences.

The "Four R's" of Moral Discipline

"I don't know what to do," Kevin's father told me. "I found a pocket video game in my eight-year-old son's closet floor, and I know it doesn't belong to him. I'm almost positive he stole it from the grocery store. He has everything he wants. Why would he do such a thing, and how do I handle it?"

Studies find that how parents react to their child's misbehavior can be destructive or productive in helping her learn right from wrong. The responsibility of responding appropriately makes a parent's job especially tricky. Here are the four *R*'s of moral discipline that I suggested to Kevin's father to help his son learn from his stealing episode. You can use these same practices with almost *any* misbehavior to help your child recognize not only why her behavior was wrong but also the consequences of her actions. Only then will she be more likely to choose the right way to act the next time. To help you recall the four easy moral discipline steps, remember that each starts with *R:*

First R—Respond calmly and assess the child's intention
Second R—Review why the behavior is wrong
Third R—Reflect on the behavior's effects
Fourth R—Right the wrong by encouraging the child to make a *reparation*

Respond Calmly and Assess the Child's Intention   The first step in confronting your child about any moral misbehavior is often the hardest: *stay calm and listen.* Try to determine not only what happened but also why she did what she did. To make sure you aren't missing anything, you'll need to gather all the facts. For example: Did she steal because she is under peer pressure and can't stand up for herself because she craves friends, is jealous, feels deprived, or is seeking attention? If the atmosphere is too tense, just call a time-out: "I want to hear what happened, but let's talk about it in half an hour," or "I'll listen only when you can use a calm voice."

Here are a few springboards to help you on your fact-finding mission: "Tell me what happened," "Why did you do it?" "What made you do it?" or "How did you think this would turn out?"

Dad: Kevin, I was picking up dirty clothes for the laundry and happened to find this video game on your closet floor. I don't think it's yours. Want to tell me how it got there?

Kevin: I took it from the grocery store. I don't think the man saw me, though.

Dad: But why did you take it, son?

Kevin: I don't know. I guess I just always wanted one.

Review Why the Behavior Is Wrong   This step is critical: you want to make sure your child clearly understands the reason what she did was wrong so that it becomes a moral lesson. Studies find that some parents skip this review stage and jump into what Dr. Martin Hoffman, a renowned authority on teaching morality, calls *power assertion:* giving the lecture about the misdeed, or the punishment. Sure we're angry, concerned, or sometimes even mystified at our kids' misbehavior, but if we lecture or punish without reviewing *why* the behavior was wrong, children may not clearly recognize the connection. Instead of fostering a stronger knowledge of right and wrong, we convey only our disapproval and the potential of punishment. So take a few minutes to discuss just what was so wrong about your child's behavior.

Start by just asking, "Was what you did right or wrong?" Try withholding your views at first so that he can freely express his opinions. Later you can calmly and clearly let your child know what you stand for and why. Here's the conversation Kevin had with his dad:

Dad: Do you think stealing is right or wrong, Kevin?

Kevin: It's wrong, Dad.

Dad: Why do you think you shouldn't take something from a store or anywhere else?

Kevin: Well, you might get caught.

Dad: That's one reason. Can you think of other reasons why a kid shouldn't steal?

Kevin: I guess I could get in big trouble with the police.

Dad: Any other reasons?

Kevin: Well, I knew you'd be pretty mad.

Dad: Why do you think I'd be upset?

Kevin: Because I'm taking something that isn't mine.

Dad: That's right, Kevin. It didn't belong to you, and you took it, and that's not right.

Studies say that conscience is learned in stages; therefore, taking time to hear to your child's explanations will give you a better understanding of her moral reasoning. For instance, Kevin's main motive for not stealing seems to be to avoid punishment; this attitude reflects that he is in the early moral stages, thinking of right and wrong in terms of either reward and punishment or what will bring him pleasure. His dad's goal is to stretch his son to a higher moral stage so that Kevin understands the full impact of his behavior, including the victim's feelings. This is your objective as well; just realize that moral growth takes place very slowly, so don't look for dramatic changes in your child overnight. Lawrence Kohlberg, a former Harvard University professor, found through extensive research that you can usually challenge a child to think only one step above her present level of reasoning. Keep this in mind and try to gear your discussions slightly above the stage your child is in.

Reflect on the Behavior's Effects Nancy Eisenberg, author of *The Caring Child,* says that one of the best moral-building practices is to point out the impact of the child's behavior on the other person ("See, you made her cry") or highlight the victim's feelings ("Now he feels bad"). Doing so enhances a child's moral growth as well as his prosocial behaviors and can be effective even with very young children. The trick is to help your child really imagine what it would be like to be in the victim's place. In his book *Raising Good Children,* Dr. Thomas Lickona suggests play-acting with very young kids how stealing might feel, using one of your child's favorite toys. After "stealing" the toy, ask your child, "How would you feel if somebody really stole that toy from you? Would it be fair? Why not?" With an older child, you could ask, "Would you want somebody to steal from you?" or "Pretend you are your friend, and you just found out somebody took his toy. How would you feel? Why? What would you want to say to the person who took the toy?" Here's what Kevin's dad said:

Dad: OK, Kevin, now let's think about the man who owns the grocery store. How do you think he feels about his property being taken?

Kevin: I guess he'd be kind of upset.

Dad: But why, Kevin?

Kevin: Because people are taking things from his store.

Dad: Sure, but who do you think has to pay for the missing groceries?

MORAL INTELLIGENCE BUILDER
The Stages of Moral Development

Lawrence Kohlberg says that reasoning about right and wrong develops in a series of stages. The more you understand your child's current moral level, the better you will be at stretching him to the next stage. Remember, you can never be sure of a child's moral level just from his chronological age; kids can fluctuate enormously depending on their experiences and abilities.

**Stage 0: Egocentric reasoning
("I should get my own way")**   **Preschool years to around age 4**
The child is very self-centered and often tries getting her way without considering the feelings or thoughts of others. *"Mommy, get off the phone. I need my dinner now!"*

**Stage 1: Avoidance of punishment
("Will I get in trouble?")**   **Preschool to kindergarten**

The child thinks of morality in terms of either reward and punishment or what will bring him pleasure, regardless of consequences. *"I'm not teasing Jena so I won't have to stay after school."*

Stage 2: "What's in it for me?" orientation   **Early elementary grades**

The child behaves morally when doing so meets the child's needs and occasionally the needs of others, and only then if there is an exchange of favors. *"I'll let you use my bike if I can use your scooter."*

Stage 3: Good boy–nice girl orientation   **Middle-to-upper elementary grades to early teens**

Good behavior is that which makes others happy and is also approved of by them. *"I'm going to be really nice to Joshua because it makes Mom happy. Then maybe she'll rent me a movie."*

Stage 4: Law-and-order orientation   **High school years, late teens**
Right behavior is doing one's duty, showing respect for authority, and following the rules to keep intact the system that the child feels a part of. *"I must follow the rules and do my work so I can graduate."*

Kevin:　　I don't know . . . the man?

Dad:　　Yep. How would you feel if you had to pay for things someone else took from you?

Kevin:　　I'd be really mad.

Dad:　　Would you feel it was fair if you had to use your own salary to pay for it?

Kevin:　　No, it's not fair.

Right the Wrong by Encouraging the Child to Make a Reparation　　The final step is to ensure that the child not only recognizes why her behavior was wrong but also, most important, *knows what to do to make it right.* That's really the whole purpose of moral discipline. With a very young child, a first-time offender, or issues that don't cause the victim distress, just reasoning with the child may be enough. For some children, setting a mild consequence may be called for to help ensure that they take your moral standards seriously. Especially when the behavior caused hurt, I would strongly suggest encouraging your child to make a reparation. Doing so helps the child recognize the consequences of her behavior and understand that she is responsible. Relevant consequences should always fit the crime and be clearly spelled out. A few examples are in the Moral Intelligence Builder that follows. Here is what Kevin's dad had his son do:

Dad: I think you know that what you did was wrong, Kevin. So let's think of what you can do to make things right. What could you do?

Kevin: I could say I was sorry.

Dad: That's one idea. Can you think of another?

Kevin: Maybe I could leave the money for the game on his counter.

Dad: I don't think it's fair to keep the game even if you pay for it. You stole the game, Kevin, and that's not right. What else can you do?

Kevin: I guess I could bring it back and say I was sorry.

Dad: That will take courage, Kevin. But that's the right thing to do. Let's talk about how you will do it and when you will take the game back.

WHAT TO DO ABOUT THE CRISIS OF CONSCIENCE

- You are your child's first and most powerful moral teacher, so make sure the moral behaviors your kids are picking up from you are ones that you want your child to copy.

- If you want your child to act morally, then expect and demand moral behaviors from her.

- Look for moral issues to talk about as they come up; your child can hear your moral beliefs, and you can assess your child's moral reasoning and stretch him to the next level.

- Take an active stand against influences toxic to your child's moral development, such as certain television shows, movies, music, video games, and Internet websites. Plainly explain your concerns to your child, set standards, and then stick to them.

MORAL INTELLIGENCE BUILDER
Reparations That Help Kids Turn Moral Wrongs into Rights

Children need to recognize that their actions can cause other people distress and that although they can't take away the hurt or undo what they did wrong, they can at least let their victims know they are sorry. So here are a few moral discipline ideas that help kids make amends for their wrong actions.

- Have the child take a cool-off time to think about what she did. Tell her when she returns that she is to explain what she could do to make her actions right: "I broke Grandpa's pipe. I could tell him I am sorry and try to buy him a new one."
- With an older child, ask her to write a letter describing what she did wrong, why it was wrong, and then how she plans to make it right: "Dear Mom, I was wrong to copy the answers from my friend's test. I will tell the teacher what I did and next time study." A younger child could draw a picture showing how he will make the person feel better.
- The child could write a note, draw a picture, call, or go to the victim to apologize: "I will go to Mr. James's house and tell him I was sorry I broke his window and that I will pay for it."
- Ask the child to name a few things he could have done instead of the misbehavior. Then have him choose one of the alternatives and go practice doing it for five minutes: "I shouldn't kick the dog when I'm mad. I could have walked away, hit my punching bag, screamed in my pillow, or shot some hoops. Next time I'll try to walk away."
- The child could bring back what was taken, redo what was done under deception, replace or repair what was broken: "I'll bring the candy back to the store and tell the manager I'm sorry."

- Use questions to expand your child's ability to take another person's perspective: "How would you feel if someone treated you that way?" "How do you think he feels because of what you did?"
- Catch your child acting morally and acknowledge her good behavior by describing what she did right and why you appreciate it.

Self-Control

**Regulating your thoughts and
actions so that you stop any
pressures from within or without and
act the way you know and feel is right**

In Richmond, California, a six-year-old boy looked longingly at his neighbor's tricycle, and then no longer could control his urge. He sneaked into the neighbor's house, apparently to steal the bike, then heard an infant crying. A litany of thoughts probably rushed through the youngster's head: "Why is he crying? Someone will hear, and I'll get caught," and "I'd like to shut that kid up." Then, perhaps imagining the only way he knew how to make the baby stop crying, the first grader acted on his second impulse: he pulled one-month old Ignacio Bermudez Jr. from his bassinet, picked up a stick, and beat the infant so savagely that it caused severe brain damage; in doing so he became the nation's youngest child charged with attempted murder.

On May 2000, in Lake Worth, Florida, thirteen-year-old Nathaniel Brazill was suspended from his middle school for throwing water balloons in the hallway on the last day of class. Sent home, Brazill, an honor student with a perfect attendance record, told a student he was thinking of bringing a gun back to school to shoot the counselor who had suspended him. His fantasy of revenge became horribly real. The boy returned to school two hours later with a gun believed stolen from his grandfather's house, but instead of walking to the counselor's office, he ended up in another teacher's classroom. When the seventh-grade English teacher asked him to leave, he impulsively pulled the semiautomatic pistol from his pocket, fired a single shot at the teacher's head, and killed him. Brazill was later indicted for murder for brutally—and apparently spontaneously—killing a teacher who had probably not even been a part of his vindictive imaginings.

Whether we want to admit it or not, we've all had sinister thoughts: "I could just kill him!" "If she does that again, I'll strangle her!" Luckily, the vast majority of us don't carry out our fantasies, and that's because a inner mechanism called *self-control* intercedes and stops us from turning those impulses into realities. Self-control is an essential virtue for moral behavior, but having it is far from guaranteed: it must be developed, inspired, and encouraged. Poorly developed self-control puts kids at a huge moral disadvantage: when harmful ideas or thoughts pop into their heads, their internal brake system is nonexistent, and instead of stopping, they barrel full speed ahead and straight into trouble. And this seems to be happening to an alarming number of kids these days.

Certainly no one variable predisposes a child to violent or immoral actions, but poorly developed self-control certainly increases the likelihood. In this day and age, considering the myriad tempting and sometimes dangerous choices that confront our kids, building this third virtue not only will improve their moral intelligence quotient but also could save their lives.

THE CRISIS OF POOR SELF-CONTROL

Self-control is what helps kids regulate their behaviors so that they are more likely to do what they know in their minds and hearts is correct. Self-control gives our kids the willpower to say no, do what's right, and choose to act morally. It's a powerful internal mechanism that guides their moral conduct so that their choices are not only safer but also wiser. That's because self-control is the moral muscle that temporarily stops potentially hurtful actions. It does so by giving kids those critical extra seconds they need in order to recognize the possible consequences of their actions and then put on the brakes, so that they don't proceed with acting on their harmful thoughts. Clearly, self-control is an essential virtue for helping kids act morally—and it's especially important for kids growing up in a sometimes violent, unpredictable world.

When all three core virtues of moral intelligence—empathy, conscience, and self-control—are absent, kids become time bombs just waiting to explode. Lacking an ability to feel for others, an inner voice to guide them to do right, and the strength to control their destructive impulses, they are left defenseless against toxic influences coming their way. And of the trio, many experts feel self-control is the one most sorely lacking. Although there are other reasons self-control is underdeveloped in youth, the four issues discussed here are especially toxic and point to a crisis in its growth.

Overworked, Stressed-Out Parents

The American family has drastically changed over the past few decades, producing a dramatic impact on the development of kids' self-control. Consider these new trends: kids living with both parents are a minority—half of all families are single-parent households, and more than two-thirds of those parents are working. Less than one in four families with children younger than age six have a parent staying at home, and almost 60 percent of mothers with children less than a year old are in the labor force. U.S. Census Bureau data released in 1999 indicate that the number of single fathers raising children increased 25 percent in just three years. In addition, the average time spent on the job has risen from 43.6 to 47.1 hours per week. The result is overworked, stressed-out parents trying hard to balance work and family; this situation has a serious impact on their kids' self-control capacities.

Here's why: the best way for kids to learn self-control is through watching others, and because parents are so stressed, they often pass that on to their kids. A recent survey by the Families and Work Institute asked one thousand children living in two-earner families, single-parent employed families, unemployed-parent families, and traditional families to grade their parents on various critical parenting skills. The survey revealed that regardless of whether their parents worked outside the home or not, children rated their moms lowest on the ability to control their temper when the children made them angry. But it isn't just anger our kids are picking up on. Here is just a sample of the kinds of impulsive behaviors children are exposed to: loss of temper, alcohol or drug consumption, gambling, smoking, overeating, excessive TV watching, impulse spending, and swearing. If the most significant person in a child's life isn't modeling self-control, how will she learn it?

In addition, what with working, sleeping, and commuting, the average parent is left with two to three hours each weekday to spend with children, which means kids are probably seeing a number of other caregivers. In fact, the Children's Defense Fund points out that every day, thirteen million U.S. preschoolers—including six million infants and toddlers—were in day care. But for discipline to be most effective at fostering self-control, it must be consistent; having many caregivers using different kinds of limit setting can take a toll on kids' behavior. Furthermore, it has been estimated that typical parents today are spending 40 percent less time communicating with their kids than their own parents did with them and eleven fewer hours with their children each week that the generation that raised families in the 1960s. It also means that parents are spending less time talking about the importance of using self-control and teaching their children appropriate ways to pause and think before they act.

Less parent time also means more unsupervised kids: nearly five million children are home alone after school each week. Coincidentally, that is precisely the time when kids' self-control seems to wane: juvenile crime peaks between the hours of 3:00 and 7:00 P.M. So our harried, stressed-out culture becomes another factor undermining self-control.

Early Abuse and Trauma

Debra Niehoff, author of *The Biology of Violence,* explains, "Behavior is the result of a dialogue between your brain and your experience." Studies say that what the brain records in children's early years can have a dramatic impact on their self-control. Bruce Perry, executive director of Civitas Child Trauma Program and chief of psychiatry at Baylor University, finds that the first three years are especially critical to self-control because this is when the cortex of the brain develops; the cortex is where higher-level thinking that controls moral reasoning and impulses takes place. Perry and his colleagues documented many damaging effects to children's brains caused by repeated doses of abuse, neglect, or terror in these early years. Among the tragic results was a diminished ability to control impulses; these children were at a drastically increased risk of acting aggressively and experiencing other learning problems throughout life.

Dorothy Lewis, a psychiatrist at New York University, contends that early brain damage may actually alter brain chemistry, making kids more prone to violent behavior and less able to control their rage. Her work echoes that of a growing number of other scientists who suggest that the answers to violence are partly genetic but also significantly environmental. One study showed that kids from violent homes were five times more likely to become delinquents. Statistics reveal that an alarming number of American kids are at risk. According to the Children's Defense Fund, more than three million children each year are reported to child-protection service agencies in the United States for abuse and neglect, and one in three victims of physical abuse is a baby less that twelve months old. These data point to a crisis of poor self-control that is certain to escalate if ignored.

Overreliance on Chemical Restraints
Instead of Self-Constraints

Pharmacists are probably among those most aware of the crisis in self-control, in that each year they fill over eleven million prescriptions for Ritalin, an FDA-approved stimulant to control such behaviors as impulsivity, hyperactivity, and attention deficiencies. And the rate at which it is being prescribed is alarming: the International Narcotics Control Board reports that the United States "accounts for approximately 90 percent of the total world manufacture and consumption of Ritalin," and children are the primary users. Currently one in thirty American youngsters between the ages of five and nineteen has a prescription for the drug, and in some U.S. schools as much as 30 to 40 percent of a class may be taking prescribed stimulants. So what's going on?

A growing number of experts feel that in many cases Ritalin is being prescribed for kids with poorly developed impulse control and thinking patterns that are due to a combination of negative social influences and poor parenting *and not for true neurologically or biologically caused impulse problems*. The danger is that these children are depending on chemicals to control behavior instead of being taught ways to restrain their impulses. And this alarming trend is affecting kids at younger and younger ages: a new study published in the *Journal of the American Medical Association* documents that prescriptions of behavior-altering medication for two- to four-year-olds has doubled and perhaps even tripled these past few years.

Glorification of Out-of-Control Behavior in Entertainment

Research also verifies what we've known all along: kids learn self-control not only from directly watching parents, teachers, and their peers but also from observing characters in books, in movies, and on television. And what they are watching is troubling; the American Academy of Pediatrics calls our media "the most violent in the world." The typical preschooler, who watches two hours of cartoons on TV daily, is exposed to ten thousand violent incidents every year. The average child will have witnessed eight thousand murders by the end of elementary school and two hundred thousand other vivid acts of violence by age eighteen. A three-year study in which four universities analyzed over ten thousand hours of television programming (excluding news and sports) discovered that *how* the violence is portrayed to our youth should be our biggest concern. Consider their findings: more than one-third of violent scenes featured "bad" characters who were never punished; 70 percent of these characters showed no remorse at the time of the violence; 50 percent of the violent acts showed victims experiencing no pain; 40 percent of all violence was combined with humor; 40 percent of the violence was perpetrated by attractive, hero-type role models; and fewer than 5 percent of the violent programs incorporated any kind of antiviolence message. One of the most critical study findings was that too often violence is portrayed as "desirable, necessary, and painless," and those lessons certainly aren't the type that build our kids' moral intelligence.

Although TV certainly isn't the only promoter of violence, it does have an impact on kids' behavior—especially on those more vulnerable because of environmental and biological stresses. Well over one thousand studies, including reports from the Surgeon General's office and the National Institute of Mental Health, have concluded that exposure to TV violence causes aggressive behavior in some children. The American Academy of Pediatrics and five other prominent medical groups have stated that "viewing entertainment violence can lead to increases in aggressive attitudes, values, and behavior, particularly in children." The American Psychological Association estimates that televised violence *by itself* contributes to as much as 15 percent of all of kids' aggressive behaviors. The Center for Media Education in Washington, D.C., found that children who watch four hours or more daily tend to favor using physical aggression to resolve conflicts and are more likely to demonstrate impulsive behavior. Considering that the *average* child under twelve watches just under twenty-two hours of television per week, the statistic should be another warning flag that all is not well in kids' self-control development.

Electronic video games are the second most popular form of home entertainment for kids these days, and nearly one-third of the top one hundred video games of 1999 had at least some sort of violent content— and that is the type of game kids apparently prefer. A survey of nine hundred fourth- through eighth-grade students found that almost half said their favorite electronic games involve violence. New research comparing violent and nonviolent video games published in the *Journal of Personality and Social Psychology* confirms that video games do boost aggressive behavior and irritability in players and even contends that "violent video game play is the most important predictor of aggressive behavior." And a recent review of the literature by military psychologist David Grossman alerts us to an especially disturbing trend. It seems that even as late as World War II, the military was concerned that only about 20 percent of American soldiers were able to point their weapon at the enemy and shoot them. The other 80 percent of our armed forces were gun-shy and posed a real problem for the military. The army's solution was simply to change their training procedures so that soldiers began shooting humanlike figures instead of bull's-eyes. And by the time of the Vietnam War, 90 percent of American soldiers were able to shoot their enemy with no hesitation. What's particularly troubling is that many of the popular video games fit the army's exact training technique that desensitized their soldiers to killing. This means that many kids are spending countless hours being desensitized to violence and are more likely to assume that acts of violence are acceptable behavior.

Of course, not every child who plays these games will become a killer, but violent video games do prepare kids to kill and even teach them to enjoy the experience. The American Academy of Pediatrics also points out that "children exposed to violent programming at a young age do have a higher tendency for violent and aggressive behavior later in life than children who are not so exposed." Each minute diminishes their impulse control even further.

These four factors all point to a crisis in poor self-control. Of course no single factor predisposes kids toward aggression: it is always the accumulation of toxic influences that reduces their defenses and can produce impulsive, destructive outcomes. But because these influences are so pervasive, it is critical that we foster self-control with passionate determination. Doing so is one of the best ways to ensure that our kids not only know and feel what is right but also choose to behave right.

WHAT IS SELF-CONTROL?

If you sat down with most kids and asked if it's right to lie, steal, cheat, or kill someone, the vast majority would emphatically tell you it was wrong. But using their heads and hearts to decipher right from wrong will take children only so far. That's why a few of those same kids would go out and commit the very act they just told us was not right. Choosing not to act on an impulsive thought requires a third ingredient of moral intelligence—self-control—and it seems to be the one virtue we may be vastly under-teaching our kids these days.

In his now classic *Emotional Intelligence,* Daniel Goleman describes a nationwide random survey in which American children seven to fourteen years old were rated by their parents and teachers in the mid-1970s; the survey was repeated in the late 1980s. The research revealed an alarming trend: on average, children declined across the board on forty-two basic indicators of emotional health and improved on none. These findings were echoed by recently released data based on pediatrician reports that found that attention deficits and hyperactivity problems have increased from 1.4 percent to 9.2 percent in two decades. Today's kids are more impulsive and disobedient, more irritable and violent, and more anxious and fearful than past generations. And their poor self-control clearly is hindering their moral growth.

Empathy helps a child feel the emotion of another, and conscience helps a child know right from wrong; self-control is what helps a child modulate or restrain his behavioral impulses so that he really does do what he knows is morally right in his heart and mind. Self-control is the virtue at the core of our kids' self-reliance: if a child has self-control, he knows he has choices and can control his actions. It is the virtue that motivates generosity and kindness, because it helps a child put aside what would give him immediate gratification and stirs his conscience to do something for someone else instead. Self-control is also what propels a child toward strong character, because it stops him from overindulging in pleasure and allows him to focus instead on his responsibilities. Self-control is what alerts a child to the potentially dangerous consequences of his actions,

MORAL INTELLIGENCE BUILDER
Signs of Strong Self-Control to Share with Kids

There are many ways people display self-control, and the more aware that kids are of what those actions look and sound like, the more likely they are to incorporate those behaviors into their daily lives. Here are a few examples of self-control to discuss and role-play with your child:

What People with Self-Control Say

"I need to calm down. I feel angry."

"I'll save my money instead of buying that toy."

"I'll raise my hand before talking."

"I understand the rule, so I won't break it."

"The cake looks so good, but it's almost dinner."

"I'd really like to go with you, but I have to study."

"I have to do my homework, so I'll watch TV later."

What People with Self-Control Do

Take three deep breaths when they feel stressed.

Wait patiently in line without pushing or cutting.

Say no to urges that they know are bad choices.

Don't lose control when angry or upset.

Behave well even when no one is watching.

Start working without procrastinating.

Plan what they will do and follow through.

because it helps him use his head to control his emotions. Experts point out that although natural temperament and biological makeup do have an impact on a child's capability for self-control, studies clearly show that kids can be taught to regulate their behaviors. This chapter shows you how to teach this third essential virtue of moral intelligence.

HOW STRONG IS YOUR CHILD'S SELF-CONTROL?

The statements that follow describe behaviors usually displayed by children who are able to regulate their behavior and resist temptations so that they do what they know and feel is right. To evaluate your child's strengths in this third virtue, write the number you think best represents your child's current level on the line following each statement and then add all the scores to get her total score. If your child scores 40 to 50, she's in great shape with this aspect of moral intelligence. If she scores 30 to 40, she could benefit from virtue enhancement. A score of 20 to 30 shows signs of potential problems. A score of 10 to 20 reveals potential danger; consider getting help to increase this essential virtue.

5 = Always 4 = Frequently 3 = Sometimes 2 = Rarely 1 = Never

A Child with Healthy Self-Control	My Child
Rarely interrupts or blurts out answers or questions.	_____
Waits her turn and rarely intrudes on or interrupts others.	_____
Is able to manage her own impulses and urges without adult help.	_____
Easily calms down when excited, frustrated, or angry.	_____
Rarely blows up, has angry outbursts, or loses control quickly.	_____
Refrains from physical aggression, such as hitting, kicking, fighting, or pushing.	_____
Rarely acts without thinking or behaves recklessly.	_____
Has the ability to wait for something, can cope with behavioral impulses.	_____
Rarely needs reminders, coaxing, or reprimands to behave appropriately.	_____
Has little difficulty bouncing back from an upsetting or frustrating situation.	_____
Total Score	_____

THREE STEPS TO BUILDING SELF-CONTROL

There are three important steps to building self-control in children. Because example is always the best way for kids to learn self-control, the first step conveys ways to tune up your behaviors so that you model for your child both self-control and the high priority you give self-control. You will also learn a few of the best parenting practices that nurture this essential virtue from the time your child is very young. The second step offers ways to help your child develop his own internal regulation system so that he can become a self-motivator. The third step offers ways to help your child use self-control in tempting or stressful times, teaching him to stop and think *before* he acts so that he is more likely to choose the safe and right way.

Here again are the three teachable steps you can use to nurture this essential third virtue in your child and build her moral intelligence:

Step 1: Model Self-Control and Make It a Priority for Your Child
Step 2: Encourage Your Child to Be Her Own Motivator
Step 3: Teach Your Child to Control His Urges and Think Before Acting

STEP 1: MODEL SELF-CONTROL AND MAKE IT A PRIORITY FOR YOUR CHILD

It was a Friday night at the St. Louis airport a few days before Christmas several years ago, and I was with dozens of other passengers trying to get home. We were experiencing every traveler's nightmare: flight attendants on TWA had called a last-minute strike, causing all their flights to be either delayed or canceled. Every passenger ticketed on that airline was somehow affected; needless to say, everyone was on edge, and tempers were flaring. So I stood that night in a line that seemed endless, slowly working my way up to the counter, when an incident occurred between a passenger and a ticket agent that I'll never forget.

A man had finally made it to the counter and was with an agent trying to get tickets home for himself and his young son standing next to him. Their encounter began amicably enough, but as soon as he was told that no tickets were available that night nor for the next few days, he'd had enough. In fact, he looked like he was ready to explode: his face turned beet red, and he began taking short shallow breaths. I could just imagine the kind of sinister thoughts that were running through his mind. It looked like he was going act on those thoughts: he clenched his fists and appeared ready to deliver a blow. But then he glanced down at his small son. That seemed to stop him momentarily, and he told the agent: "Excuse me. I need a minute to myself, before I do something I may regret."

Several passengers glanced nervously at one another, and the ticket agent turned white—probably assuming mayhem would break out in the next minutes. All eyes were tensely glued on the man, and we saw him turn around so that his back was facing the agent. He paused and took a few deep, slow breaths, apparently to calm down; then slowly he turned back to the counter and looked square at the agent calmly. He said, "OK, I'm back in control. Now let's work this out so my son can get home in time for Santa."

The reaction from the group waiting in line was rather unusual: they applauded! Seeing self-control is a rarity among air passengers these days—more common is basic incivility, vulgarity, and even rage—so this was an amazing moment. But the absolutely best reaction was from the man's son. The little guy had quietly watched the whole episode and was beaming ear to ear with pride for his dad—and he was also clapping the loudest. It just goes to show that our kids are watching and that our actions really do speak louder than our words.

This first step shows you how to begin nurturing self-control in your child so that you can help her recognize the importance of this most essential virtue. Because example clearly is the best way for our kids to learn, this section also offers a few of the most effective parenting behaviors that model self-control for you to tune up in your own behavior. The earlier we begin inspiring self-control in our kids, the better the odds that the virtue will become a moral habit that directs their conduct for life.

How Well Are You Modeling Self-Control for Your Kids?

Several years ago my husband and I decided it was time to renovate our house. Our three boys were getting bigger, and we had outgrown our small kitchen space. We hired a contractor, and the kitchen walls came tumbling down so that a family room area could be built. After a few hectic weeks, the job was almost done; the only task remaining was to paint the room. We were so anxious to move the furniture back into the room that my husband volunteered to paint. He started as soon as he came home from work and continued until he finished sometime after midnight. I'd been at a meeting so had come in late, complimented his tenacity, and went to bed elated that everything was finally done.

The last thing I expected to see the next morning was for the walls to be two different colors. My husband—who is horribly color-blind—had logically used the paint left around; because the cans looked identical, he had assumed the colors were also. He had spent the night painting half the room violet and the other half peach.

Well, my sons and their two friends who had stayed overnight sure recognized the difference. They walked into that room, and five kids had the same shocked look. Then they heard their dad coming toward the room, and their shock turned to fear. I'm sure I shared the exact thoughts: how was he going to react to the news? But my biggest concern was that five impressionable kids were watching; two were sure to go home and relay my husband's reaction to their parents. He walked in, and from the looks on everyone's faces instantly surmised that something was up, but he didn't have a clue as to what. I had to break the news:

"Craig, your painting job is fabulous," I began. "But there's one little problem: the walls are two different colors." As color began to drain from his face, I noticed that all five kids were frozen, waiting for his next response. But before he could say a word—which probably wouldn't have been the most civil—I quickly said, "You must be so upset, and these five kids are watching you very closely to see how well you cope with your anger." My comment was enough to break his urge to say or do the unthinkable. He turned toward the kids; he could see my point. He took a slow, deep breath and told us all: "I can't believe I used two different colors. I guess I'll have to paint again tonight." Five kids had seen the virtue of self-control in real life and, like me, probably won't forget it for a long time.

Building Moral Intelligence

Robert Coles, the renowned Harvard psychologist, stated in his elegant book *The Moral Intelligence of Children* that the best way for kids to acquire a moral compass is by watching their parents. Our good example is one of the best ways of ensuring that our kids will acquire the moral virtue of self-control. Before you try building your child's self-control, seriously reflect on your own behaviors and assess how well you are modeling the virtue. After all, your behavior is a living textbook to your child, so ask yourself what lessons she might be learning from your actions. The following are questions about some of the key issues of self-control for you to ponder:

- How do I act in front of my kids after a hard day and my patience is lacking?
- How do I control my own anger and stress?
- In middle of an argument, am I able to stop and say, "Let's get calm"?
- Am I doing anything in excess—drinking, gambling, eating, smoking, swearing, spending, working, or playing—that might be sending a mixed message to my kid?
- Do I restrain my urge to drive over the speed limit?
- Do I model fiscal prudence or buy things impulsively?

Take time to tune up your own self-control behaviors to ensure you really are walking the moral talk. Your child is watching.

Four Family Practices That Nurture Self-Control

I'm sure most of us would agree there are some "givens" we can't change about our kids, such as their genetic makeup and their innate temperament. But even those are not etched in stone: we can still modify or enhance those characteristics, and that was recently verified by a twelve-year study of 720 pairs of adolescents with varying degrees of genetic relatedness (from identical twins to stepsiblings). "Biology is not destiny," discovered David Reiss, researcher and coauthor of *The Relationship Code.* "Many genetic factors, powerful as they may be in psychological development, exert their influence only through the good offices of the family." Reiss's study found that genetic tendencies can be either encouraged or stifled by specific parental responses, which means that how parents treat their children does make a difference in how those kids turn out.

Sure, we can't change an impulsive child into one who is passive, but we can teach him how to temper his aggressiveness so that he can react more calmly. Many of the most important skills of self-control are learned, not inherited; and the very best training ground for teaching those skills is our homes. What follows are four of the best parenting practices you can use to nurture self-control in your kids.

1. Teach the meaning and value of self-control. If you want your kids to develop self-control, then take time to explain the meaning of the virtue: "Self-control means making your body and mind have the power to do what you know you should do. It's what helps you make the right choices in tempting situations, even when bad ideas or thoughts pop into your head. Self-control is what helps you stop and think about what might happen if you made those harmful choices. It keeps you out of trouble and helps you act right."

Emphasize that there are often lots of things we may want to do instead of what we should, so using self-control isn't always easy. Sometimes it takes strength and even courage. You might ask your child what things are hard for her to put off: eating dessert before dinner, saving money, watching TV before doing homework, punching someone who makes her mad, sticking her tongue out at the person who insulted her, or saying no to what a friend wants her to do. Then use the term *self-control* frequently to help your child understand how important the virtue is in her life. And when your child successfully resists temptation, point it out and reinforce it: "That's self-control. You didn't give in, and you did what you knew was right. Good for you!"

2. Commit yourself to raising your kids to have self-control. How important is it to you for your kids to have strong self-control? It's an important question to ask, because research finds that parents who feel strongly about their kids showing self-restraint usually succeed *because they committed themselves to that effort.* If you really want your child to be someone who is self-controlled, make a personal commitment to strengthening that quality in him. Then you *must* follow through on your commitment so that your child does improve.

A mother in one of my parenting workshops shared that she always tells someone she trusts about her parenting plans. It helps her stick to her commitment, because the person asks her from time to time to tell about the progress she's making with her child. It also helps her think about other strategies she could try. Another mom explained that she keeps a parenting journal and each month writes down the virtue she really wants to inspire in her kids. Every day she rereads the journal and jots down any progress she's seen: "Today Jerry really tried to stop and calm himself before confronting his brother. I need to keep practicing taking deep breaths with him when he starts to get upset. It seems to be working." Or, "For the first time, Jenny didn't run out and spend all her allowance. She actually decided to save some. Progress!" The notes reinforce her parenting efforts and encourage her to keep the promise she's made to herself to improve her children's self-control.

3. Create a family self-control motto. A father in Orlando told me he was so concerned about the poor self-control of a few of his sons' friends that he spent an afternoon brainstorming mottoes about the virtue with his kids. They wrote them on index cards, then taped them on their bedroom walls and refrigerator. Here are a few they created (or borrowed from a few famous Americans): "Think then act." "He that can have patience can have what he will." "You get the chicken by hatching the egg, not by smashing it." "Nothing valuable can be lost by taking time." "The best remedy for a short temper is a long walk." Develop your own family motto to help remind your kids that always staying in control is an important part of the best code of behavior.

4. Set a rule to talk only when in control. An excellent idea adopted by many families is to establish this rule: "We only talk when we are in control." Whenever someone feels in danger of losing control, she calls a time-out: it means she needs to calm down, so she walks away and returns when she's in control. Explain the concept to your family, then discuss ways to gain control during the time-out: taking a walk, shooting some baskets, talking to another family member, going to another room and taking deep breaths, and so on. Do emphasize that once the rule is agreed on, it must be honored: if someone calls a time-out, there should be no questions asked and no judgments passed. This rule is particularly valuable for kids with persistent self-control problems or if you have an emotional adolescent at home.

MORAL INTELLIGENCE BUILDER
A Story to Tell Kids About Self-Control

Growing up in America in the 1960s was different than it is now. There were no computers, VCRs, or video games, but an even more important difference was that black children living in the South had no rights. Black people were not allowed to socialize with white people just because their skin color wasn't white: they couldn't use the same drinking fountains, restaurants, or bathrooms, and black children weren't allowed to go to the same schools. Of course it wasn't fair, but in those days that was the law, although some people knew it wasn't right and wanted the laws changed. In November 1960, the U.S. federal government ordered the schools of New Orleans to be integrated so that black and white children went to school together.

A judge ordered four black girls to go to two white schools. Ruby Bridges, a six-year-old black girl who lived in New Orleans, was one of those children. Three of the girls were sent to one school; Ruby was sent to another. And, not knowing anyone, she went to her new first grade at William Frantz Elementary School as the only black child in an all-white school. Instead of being welcomed, she was greeted by a crowd of angry white people upset that a black child was coming to their white school. They carried signs that told her to go home, screamed unkind words, and called her names. Some people were afraid Ruby would be hurt, so the president of the United States ordered federal marshals to protect her with guns.

Charles Burks, one of the U.S. marshals who escorted her, remembered, "For a little girl six years old going into a strange school with four strange deputy marshals, a place she had never been before, she showed a lot of courage. She never cried. She didn't whimper. She just marched along like a little soldier."

If anyone should have felt angry, it should have been Ruby. But she used tremendous self-control: every day she kept her feelings and thoughts to herself, stayed in control, and walked calmly to class. Once inside she always sat by herself, because the white people refused to send their children to school with a black child. So Ruby learned to read and write with only the company of her teacher.

Her teacher, Barbara Hurley, watched Ruby each day from her classroom window and wondered how she could keep so cool and have such self-control under

(Continued)

such pressure. "She didn't seem nervous or anxious or irritable or scared," the teacher said. "She seemed as normal and relaxed as any child I've ever taught."

One morning Miss Hurley saw Ruby walk through the screaming mob and stop right in the middle of them. She seemed to be talking to them! The crowd became so furious that even the marshals were concerned. Then Ruby finished and walked calmly to her class. The teacher asked her what she had said to the crowd. Ruby explained that she hadn't said anything; she had prayed, and did so before and after school each day to help her get through the day. It was how she kept herself in control. She prayed for God to forgive those people for saying such bad things.

The angry mobs remained for weeks as Ruby went to first grade. Then white parents gradually began to send their children back to school, and slowly the unfair segregation laws began to change. Today every child growing up in America has the right to an education regardless of their race or beliefs. And forty years ago, when she was only six years old and barely three feet tall, Ruby Bridges helped make that change possible. Today people remember her for her courage, but they also remember her for how she faced those angry mobs each day using tremendous self-control.

Ruby Bridges still leaves in New Orleans and has four sons of her own. She established a foundation to increase parent involvement in schools. To contact Ms. Bridges and find out further information about her foundation, write: The Ruby Bridges Educational Foundation, P.O. Box 870248, New Orleans, LA 70187. You can also read more about Ruby's experience in a wonderful book called *The Story of Ruby Bridges,* by Robert Coles (New York: Scholastic, 1995), from which much of this story was adapted, or *Through My Eyes,* written by Ruby Bridges (New York: Scholastic, 1999).

STEP 2: ENCOURAGE YOUR CHILD TO BE HER OWN MOTIVATOR

One of the best baby shower presents I was ever given was a red dinner plate that was engraved along the edge with the words "You Are Special." Through the years my family has loved it. Anytime someone does something deserving special recognition—such as working hard at a task, doing a special kind deed, putting in extra effort to improve a behavior—he is served dinner on the plate. My husband and I always tried hard to make sure that we put more emphasis on celebrating the effort made rather than the final product (the grade, test score, or soccer goal). We wanted our sons to recognize that they had control over their lives—it was all a matter of what choices they made and how hard they worked.

Not long after we began this tradition, each child would tell me sometime during the day about a special deed he had done that deserved the red plate, and I'd always be sure the table was set with it waiting there for the recipient to receive the "royal treatment." We began to notice that the kids never expected material rewards or even praise for their feats: being able to tell the rest of us that night about their accomplishment was reward enough.

One day, when my oldest child was in the third grade, the plate played a role in an unexpected scenario. My son came home with his best friend, David, who rode over on a new scooter. It was the exact one my son had been saving his money for weeks to buy. David explained that he had passed his multiplication tests, so his parents rewarded him. My son had been studying all year every night for hours and had passed almost every test. David's mom had told me that he had been failing most of his because he wouldn't study. The scooter turned out to be David's incentive to study.

I could see that my son saw the whole thing as a huge injustice: after all, he'd worked his tail off studying, passed most of the tests, and was still having to save his money. I'm sure he figured it was his bad luck to have parents who had long ago decided that doing your best should be a reward in itself; getting a scooter for passing a math test was never even remotely possible. Though I knew my next words weren't the ones he wanted to hear, they were what I believed, so I said them: "I know how upset you must be, especially since you've worked so hard. And that's what dad and I are most proud of." Then I joking-ly added, "Besides, think how lucky you are: you get to eat off the red plate."

His reaction amazed me. It wasn't at all what I expected. He looked at the scooter awhile and at his friend, then quietly said, so David couldn't hear,

"You're right, Mom, the red plate is better. But that's because you have to really earn it." And he ran off to play while I stood stunned. Maybe all our efforts were paying off after all.

One of our most important parenting tasks is to help our children become self-reliant. Although we may relish the role of cheering our kids on to success, in the end our kids have to be their own cheerleaders and learn to count on themselves and not on us. That's a big part of what self-control is all about. Our goal is to help our kids recognize that they do have control over their lives and the choices they make.

Of course, self-control develops slowly over time, but we can help our kids when they are young by weaning them from expecting rewards or social approval for being good. And that alone is a big step. It seems as though kids these days are being raised from an early age to expect rewards and incentives for acting right or performing well. The danger is that they get hooked on the praise and learn to expect the gold stars, stickers, or monetary prizes for a job well done. Instead of developing internal control, they end up with a highly developed external control system that relies on someone else to acknowledge (or reprimand) their actions.

Morally intelligent kids choose to act well because they know it's the right thing to do *and because that in itself is reward enough.* The more our kids recognize that they need to rely on themselves, the more they will develop good old inner strength and control—willpower. This second step offers you strategies to help your child develop her own internal regulatory system that will enhance her self-control—the essential third virtue of moral intelligence.

Five Simple Ways to Help Kids Reinforce Themselves for a Job Well Done

The deadliest scenario for moral development is one in which the child grows up believing that she should do something only if she's given something in return: "I'll share my toy with Sally because Mommy will think

I'm a good girl." "I'm going to tell Johnny I'm sorry I hit him. Daddy will like me more." "If I'm really good and stay quiet, Granny will buy me a treat." Instead of behaving the right way because inside the child knows it's right—being self-controlled—she acts in ways that are contingent on our response: "other-controlled." The following strategies are simple ways to help kids begin to become responsible for regulating their own actions.

1. Switch your pronouns from "I" to "you." One of the easiest ways to wean kids away from external control is simply to change the pronouns in your praise: just switch your "I" to "you." The simple pronoun switch takes the emphasis off of your approval and puts more on the child's acknowledging her appropriate actions. It also helps kids begin to regulate their own actions.

"I" statement: I'm really proud of how hard you worked today.

"You" statement: You must be really proud of how hard you worked today.

2. Encourage internal praise. We can tell our kids from morning till night how proud we are of them, but in the end they need to rely on themselves as their own reinforcers. I find that a lot of children, though, have become so dependent on our approval that they don't know how to acknowledge themselves. A simple way to help them is by pointing out what they did that deserved merit and then reminding them to acknowledge themselves internally (to use "self-talk").

Here's how it works: suppose your son has had difficulty controlling his temper whenever he loses his soccer games. This time you noticed that he really made an effort to use self-control and not blame everyone for the loss. At a private moment, encourage him to acknowledge his success: "John, you really made an effort not to say anything negative about the other team today. You used good self-control. Did you remember to tell yourself that you did a great job?"

3. Ask the child to acknowledge herself. I was observing a fourth-grade teacher in Atlanta and saw her do one of the easiest but most powerful reinforcement techniques I've ever witnessed. One of her students seemed to always get in trouble for saying negative, unkind comments to his peers. The teacher had tried all types of behavior management approaches and admitted that none had been very successful. Then during a team assignment for science, the boy had been not only cooperative but also encouraging to his teammates. The teacher called him over to her desk and handed him an envelope and piece of paper and said, "You did a fabulous job in your science team today, Eli. You were cooperative and said encouraging comments to your team members. You write your mom and dad a letter right now and tell them what you did and what a great kid you are, and I'll sign it. Then we'll go put it in the mail." The beam on his face was priceless. Eli's teacher praised his efforts and specifically told him what he did to deserve the recognition, but she also had Eli be his own reinforcer. In doing so, she enhanced his self-control.

4. Keep an accomplishment journal. A foster mom shared with me another way to help kids learn to reinforce their own behavior. She says her children are so starved for approval that they often overlook their own efforts and accomplishments. So one thing she gives each child when he is placed with her is a small journal. At least once a week she asks each child to spend a few minutes writing (or drawing) his successes. The mom also explained that she always tells her kids that the true definition of success is a four-letter word spelled *g-a-i-n*. It is any improvement—big or small—that the child thinks he has made. The simple routine helps her children slowly recognize that they do have control over their own lives.

5. Design a certificate. A third-grade teacher in Aurora, Colorado, has an award center set up in her classroom where kids are free to go and make themselves or a deserving peer an award. She leaves an assortment of art supplies—marking pens, a hole-punch, stickers, construction paper, letter stamps, stencils, glue—in a box, and then whenever a student is "caught" doing some behavior that the teacher is reinforcing (positive comments, kindness, sharing, truthfulness, quality effort), the student is sent to the center to make her own certificate. The teacher's only rules are that the child must identify the behavior and describe what she did to earn the certificate and that it must be signed by the teacher before it goes home.

The teacher explained that she started the center because her students had become so used to receiving certificates and awards from other teachers that they were forever asking when she would be giving them out. By having students design their own certificates, she gradually weaned them away from expecting recognition from her and begin reinforcing themselves instead.

MORAL INTELLIGENCE BUILDER
Eight Ways to Help Kids Control Their Spending Urges

Studies find that today's kids don't have the self-control to save money, and a recent survey found that nearly two out of three parents felt that their children measure their self-worth more by possessions than they themselves did at the same age. We need to help kids fight their spending urges and teach them money management skills when they are young. Here are eight ways:

1. Give a weekly or monthly allowance (depending on age) so that she can learn to budget money.
2. Buy her a piggy bank to save coins. Make a rule that it must be filled before the money is spent.
3. Make her draw or write down her intended purchase and post it for a few days before she buys it.
4. Require her to spend her own money on entertainment and nonessential items. Don't give out loans.
5. Help her open up a savings or checking account so that she can monitor her money and spending.
6. Require that a portion of her allowance go to a charity of her choice.
7. Require a set portion of her allowance to be saved.
8. Say no to frivolous, rash buying—*and don't give in.*

Scout leaders as well as parents have told me that they've used the idea with their kids and the kids love it.

Praise That Nurtures Self-Reliance

Praise is one of the oldest strategies parents use to encourage their kids' good behavior. But does it really enhance the child's moral conduct? That's what psychologist Joan Grusec wanted to find out. She and a team of researchers observed young children and found that those who were frequently praised by their mothers whenever they displayed generous behavior actually tended to be *less* generous on a day-to-day basis than other children.

So what's going on here? Shouldn't the kids have become more generous because their parents were praising those behaviors? Not necessarily, researchers say, and for a simple reason: more than likely the children weren't personally committed to the trait—in this case, generosity—that their moms were praising them for. Without their moms' encouraging words, there was really no reason for them to continue doing generous actions on their own, because their good behavior was guided by social approval and not on their own internal convictions.

That doesn't imply we should stop encouraging our kids' good behaviors: *it just means we need to be more conscious of how we encourage and what we say.* And we need to make sure that the goal of our encouragement is to nurture our children's self-reliance instead of their reliance on us. Alfie Kohn, author of *Punished by Rewards*, explains: "With every comment we make—and specifically, every compliment we give—we need to ask whether we are helping that individual to feel a sense of control over his life." There are four points that make encouragement more effective in enhancing moral behaviors and less likely to "hook" our kids on depending on our approval. The good news is that you can use them immediately to begin nurturing your child's inner motivation.

1. Praise the action, not the child. The real goal of effective praise is to help the child learn right from wrong and discover how to improve her behavior. So it makes sense that we should be focusing our praise on the child's *behavior* and *not the child.* Notice how the statement "You're such a good kid" really addresses the child and makes a sweeping comment about what she is like as a person. More effective praise focuses on what the child did: "That was so kind when you shared your toys with Mariettza."

2. Make the praise as specific as possible. When you observe behavior that you would like to encourage, word your message so that your child knows exactly what was done well. For example, if you see your child displaying self-control, tell him specifically what was worthy of notice: "You didn't push Kim but used your words. That was using good self-control." Or "Hey, good job! I know it was hard waiting so long in line, but you showed great self-control."

3. The praise should be deserved. Children know when they have really earned the praise they receive, so be sure the praise you give is deserved: "You took time on your homework and didn't rush: it looks so much neater."

4. The praise should be genuine. The best reinforcement is always sincere and genuine and lets the child know exactly what she did that was right: "It took effort to stay in control, but you did it! Very good!" Kids know instantly when we're not being sincere. One of my boys' middle school teachers was very poor at classroom management and tried to get the students in line with her praise. The problem was that she used a very phony, saccharine-sounding voice. And to top it off, her praise was so juvenile—"Oh, I just *love* the way Humberto is sitting!"—that it backfired. Instead of appreciating her intentions, they saw right through her praise.

STEP 3: TEACH YOUR CHILD TO CONTROL HIS URGES AND THINK BEFORE ACTING

It's hard finding a parent these days not worried about violence. Consider these alarming statistics about today's youth:

- The American Academy of Pediatrics reports that among the twenty-six wealthiest nations in the world, the United States has the highest youth homicide and suicide rates. Although the overall rate of homicides and violent crimes has dropped in recent years, two disturbing trends remain: gun killings by young people have increased, and the rate of homicides among small town and rural youth rose by 38 percent in 1997.

- Rates of violence demonstrated by adolescents are considerably higher in the United States than in other countries. For example, American youths are ten times more likely to commit murder than comparably aged youths in Canada, and the homicide rate among adolescent males is twelve times higher in the United States than in most other industrialized societies.

- A major study by the Carnegie Corporation found that by age seventeen, one-quarter of American adolescents have "engaged in behavior that is harmful to themselves and others." A 1998 national survey found that almost one in every four middle school and high school males said they had hit a person in the past twelve months "because they were angry," and 24 percent of male high school students admitted bringing a weapon (gun, knife, or club) to school at least once in the past year.

These are scary times to raise kids. In my work as a consultant in schools, one of the biggest trends I'm seeing with *all* kids is an increase in out-of-control behaviors such as impulsivity, aggression, and anger. And data confirm this trend: surveys based on pediatrician reports found that the number of diagnoses of hyperactivity and attention deficits has risen *more than 700 percent in twenty years.* Although there are many reasons for the increase, what should not be overlooked is that many kids have not learned how to deal effectively with their strong feelings and use self-control in stressful situations. Whether we care to admit it or not, the steady onslaught of violent images and words—on television, video games, the

Building Moral Intelligence

Internet, and movies and in our newspapers and pop music lyrics—is hurting our children and steadily bombarding them with the message that aggression is the only way to solve a problem. And if we aren't modeling calm ways to handle frustrations, then our kids' only examples will be negative ones. This final section offers strategies on how to help kids learn to use self-control in stressful or tempting situations—to *think before they act*. In this day and age, these may well be some of the most important skills to teach your child.

Four Anger-Control Strategies That Help Kids Cope in Stressful Situations

In 1960, Walter Mischel, a psychologist at Stanford University, conducted the now famous Marshmallow Test. Mischel challenged a group of four-year-olds: Did they want a marshmallow immediately, or could they wait a few minutes until a researcher returned, at which point they could have

MORAL INTELLIGENCE BUILDER
Talking About Self-Control with Kids

Here are some questions to help kids think about the value of learning self-control and using it in their lives.

- What is self-control? What does it mean when somebody has self-control? Why do you think some people have more self-control than others?
- Have you seen somebody lose self-control? What did he or she do?
- What makes people lose control? What would make you lose control?
- What things can people do or say that would make them have more control? Can you name some things you could do or say that might help a person regain control?
- Can you think of a time when you felt very upset or frustrated and used self-control? How do you feel when you get angry? Does your body give you any signals right before you get angry? What helps you get back in control?

two marshmallows? Mischel's researchers then followed up on the children upon their high school graduation and found that those who had been able to wait for those marshmallows years before at age four were now more socially competent: more personally effective, more self-assertive, and better able to cope with the frustrations of life. The third who waited longest also had significantly higher combined SAT scores (by an average of two hundred points) than the teens who at four couldn't wait. Those results clearly revealed the importance of helping kids develop the ability to cope with behavioral impulses and learn self-control.

Teaching children a new way to cope with their intense feelings is not easy—especially if they have only practiced aggressive ways of dealing with their frustrations. The good news is that *although violence is learned, so too is staying in control.* Here are four ways to help your kids deal with their strong feelings and use self-control in stressful situations. Teaching them how to use self-control may be the best way to stem the onslaught of violence and help our kids lead more moral and peaceful lives.

1. Develop a feeling vocabulary. Many kids display aggression because they simply don't know how to express their frustrations any other way. Kicking, screaming, swearing, hitting, or throwing things may be the only way they know how to show their feelings. Kids need an emotion vocabulary to express how they feel, and you can help your child develop one by creating a "feeling word" poster together. You might say, "Let's think of all the words we could use that tell others we're really angry or starting to get upset," then list his ideas. Here are a few: angry, upset, mad, frustrated, agitated, furious, apprehensive, tense, nervous, anxious, irritated, ticked off, irate, incensed. Write them on a chart, hang it up, and when your child is angry, use the words so that he can apply them to real life: "Looks like you're really angry. Want to talk about it?" "You seem really irritated. Do you need to walk it off?" Then keep adding emotion words to the list whenever new ones come up in those great "teachable moments" that come up throughout the day.

2. Identify anger warning signs. Explain to your child that we all have our own little signs that warn us we're getting angry, and that we should listen to them because they can help us stay out of trouble. Next, help your child recognize what specific warning signs she may have that tell her she's starting to get upset. For example, "I talk louder. My cheeks get flushed. I clench my fists. My heart pounds. My mouth gets dry. I breathe faster." Once she's aware of her signs, start pointing them out to her whenever she *first* starts to get frustrated: "Looks like you're starting to get out of control." "Your hands are in a fist now. Do you feel yourself starting to get angry?" The more we help kids recognize those early warning signs when their anger is first triggered—usually when they first show signs of tension and stress—the better able they will be to calm themselves down and learn to regulate their own behavior. Anger escalates very quickly, and if a child waits until he's in meltdown to try to regain control, it's too late.

3. Use self-talk to stay in control. Experts suggest that another way to help kids stay in control is to teach them to say affirmations—simple, positive messages—to themselves in stressful situations. Here are a few that kids can learn: "Stop and calm down," "Stay in control," "Take a deep breath," and "I can handle this." Suggest a few phrases to your child, then have her choose the one she feels most comfortable saying; help her rehearse it a few times each day. You might post the words she chooses throughout the house as a reminder. The more your child practices the affirmation, the greater the likelihood she will use it during a difficult situation in which she needs to stay cool and in control.

4. Teach abdominal breath control. Learning to breathe the right way—especially in stressful situations—is one of the most effective ways to stay in control, so it's an important technique to teach kids. John Dacey and Lisa Fiore, child development experts and the authors of *Your Anxious Child,* advise you to teach the relaxation method with your child sitting in a comfortable position, her back straight and pressed into a chair for support. Then show your child how to inhale slowly to a count of five ("one Mississippi, two Mississippi," and so on), pause for two counts, then slowly breathe out the same way, again counting to five. Repeating the sequence creates maximum relaxation. One of my students called it twelve-count breathing because there are twelve counts altogether. The name stuck, and I've used the term with kids ever since.

It also helps if your child places her hand on her belly to make her hand move out as she breathes deeply into her abdomen. Dacey and Fiore suggest telling your child to make her tummy stick out as though it has a watermelon in it. A foster parent told me she has her kids lie down with their back on the floor so that they can feel their stomach rise with each breath. The trick is to help your child learn to breathe very slowly and deeply and then practice it over and over in a calm, relaxed setting so that she can remember to use the technique during a stressful time.

A Three-Part Formula to Help Kids Control Impulsive Urges

Michael Schulman and Eva Mekler, authors of *Bringing Up a Moral Child*, explain that what a child learns to say to himself during moments of temptation is a significant determinant of whether he is able to say no to

MORAL INTELLIGENCE BUILDER
The Stages of Self-Control Development

Researchers find that self-control develops slowly for children in a series of predictable stages, although they caution that you can never be sure of a child's stage just from his chronological age. Children vary enormously depending on their experiences and abilities. The more you understand your child's current self-control level, the better you will be at helping him move to the next stage. The following stages are adapted from the work of Michael Bloomquist, a child psychologist and the author of *Skills Training for Children with Behavior Disorders.*

Stage 1: Formation of a secure base   Infancy (birth to 1 year)

The baby is very self-centered and explores his environment using his caregivers as a security base. *The baby crawled toward the stuffed animal and then turned to make sure his daddy was still in the room.*

Stage 2: External control orientation   Toddler (1 to 3 years)

The child responds to the external control of adults and complies with their requests. *"OK, Mommy, I'll go pick up my toys."*

Stage 3: Rigid rule-following   Preschool (3 to 6 years)

The child follows the rules set by the adults in charge and often talks out loud as a means of controlling her behavior. *"I better not eat the candy because dinner is soon and Mom doesn't want me to eat snacks."*

Stage 4: Awareness of impulses   Elementary school (6 to 12 years)

The child uses inner thoughts to direct his behavior and manage impulses. He learns beginning problem-solving skills and develops a stronger awareness of his behavior. *The boy looked at the bully and said to himself, "I need to stay calm. I always lose it when he starts teasing me."*

Stage 5: Internal control orientation   Adolescence (12 to 20 years)

The child acquires more sophisticated problem-solving skills and is much more aware of her own behavioral urges and triggers. *Kevin knew his friends would ask him to smoke, so he planned a strategy: "I could tell them I'm sick or tell them about the pledge I made to my parents not to smoke. I'll tell them the truth."*

impulsive urges. Psychologists call the technique *self-instruction,* and we can teach it to our kids. The three parts of the lesson that follows teach kids to be less impulsive and to use self-control, particularly in stressful times; kids learn to stop to think *before* they act, so that when they do act, they act properly. Each part is a critical step in learning to restrain their impulses. The three parts are (1) *s*top, (2) *t*hink, and (3) *a*ct *r*ight. My students used to call the lesson by the first initials of each part, so it became the "STAR" way to remember how to stay out of trouble and act right.

1. **Stop** *Sally's five-year-old son, Sean, was playing Legos with Kenny, who lived next door. Sally glanced over and noticed that Sean seemed to be getting upset and then saw why: Kenny was hiding some of the Legos in his pocket. Sean looked ready to explode as he barreled toward Kenny. Sally quickly got to Sean and firmly put her hands on his shoulders and said, "Stop and freeze."*

The first part to helping your child restrain impulses is the most important: she must learn to stop and freeze *before acting.* The split second she takes to freeze and *not* act on an impulse can make a critical difference—especially in stressful or potentially dangerous situations. And stopping is not easy for many kids to learn, particularly for those who are younger or more impulsive. So when you first begin, you may have to physically restrain your child by gently but firmly putting your hands on her shoulders and saying, "Stop and freeze." Continue doing so as situations arise until she can stop on her own. Another idea is to help her develop a special response that reminds her to freeze, such as saying to herself, "One Mississippi, two Mississippi," taking a slow deep breath, putting a pretend stop sign in front of her eyes, or just saying "Stop and freeze" inside her head. The child must then practice freezing using the chosen technique—over and over and over—until it becomes second nature; this is the only way she will be able to actually stop to think during a trying time. Remember: you're helping your child learn a new habit, and the best way to do so is through frequent practice.

Building Moral Intelligence

2. Think   *Sally then whispered to Sean: "Think, Sean, is this a good idea? What might happen?" She could see that Sean was starting to get back in control and think about what the outcome of his actions might be.*

"But he took my Legos," Sean yelled, "and I'm really mad."

Sally replied, "I can see you are mad, but you looked like you were going to hit him. What would happen then?"

"I'd get in big trouble," Sean answered, "and Kenny could get hurt."

The second part of helping kids control impulses is getting them to think about their stressful situation and the possible consequences of a wrong choice. The easiest way to train thinking is to teach your child to quickly look around him, see what's happening, and then ask himself such questions as "Is this right or wrong?" "Is this a good idea?" "Might someone get hurt?" "Is this safe?" "Could I get in trouble?" Even very young kids can learn this step. Of course, your child will need you at the beginning to remind him of the questions, so you will need to repeatedly ask your child the questions at first. When he hears you asking the same question or two over and over, he will begin using them inside his own head without your prodding.

Predicting how decisions will turn out is not easy for many adults, let alone children, but is an important part of helping kids handle impulses so they do act right. Without your guidance to help them think through where their behavior might lead, many kids make rash and sometimes disastrous choices. One way to help your child think about possible outcomes is to teach her to ask herself, "If I did that, would I still feel OK about it tomorrow?" A fun idea to use with a younger child is to tell her to pretend she is a fortune-teller who can see into the future. Then ask, "What do you see happening if you did that?" Remind your child that if she ever feels that she may later regret making a particular decision, she should always eliminate that choice. Once she's comfortable with her answer, she'll most likely make an appropriate behavior choice.

3. Act Right Usually Sally stepped in anytime her son was having a conflict with another child, but this time she stopped herself from doing so. She knew that Sean would have to start learning to make choices by himself. That also meant that he would have to learn to deal with the outcome of his decisions. So Sally waited to see what her son would do next.

Sean turned to Kenny and said, "I'm really mad. You took my Legos, and I want you to give them back."

Sally smiled: this was a big step for Sean. Usually when he got upset he would resort to hitting, and this was the first time he had stopped to think through his actions. He still needed help controlling his urge to hit, but Sally could see signs of improvement. He was starting to monitor his own behavior.

The first two steps help your child stop, calm down, and think about what might happen if she continued with her behavior. Once she proceeds, there is no turning back—she is stuck with the outcome of her decision. This last step helps your child recognize that she alone is ultimately responsible for her actions, and it's an important part of developing moral intelligence. Morally intelligent people not only *think before they act* but also *take responsibility for their actions.* And they do so by accepting whatever happens, without making excuses, blaming, or spouting out rationalizations, even if the outcome turned out to be unsafe or unwise.

The point is, all kids are bound to make unwise decisions sometimes; that's just part of life. If your child *did* make an unwise choice, use it as an opportunity to help her think through what she did wrong so that she can make a better choice the next time. Your aim is not to lecture but to guide her so that she recognizes at what point her actions took a wrong turn and then help her think about what she might have done instead. After all, in the end, your child must learn to control her impulses and rely on herself to make the best decision. What follows are a few questions you can use with your child during a relaxed time to calmly help her sort out what happened.

• What did you want to happen? What happened instead?

• At what point did you think it might turn out wrong?

MORAL INTELLIGENCE BUILDER
Behavior Report

1. Filed by _____ Date _____

2. Who was involved?

_____

3. Where did it happen?

_____

4. Tell what happened.

_____

5. What did you want to happen?

_____

6. At what point did things go wrong?

_____

7. How do you feel about what happened?

_____

8. How do you think the other person feels, and why do you think the person feels that way?

_____

9. Name something you could have done so that it might not have happened.

_____

10. What will you do the next time this happens?

_____

Developed by Michele Borba. *Self-Esteem: A Classroom Affair, Vol. 2.* San Francisco: HarperSanFrancisco, 1982.

- Did you think about saying no? What made you keep going?
- What could you do the next time so it won't happen again?

The Moral Intelligence Builder on the prevous page is a strategy to use with your child when another person was involved in the problem. Duplicate the form, and your child can use it to write what happened and to develop a plan to remedy the situation; younger children can dictate their answers. I designed it when teaching several years ago to help my students see not only that they are responsible for their own behavior but also that there are ways to change behavior. I shared the strategy with hundreds of teachers at my workshops, and dozens of schools across the country are now using it with their students to help them develop self-control.

WHAT TO DO ABOUT THE CRISIS OF POOR SELF-CONTROL

- To teach kids self-control, you must show kids self-control, so be a living example of self-control.

- Be aware of the ratings for violence on television, music, movies, and video games, then set clear standards for your child and stick to them.

- Refrain from always giving tangible rewards for your child's efforts. Help her develop her own internal reward system in which she acknowledges herself for a job well done.

- Your home is the best place for your child to learn by trial and error how to control his impulses and deal with stressful situations. Reinforce his efforts until he is confident doing so on his own.

- Kids need to practice making moral decisions, so help your child think through the possible outcomes and then guide her toward making safe and right choices; this way, she will eventually learn to act right without your help.

THE 4th ESSENTIAL VIRTUE

Respect

Showing you value others by treating them in a courteous and considerate way

I was in Hong Kong at an educational conference a few years ago to present a keynote address and conduct workshops about improving students' emotional health. One session was quite memorable: the educators worked at various international schools in Asia and the Pacific Rim with students from all over the world. Gradually I realized that several of these teachers had been assigned to U.S. schools but had left before they'd finished the year. Apparently they just couldn't continue and had to cut short their commitment. I was surprised and curious: what was it about the American schools that had been so negative that they'd had to change their plans, break off the year early, and ask for reassignment?

So I tried to catch a few of the teachers alone and find out what had really happened. One Australian teacher who'd just come back early from California told me confidentially that it wasn't the schools or the parents or the other teachers. No, it was the kids themselves.

"The kids?" I was really concerned by now. "What was wrong with our kids?"

"I couldn't teach them. They had no self-respect!"

119

Self-respect! That's why this teacher went home early? I had to check around more. So I cornered a young woman from Singapore who had also shortened her U.S. teaching experience.

"Your students don't respect themselves, but they also don't respect authority: not all of them, but enough to make it really tough in a classroom," she explained. "If they weren't going to value my opinions—let alone listen to them—then how could I teach them? That's why I left."

A Taiwanese teacher overhearing us added, "But they're just as disrespectful to their peers: I stopped having class discussions because some were so rude to each other. They didn't have enough courtesy to be quiet and listen to their classmates."

"I've seen them treat their parents like that too," said another teacher, "and it's a lot worse than how they treat us. They can be very flippant and even insolent."

"But what does all this have to do with lacking self-respect?" I asked.

An Australian educator explained to me: "Many of your students seem sad or even angry. Oh, they can sound like they're confident, but deep down I think a lot of them feel empty. They're just treating others the way they really feel about themselves."

The group of teachers all agreed they'd encountered the same problem: American students lacked self-respect, and it was showing up in how they treated others. As one teacher pointed out, "How can you treat others respectfully if you don't respect yourself?"

A group of foreign educators hundreds of miles away had discerned a major issue troubling many of our kids, while most Americans remain baffled. It centered on our children's craving for respect: an essential moral virtue and one critical for the attainment of solid character. Data seem to confirm these teachers' perspectives: our children's self-respect has steadily decreased over the past decades, and this decrease in self-respect leads them to act disrespectfully toward others as well as themselves and to engage in such disrespectful behaviors as incivility, discourtesy, thoughtlessness, flouting of authority, rudeness, and vulgarity. Without a foundation of respect, the development of self-respect is imperiled. After all, a decent and moral life begins with the recognition of the infinite value of each and every human being, and to achieve that recognition, our children must learn first to respect themselves. Only then can they really respect others by treating them with consideration, thoughtfulness, and honor. Nurturing this fourth essential virtue not only will improve our kids' moral intelligence quotient but also will create a more civil, tolerant, and moral atmosphere in which to live. And it will help children gain what so many long for: self-respect.

THE CRISIS OF DISRESPECT

Respect means showing regard for the worth of someone or something. It's the quality that presses us to treat others with consideration and to value human life, so it's an essential virtue of moral intelligence. And that's why it's so disturbing to find such widespread agreement—from child development authorities, parents, educators, lawmakers, and the general public—that this core moral trait is deteriorating in our youth. Here are a few examples indicating a growing national crisis of disrespect:

- In a survey quoted in *Child* magazine, only 12 percent of the two thousand adults polled felt that kids commonly treat others with respect; most described them as "rude," "irresponsible," and "lacking in discipline."

- Dr. Thomas Lickona, renowned educator and the author of *Educating for Character,* cites the large numbers of children showing attitudes of disrespect and defiance toward authority as one of the ten most troubling youth trends and warns that it is a clear a sign of moral decline.

- A nationwide survey published in the *New York Times* showed that 93 percent of responding adults believed parents have failed to teach children honesty, respect, and responsibility.

- Louisiana lawmakers were so concerned with the breakdown of basic civility in school kids that they recently passed legislation making the saying of "Yes, ma'am" and "Yes, sir" expected student behavior. Failure to address a teacher respectfully is now considered a minor offense that can bring detention.

Although there is no one factor responsible for this crisis of disrespect, the six described here are especially toxic in thwarting the development of this essential virtue of moral intelligence.

The Impact of Treating Kids Disrespectfully

The development of respect is based on one critical premise: in order for a child to respect others, she must first learn to value herself, *and she can do that only if she has been treated with respect.* Researchers find that a warm, cordial, and *respectful* relationship with parents is critical for nurturing respect. Perhaps therein lies one of the greatest reasons respect is disintegrating in our kids: far too many are treated disrespectfully by adults—parents as well as other significant caregivers. And numerous data attest to the problem.

Research shows, for instance, that the *average* parent makes eighteen disrespectful comments to his child for every respectful comment, and reports continue to reveal an alarming upsurge in child abuse committed by parents. A study of 991 parents by sociologist Murray A. Straus, codirector of the Family Research Lab at the University of New Hampshire, found that half of parents surveyed had screamed, yelled, or shouted in rage at their infants. By the time a child reaches seven years of age, 98 percent of parents have verbally lashed out at them. A telephone survey of parents revealed that one out of five threatened to kick a teen out of the house in the past year and that one out of three called his children belittling names and swore at them. All of us can confirm this by listening to how our fellow adults talk to their kids. I did so this weekend and was appalled at how parents spoke to their kids: "If you don't sit in this cart, I'm going to smack you good."

"You're such a pain—I'd like to leave you here and see if anyone would put up with you." "I'm tired of listening to you. Shut up!" The fact is that far too many kids are receiving a preponderance of sarcastic, disrespectful, negative messages from grown-ups. No adult would put up with such rudeness from another adult, but kids don't often have a choice.

Do keep one critical point in mind: *this disrespectful treatment affects your child's ability to attain respect even if these statistics don't apply to your own home life.* That's because your child isn't influenced by you alone: there are myriad people in her life—teachers, coaches, baby-sitters, day-care workers, nannies, relatives, peers, scout leaders—who help weave her internal moral fabric. So that old proverb, "What goes around, comes around," applies to the development of respect. After all, if kids aren't treated respectfully, how can they possibly learn to respect others?

The Decline of Civility

Civility and common courtesy are traditional hallmarks of respect, and both are on a sharp descent in our culture. A survey conducted by *U.S. News & World Report* found that nine out of ten Americans feel that the breakdown of civility is a problem and nearly half rate the problem as extremely serious. More than 90 percent of those polled felt the decline of social graces significantly increases the opportunities for violence and erodes healthy moral values like respect for others. Four out of five adults believe incivility has gotten worse in the past ten years, and a number of signs confirm those perceptions. The following is just a sampling.

Let's start with basic driving etiquette these days. You wonder if earplugs should be required along with seat belts, considering the way some drivers scream out obscenities to one another on the road. An "every man for himself" mentality prevails; respect for the driver in the next car may be a rule written in the driver's handbook, but it isn't being enacted on the road. A recent *USA Today* poll found that of those surveyed, 93 percent of men and 87 percent of women admitted to committing one or more acts of aggressive driving in the past month.

But incivility isn't just happening on the road. If you haven't heard, there's a whole new phenomenon known as "air rage," expressed by airline passengers whose behaviors range from rudeness, insolence, and verbal abuse to outright violence. Airline officials worry that these abominable displays of disrespect are dramatically increasing and could become one of the most significant hazards of air travel.

If you need further proof that civility is eroding, read on: apparently the lack of civility in the Senate and House has reached the point where even our politicians are concerned with how it is impeding their legislative work. During the Clinton presidency, the Republican and Democratic members of both congressional bodies held two joint off-site retreats led by professional conflict resolution mediators to help these politicians learn new skills for working together more respectfully.

Perhaps the most disturbing new trend of incivility is to be found not among our kids but among their parents—at their children's athletic events. The National Association of Sports Officials told the Associated Press that it receives two to three calls a week from an umpire or referee who has been assaulted by a parent or spectator. The complaints range from verbal abuse to the official's having his car run off the road by an irate parent. Youth sports programs in at least 163 cities are so concerned about the trend of parental incivility that they now require parents to sign a pledge of proper conduct while attending their kids' games. Some sports programs ask parents to watch a thirty-minute video on civility, and others have gone so far as to have a silence day, when any parent who even opens his or her mouth at the game is ejected. If the parents can't act civilly, how can we expect the kids to?

The Price of Fear and Suspicion

Without a doubt, these are scary times to raise kids. Surveys repeatedly show that a top parental concern is for children's safety, and we are reacting to that concern. One of the first things we teach our kids is to be suspicious of people. So children learn early to never say their parents are not home, to always lock doors, to never give out personal information that could find its way to predators, and not to befriend strangers. Of course our kids do need to be cautious—they are growing up in an unpredictable, sometimes violent world—but all the emphasis on suspicion toward strangers may be taking a toll on kids' attainment of respect. A common trait of people who behave morally is that they stand up for the rights of others. But how can you show positive regard toward other people if you distrust their intentions?

For the past two summers, I've been invited by the Finnish ministry of education to conduct teacher trainings in Helsinki. I've loved spending time with their educators talking about differences between America and Finland. One conversation was fascinating: a few Finnish teachers had recently taught in our country on exchange programs, and each commented on how much safer their children feel living in Finland. Many asked me, "How can your children learn to be confident around adults if they're always taught to be afraid of them? In our country, our children respect grown-ups because they can trust them." Their point was well taken. By admonishing our kids to be suspicious of their fellow beings, we may be training them to become leery of doing the very kinds of considerate, helpful behaviors that express respect.

The Decrease of Prominent Role Models

Example is always one of the best teaching strategies, which is why it's especially troubling that over the past few years we've witnessed a decline in the number of adults modeling respect for life, property, and our basic rights and laws. It seems that the disintegration has hit every realm of our children's lives: for example, police officers charged with racial brutality, clergymen accused of adultery, teachers arrested for sexual crimes with students, elected officials indicted for endless numbers of crimes, and even the president of the United States charged with perjury.

Although we may try to protect our kids from such incidents, wide media coverage makes it an almost impossible feat, so our children are exposed to images directly countering respect. And because those disrespectful images are flashed before kids at an unending pace, the crisis just keeps escalating. Perhaps most disturbing is that these disrespectful acts are perpetrated by adults in powerful positions who are supposed to be—at least in children's eyes—models of solid moral conduct. Research tells us that the more significant the child perceives the individual to be, the greater that person's influence on the child's moral growth. Because of their immense visibility and seemingly prestigious positions, athletes, actors, and rock stars top many impressionable young kids' lists of heroes. Although many of these individuals are atrocious as moral models, they *do* influence our kids, so let's examine a few of the more conspicuous of them, and their role in widening the crisis of disrespect.

Here is just a sampling of athletes that should be members of the "Hall of Shame" for their recent national displays of disrespect: within a month of each other, linebacker Ray Lewis of the Baltimore Ravens was taken into custody for a double homicide, and Carolina Panther receiver Rae Carruth was arrested for arranging the murder of a pregnant girlfriend. John Rocker of the Atlanta Braves is best known not for his pitching but as the player with the foulest and most bigoted mouth. Football player Tito Wooten was signed to an $8 million deal with the New York Giants less than a month after a girlfriend who had accused him of beating her up committed suicide in his garage. Certainly none of these people create the kinds of images that boost our kids' respect for human life.

The prestigious Wimbledon tennis tournament is generally considered to be the most civil of all sports affairs, but the behavior of some of the competitors at the recent event presents quite a different image. *Newsweek* magazine chronicled these incidents: Anna Smashnova, the fifty-ninth-ranked Israeli, smashed a ball at her opponent's husband and missed, hitting a spectator in the face. South African Wayne Ferreira broke his racquet in half over what he called the umpire's "f——ing airs and graces." Following her second-round loss, Alexandra Stevenson was heard issuing a litany of names at her competition. And Jeff Tarango was booed off the court after his five-set loss for refusing to shake hands with his opponent and the umpire. So much for respectful conduct on the courts.

In case you're not aware of it, one of the fastest-growing kid crazes these days is the World Wrestling Federation (WWF)—now airing four nights a week (and *no repeats!*). And this is serious business: WWF videos now rank number one in sports, its action figures outsell Pokémon, and the company projected sales of $340 million for the year 2000. The problem is that these new "heroes" are the epitome of disrespect: they wear raunchy clothes (tights, spikes, black boots), carry sledgehammers and other weapons, and talk "trash talk." Here's a sample from WWF's Screamin' Norman, aired coast to coast: "Get your ass down here right now and fight me," and "I want to puke my guts out." Perhaps most troubling is that our kids are *copying* the behaviors of these performers. One of the most disturbing kid trends that concerns pediatricians is "backyard wrestling." And serious injuries to children are resulting from such sophisticated wrestling techniques as body slamming one another onto concrete; setting their opponents on fire; and hitting one another with metal chairs, cheese graters, and barbed wire—all so they can try to be like their WWF idols.

Sure, athletes are "only human." But these individuals are nationally known, many of their faces are on cards kids are trading, and all are making hundreds of thousands (and even millions) of dollars a year. How do you explain their behavior to kids? And how do you justify why they are allowed to get away with their atrocious displays of disrespect? After all, they are adults, and they are in tremendously prestigious positions.

The Increase in Obscene Language

One way people show their respect for others is through their choice of words. Thomas Lickona explains, "Language is an index of civilization; changes in language are socially significant." So the casual and prevalent use of bad language—especially among our youth—would certainly suggest yet another sign of moral decline and a crisis of disrespect, and data support that idea. Consider these facts. The use of swearing and obscene gestures is increasing dramatically on school campuses. A recent *USA Today* poll of high school principals found that 89 percent deal on a regular basis with profane language and provocative insults toward teachers or other students. A Harvard University study of schools reported that 59 percent of teachers in urban schools and 40 percent in rural areas said they face swearing and obscene gestures from students. And the American public doesn't feel the prospects are getting any better. *ABC Nightly News* reported that 80 percent of Americans polled in a national survey feel vulgarity is only getting worse. It's just one more reason we need to fervently work to instill this fourth essential virtue in our kids.

Crudeness, Rudeness, and Raunchiness Flaunted by the Media

There is one factor that no other generation of youth has faced: the number of media influences that are continually bombarding our kids with messages that *directly counter the development of respect*. Data show that over the past decade the use of foul language on network programming has skyrocketed. The Parents Television Council looked at four weeks of programming during the 1999 fall season in the 8:00 P.M. to 11:00 P.M. time slot and totted up 1,173 vulgarities—nearly five times more than in 1989.

Movies are another obvious source of disrespectful language, but vulgarities are no longer restricted to those rated NC-17. A review by *Preview Family Movie and TV Review* of 209 films released in 1996 found that of the PG films ("Parental guidance suggested; some material may not be suitable for children"), 89 percent featured crude language, and 59 percent used obscene language.

Many popular CDs contain some of the most vulgar and obscene lyrics ever recorded and are also among the most popular with today's kids. One of the foulest-mouthed rappers, Eminem, recently walked away with the 2000 MTV Video Music Award for top male video and best video of the year, "The Real Slim Shady"; his crude, vulgar lyrics promote violence against women and homosexuals.

The Internet, admittedly an extraordinary vehicle for expanding our children's knowledge, has a dark and dangerous side: hundreds of easily accessible sites contain obscene language and pornographic materials.

It isn't just vulgar language the media are flaunting: crudeness and blatant disrespect have become commonplace. One of the biggest culprits contributing to the upswing of rudeness is television, and that's perhaps because it is so accessible: the average child is viewing almost three hours of television daily. What children are watching should concern us because of its slow yet insidious impact on civility. Name-calling, discourtesy, cynicism, and nastiness seem to have become the accepted ways for characters to interact on popular sitcoms. The huge popularity of voyeur TV—such shows as *Survivor, Real World,* and *Big Brother,* in which real people are recorded in their most personal moments so all the world can watch—is just another sign that decency and respect for privacy are things of the past.

Daytime talk shows have hit an all-time low with some of the most dysfunctional and crude guests producers can find. Here's a sampling of show topics aired in a one-week span: on Jerry Springer, "Affairs with Transsexuals" and "Lesbian Romances"; on Ricki Lake, "Virgins Offer to Sell Their Virtue"; on Jenny Jones, "Promiscuous Mothers and Daughters"; and on Sally Jesse Raphael, "Updates on Cheating Husbands." Remember, this is *daytime* television; with the push of a button, any child can access profound raunchiness. And even if you've prohibited your kids from watching the programs themselves, chances are they'll still see tantalizing thirty-second promos aired throughout the day. The constant media onslaught of rudeness, raunchiness, and vulgarity is just one more toxic influence hindering the development of respect in our kids.

All the facts point to a disturbing trend: today's children are far less respectful toward themselves and others than previous generations, and we need to commit ourselves fervently to nurturing this essential virtue back into our children. Not doing so will greatly reduce their chances for living in a moral society, because people who haven't achieved respect don't treat themselves or others morally. As the crisis increases, disrespectful behaviors such as rudeness, incivility, vulgarity, abusiveness, and even violence will become more commonplace. Consequently, respect is an essential virtue of moral intelligence that must be nurtured if our children are to behave morally. And we haven't a moment to lose.

WHAT IS RESPECT?

Respect is the virtue that enforces the Golden Rule; when we treat others the way we would like to be treated, it helps make the world a more moral place. Children who make respect a part of their daily life are kids who are more likely to care about the rights of others. Because they do, these kids show respect for themselves, too. Teachers always comment on how pleasant these students are to have in classrooms because they are able to think about other people in a more positive, caring way. Scout leaders, baby-sitters, neighbors, coaches, and other adults describe these children as their "favorites" because they are so courteous and well mannered.

The fourth virtue of moral intelligence extends far beyond our homes, scout troops, soccer fields, and classrooms: nurturing respect is also vital for developing solid citizenship and decent interpersonal relationships. And because respect is based on the premise that *all* people should be treated with inherent worth and dignity, it is the cornerstone to preventing violence, injustice, and hatred. In fact, this virtue is vital for success in *every* arena of our children's life now as well as in their future. And respect is a virtue that can be taught. This chapter shows you how to help your children understand the meaning, value, and behaviors of respect so that they can display them on their own and make them a part of their lives without our prompting and reinforcement.

HOW RESPECTFUL IS YOUR CHILD?

The statements that follow describe behaviors usually displayed by children who show they value others by acting respectfully. To evaluate your child's strengths in this fourth virtue, write the number you think best represents the child's current level on the line following each statement

Signs of Strong Respect to Share with Kids

There are many ways people show respect to others, and the more aware that kids are of what those actions look and sound like, the more likely they are to incorporate those behaviors into their daily lives. What follows are examples of respectful behavior to discuss and role-play with your child. One way to share them would be to make the list into a chart to add to as your child offers more ways to practice respect.

What Respectful People Say

"Pardon me."

"Excuse me."

"That's an interesting point of view."

"Thank you."

"I'm sorry I offended you."

"I understand you feel differently."

"I didn't mean to interrupt."

"I don't want to infringe on your privacy."

"That's gossiping. It's not nice to talk about someone behind her back."

"May I borrow this, please?"

What Respectful People Do

Wait for a speaker to finish before talking.

Open the door for women or older people.

Don't talk back, whine, or sass.

Treat the environment with care and consideration.

Listen without interrupting.

Listen to someone's opinion with ears and heart.

Observe someone's need for privacy.

Are careful with someone else's belongings.

Obey their parents and teachers even when they don't feel like it.

Don't use obscenities.

Are patient and considerate to the elderly and to people with disabilities.

and then add all the scores to get his total score. If your child scores 40 to 50, he's in great shape with this aspect of moral intelligence. If he scores 30 to 40, he could benefit from virtue enhancement. A score of 20 to 30 shows signs of potential problems. A score of 10 to 20 reveals potential danger; consider getting help to increase this essential virtue.

5 = Always 4 = Frequently 3 = Sometimes 2 = Rarely 1 = Never

A Child with Healthy Respect	My Child
Treats others respectfully regardless of age, beliefs, culture, or gender.	_____
Uses a respectful tone of voice and refrains from back talk and sassiness.	_____
Treats himself in a respectful manner.	_____
Respects the privacy of others; knocks before entering a room.	_____
Refrains from gossiping or talking about people unkindly.	_____
Treats his possessions and the property of others respectfully.	_____
Uses respectful posture when listening to others (no smirking, rolling eyes, shaking head, turning away).	_____
Is well mannered and uses courteous phrases such as "Excuse me," "Please," and "Pardon me" without reminders.	_____
Listens to ideas openly and does so without interrupting.	_____
Refrains from swearing or using obscene gestures.	_____
Total Score	_____

THREE STEPS TO BUILDING RESPECT

There are three steps to building respect. Each step nurtures your child's sense of consideration, courtesy, and civility. Because respectful behaviors are best taught not by telling our kids about them but by showing them with our own behavior, the first step shows ways to tune up your own respectful behaviors so as to show your child not only how much you value the virtue but also how much you value her. The second step is to help your child realize the consequences of disrespectful behaviors and to take an active stand to squelch back talk, sassiness, and rudeness. Because respectful children are found to be more courteous and polite, the last step helps tune up your child's manners so that she can extend respect as well as receive it from others. The more your child practices respectful behaviors, the better she will feel about herself and the better others will feel about her.

Here again are the three teachable steps you can use to nurture this essential fourth virtue in your child and build his moral intelligence:

Step 1: Convey the Meaning of Respect by Modeling and Teaching It
Step 2: Enhance Respect for Authority and Squelch Rudeness
Step 3: Emphasize Good Manners and Courtesy—They *Do* Count!

STEP 1: CONVEY THE MEANING OF RESPECT BY MODELING AND TEACHING IT

I can still remember a lecture given by a psychology professor at Santa Clara University. It was probably the best talk about parenting I've ever heard. He began by reading a quotation from the work of James Baldwin: "Children have never been good at listening to their elders, but they have never failed to imitate them." For the next hour, the professor entertained us by acting out parent-child interactions, quickly switching between the roles of parent and child. Each brief scene—and there must have been at least twenty— showed a parent acting hypocritically and illustrated the message that the behavior taught the child. Here are a few of the kinds of scenes he portrayed:

Scene 1: A mother tells her child how wrong it is to talk behind some-one's back. Then the child overhears her mother the next day gossiping about their neighbor to her friend.

Scene 2: A father fines his son for swearing. The son walks into his dad's office and hears a conversation in which his dad is swearing about his boss to a coworker.

Scene 3: A father lectures his daughter about how she never listens when he's talking to her. The daughter later tries to tell him about a school problem, and he asks her not to interrupt him because he's watching a football game.

Scene 4: A mother gives her son a time-out for talking rudely to her. Later the boy hears her phone conversation with his grandmother, in which she's blatantly disrespectful.

Scene 5: A mother tells her daughter how wrong it is to read people's mail. Later the daughter finds her mom reading her diary.

The professor's lecture brilliantly conveyed an essential parenting premise: our behavior is a living textbook for our kids. If we're not careful, the only lesson our kids learn from us is "Do as I say—not as I do." Perhaps that is why many children are so disrespectful. They may have been told to be respectful, but the way they are treated or the way they see others treated often opposes that message. If we really want our children to be respectful, then we need to tune up our behaviors to ensure that they see what we want them to imitate. That's what this step is about.

Seven Parenting Practices That Nurture Respect and Love

One of the best ways to ensure that our kids are respectful is to treat them respectfully. Here are seven parenting practices that help children see themselves as valuable human beings because your actions let them know you love, respect, and value them.

1. Treat your child as the most important person in the world. Stephanie Marston, author of *The Magic of Encouragement*, suggests that you ask yourself often, "If I treated my friends the way I treat my child, would I have any friends left?" Marston says that very often we say and do things to our children that our friends would never tolerate. If you want your children to feel valued, treat them as though they are the most important people in the world. One mom told me she asked herself the question so often it became a nighttime habit. It also helped her remember throughout the day to treat her children respectfully.

MORAL INTELLIGENCE BUILDER

A Story to Tell Kids About Respect

When Kanésha Sonée Johnson started fifth grade in Hawthorne, California, she saw that the African American kids in her class often taunted the Vietnamese students. She also noticed that the two different cultures kept to themselves and rarely interacted except to torment the other. Kanésha, an African American, thought that was wrong and believed people should get along. She began making friends with the Asian students who couldn't speak English. She helped them with their homework and stood up for them by telling the other students to stop harassing them.

Kanésha explained, "I just decided to, because I know how it feels when people laugh at you." She added some wise advice: "That old poem says, 'Sticks and stones may break my bones but names can never hurt me,' but some words do hurt."

Kanésha strongly believed that people must respect each other regardless of their differences. So she held her ground, refusing to give in even when she was called a lot of names. Kanésha cried when she was home where her tormentors couldn't see her, but she didn't give up.

The eleven-year-old girl succeeded in her efforts. After seeing blacks and Asians choose only each other for their teams, Kanésha convinced them they should play all together. Because of her efforts, the class teams are now integrated. And she got them working together in class, respecting each other for what they had in common—being real kids and not thinking of themselves as just the "African Americans" or the "Asians."

What would you do if someone called your friend a name or ridiculed her culture? Respectful people like Kanésha always follow one simple rule to avoid hurting other people's feelings: *treat others as you would like to be treated.* If you want to see a picture of Kanésha and read more about her and other children like her who are making a difference, check out the Internet site called "The Giraffe Project," at http:www.giraffe.org/giraffe. It recognizes compassionate people like Kanésha who stick their necks out for the common good and in doing so are making the world a better place. The website may also give you ideas of ways you can help make the world a better place.

2. Give love with no strings attached. No child should have to earn our respect and love; it should be guaranteed with birth. Unconditional love is loving your kids with no strings attached and is the kind of love that says, "I'll never stop loving you, no matter what you do." Of course, that doesn't mean we're going to necessarily approve of all our children's behaviors. In some cases, when our kids' actions are inappropriate, we may need to respond with clear and sometimes passionate correction. But our kids know we'll always be there for them no matter what—and that's the kind of love kids need to feel they are genuinely respected and valued. Make sure the love you give your child is unconditional and guaranteed, so that no matter what, he knows you love him.

3. Listen attentively and respectfully. Kids tell researchers that the one behavior they wish their parents would do more is *listen*—really listen—to them. Attentive listening is a wonderful way to convey respect. When your child talks, stop everything and focus completely so that she feels you really value her opinions and want to hear her thoughts.

I remember a mother of one of my students who conveyed respect to her child beautifully while listening to him. I watched her several times during the year on our field trips and class parties and saw that each time her child would talk, she'd stop everything, look into her son's eyes and listen with genuine interest. Her words usually were nothing more than repeating back small tidbits of what he just said, to let him know she was hearing him. Occasionally she'd add, "Uh-huh" or "Really?" She acknowledged him simply by saying how she thought he was feeling: "You seem so happy" or "Wow, you look proud." The effect on her son was dramatic: his whole demeanor brightened when he realized his mom really heard what he had to say. I always wished I could have videotaped her listening skills to play back to other parents. Her behaviors were so simple but always conveyed respect to her child. It wasn't any surprise that her child turned out to be one of my most respectful students.

4. Communicate respect with your whole body, not just with your words. Most of the time our kids aren't listening to our words nearly as much as they are watching our posture, gestures, and facial expressions and hearing the tone of our voice. So make sure your whole body is communicating respect when you talk to your child. You may say, "I want to hear your ideas," but if your child sees you shrug your shoulders, raise your eyebrows, smirk, or roll your eyes, he is likely to pick up a whole different meaning. I've yet to meet parents who want their kids to think they aren't interested in their ideas or don't respect their kids' feelings. Yet those are the messages children pick up, all because of how parents react when their children talk.

5. Build positive self-concepts. Labeling children with such terms as *shy, stubborn, hyper,* or *clumsy* can diminish self-esteem and become daily reminders of unworthiness. They can also become self-fulfilling prophecies. Regardless of whether the labels are true or not, when children hear them they believe them. So use only labels that build positive self-concepts. One good rule to remember about labeling is, If the nickname is not respectful, it's best not to use it.

6. Tell them often why you love and cherish them. The more you show your child you love her, the more your child learns to value and love herself. So tell your child often that you love her, but also tell her what you love about her and express your gratitude that she is your child. "I love that you are so kind." "I'm so glad I have the fortune of being your mom." "I love you just the way you are." "I respect the way you never give up." Never assume that your child knows what feelings about her you hold in your heart. Tell her.

The moderator of a parenting talk show on which I appeared told me he was a single dad with a thirteen-year-old son and a frantic work schedule that often didn't leave much time at home. He started a tradition three years earlier of every day leaving a small note on his son's pillow reminding him how much he loved him and wishing him a great day. And though his son never said anything about those notes, the father never stopped writing them. One day he was looking for the shoes his son had borrowed, and while searching under the bed he happened upon an old cigar box.

When he opened it he found it filled with all the notes he had written: his son had saved every one! His story was a wonderful reminder of how we often take for granted the words we say to our kids. There's nothing more our kids want to be reminded of than how glad they are ours and how much we love them.

7. Enjoy being together. One of the best ways to help a child feel respected is to let her know how much you enjoy being with her. Put your child at the top of your schedule and set aside relaxed times together during which you can really know who your child is. Only then will you be able to let her know why you value, love, and respect her so.

Three Ways to Teach Kids the Meaning of Respect

I walked into Lakeview School in Robbinsdale, Minnesota, and instantly knew the teachers were emphasizing respect. Huge hand-printed signs were posted everywhere with the word "Respect" and its definition: "Treat others the way you would like to be treated." Charts were posted in every classroom describing the kinds of things respectful people say and do. The library had a table covered with children's books addressing the theme of respect. The bulletin board in front of the principal's office was filled with photographs of students who had been "caught" acting respectfully sometime during the month. An index card under each photo listed the child's name and what specific behavior that demonstrated respect the child was honored for. And blaring in the background as the students walked to class was Aretha Franklin singing out "R-E-S-P-E-C-T, find out what it means to me." I had no doubt those students would learn this critical virtue because the teachers were making very sure the children understood its meaning.

The following techniques are designed to help your child understand the meaning of respect and why it is an important virtue to acquire. Like Lakeview School's techniques, these ideas are simple and best mastered if you constantly reinforce them for at least three weeks, so that your child has enough practice time that he can really incorporate the virtue into his daily life.

MORAL INTELLIGENCE BUILDER

Eight Simple Ways to Show Your Children You
Respect and Cherish Them

Here are eight ways to show your children know how much you respect and value them. It's one of the greatest gifts you can ever bestow on them.

1. With your child, mark a spot on the calendar that's just for "special together time." Ask your child to choose what special thing she wants to do with you, then do it.
2. Put a note under your child's pillow telling her why she is special and how glad you are that she's yours.
3. Give him a small personal photo album just of pictures of the two of you.
4. Buy a special candle and holder; light it together for a nightly tradition of just talking and reading together.
5. Write a letter each year about why you're glad your child is part of your life, and read it together. Save all the letters and give them to her as a special twenty-first birthday present.
6. Make a memory box together: cover a shoe box with magazine cutouts, photos, and words that show the qualities you love in your child. Use it to store your child's special mementos.
7. Tell him five unique strengths that you value in him. Now hold his hand and print one strength on each of his fingers using a watercolor pen. He'll *never* want to wash his hand.
8. Deliberately say positive comments about your child to someone else, making sure your child overhears you without her knowing she is supposed to.

1. Define respect. Take time to clearly explain what you mean by acting respectfully. You might say, "Respect means that you value or admire someone or something by treating them in a considerate, courteous, and polite manner. How you treat people can let them know you think they are special. It can also let them know you *don't* value them. It's all in how you act. I expect you to act respectfully because it's one way to make our world a better place." I asked a group of third graders recently what they thought respect was; here are a few of their responses: treating people nicely, being polite, letting the other person know you think he's special, listening to the person's ideas, looking up to someone because you want to be like her, making other people feel good inside. Many teachers and parents write the agreed-on definition on a chart and post it to remind children of the virtue's importance.

2. Ask the Golden Rule question. Tell your child that there is one rule that has guided many civilizations for centuries, called the Golden Rule, and it says: "Treat others as you want to be treated." Explain that a simple way to determine if you are acting respectfully is to always ask yourself before you act, Would I want someone to treat me like that? You may need to use a few examples of disrespectful behavior so that your child gets the idea: "Would you want someone to gossip about you behind your back?" "Would you want someone to read your diary without your permission?" "Would you want someone to take your bike without asking you?" "Would you want someone to always interrupt you while you are speaking?" Once your child understands the meaning of the question, use it any time her behavior is disrespectful: "Are you using the Golden Rule?" It will help her think about her behavior and its consequences in terms of other people's feelings. I used the question so often when my own kids were young that they began to say it faster than I could. "I know," they would say, "it wasn't how I'd like to be treated. I'll try not to do it again." Just remember, the question is always most effective when used consistently.

3. Instill respectful rules. Many families, scout troops, clubs, classrooms, and schools develop a set of rules that everyone agrees will govern how they treat one another. All the rules are based on respect and are almost always ones you would choose yourself, but because the children have a voice in determining them, they become "their" rules not "yours" (so they're much easier to enforce). Begin by gathering everyone together and asking, "What rules should guide how we treat one another in our family [classroom, or other setting]?" Write all suggestions on paper and then use the democratic process and vote. The top suggestions become the Family Constitution or Classroom Guidelines. Here are a few family guidelines parents have shared with me: don't borrow without asking; listen to one another; don't pass on to others what is said in confidence; treat one another like you'd like to be treated; be considerate of one another; use calm, pleasant voices; only say things that build people up; and respect each other's privacy. Many families make their final version into a chart, have all members sign it, and post it as a continual reminder.

STEP 2: ENHANCE RESPECT FOR AUTHORITY AND SQUELCH RUDENESS

Ask *any* teacher who has been in education ten years or more, "What's different about the students you're teaching now?" I can almost guarantee they'll say, "They're more disrespectful." I know it because they tell me their concerns at every one of my workshops. It's their contention that far too many kids lack a basic respect for authority, and facts are supporting their view. Children learn respect by observing what is modeled to them, and too frequently our kids are being bombarded with messages that oppose the value of respect. It is absolutely critical that we squelch rudeness and swearing and demand that kids show respect for authority. This second step will show you how.

How to Get Rid of Disrespectful Behavior

"I don't know how to get my son to stop talking back. It's driving me crazy!" the mother told me. "It seems like the only way Kevin knows how to talk is sarcastically. And it's like he always seems to want to get in the last word. It sounds so disrespectful. If somebody ever heard the way he talks to me, I'd just die."

"What have you done to try and get him to stop talking back?" I asked.

"Well," said the mother. "I tell him over and over to stop. I say it's rude! I tell him kids shouldn't talk like that to their parents, but he doesn't listen. Lately it's gotten so bad, I find myself yelling at him all the time, but he just talks back more. How do I get him to stop?"

Back talk and sass are on the rise, and these behaviors seem to get to every adult. If back talk is allowed to continue, it can have very negative social results. Believe me: no teacher, coach, scout leader, or other child's parent appreciates a disrespectful kid. Rude kids quickly earn bad reputations that are hard to rebuild. Luckily, disrespectful behaviors such as whining, back talk, sassiness, and swearing are some of the easiest inappropriate behaviors to get rid of. There are two important secrets to ending rude behavior: first, catch it early before it becomes a habit; second, once you decide to squelch it, *be consistent and don't back down.* So what should you do if your child is disrespectful? You can use the following five steps to guide you in reducing disrespect.

Step 1. Call Out the Rude Behavior on the Spot   The first step in eliminating rudeness is to determine which behaviors you consider disrespectful, so that your child is clear on what you expect. All kids slip every once in a while, but is there a disrespectful word, tone, or body gesture your child is using fairly frequently? That's the behavior you can target. And whenever your child does display the rude behavior, name it on the spot. Here are a few examples of how parents pointed out rude behavior. Notice how their message addresses only the disrespectful behavior and *not* the child's character.

- "I notice that when I talk to you, you roll your eyes. It looks disrespectful, and you need to stop."
- "Telling me to 'chill out' when I am talking to you is disrespectful. You may not talk that way."
- "When you want something, you are using a whining voice. You need to use a respectful voice."
- "Saying 'shit' is not acceptable. That's swearing, and it's not allowed in this house."

Step 2. Refuse to Engage When Treated Disrespectfully Studies in child development find that children are much more likely to stop rude behavior if they see it is ineffective in getting our attention or other results. So stay neutral and don't respond. Don't sigh, roll your eyes, shrug your shoulders, or look exasperated. Also do not coax, bribe, or scold; such tactics almost never work and probably will just escalate the behavior. If you must, look at something else or, if all else fails, go lock yourself in the bathroom. *Just clearly refuse to continue the conversation until your child stops the rude behavior—and do it every time your child is disrespectful.* Usually when kids see you're not going to give in, they will stop. Here are a few examples:

- "Stop. That's a disrespectful tone. We'll talk when you use a respectful tone."
- "I can't understand that voice. I listen only to nice voices."

- "I don't listen to sass. If you want to talk to me, talk respectfully. I'll be in the other room."
- "We'll talk when you can listen respectfully without rolling your eyes and smirking."

Step 3. If Rudeness Continues, Set a Consequence   Suppose that you've been clear with your expectations, yet the disrespectful words and gestures still continue. Then it's time to set a consequence for the rudeness. Effective consequences are clear to the child, have a specified time, directly relate to the disrespectful deed, *and* fit the child. Once you set it, consistently enforce it *and don't back down!* For "repeat offenders" it's best to develop a written plan that is signed by all involved and readily accessible. One more thought: do consider letting your child participate in creating her own consequences—they often are much harsher than ones you would set. Here are a few examples of consequences for different ages:

- *Swear jar.* Establish a swear jar—any jar with a lid that's set aside just for swearing behavior (although it can also be used for some rude behaviors). Clearly define what swearing behavior is and set a fine. For kids short on money, make and post a list of chores that can be done to work off the fine. Each time the child swears, he is fined and must put the set amount of money in the jar. When the jar is filled, donate the money to a charity of your choice.
- *Time-out.* Younger kids who whine and sass can be removed from the room until they can talk respectfully: "Lydia, that was sassing. Go to time-out for five minutes." Make sure the area is one where she may not receive attention. The simplest rule for determining the time length is one minute for each year of the child's age (five years equals five minutes, ten years equals ten minutes, and so on). Some parents call the location the thinking chair or the cool-down corner.

Building Moral Intelligence

- *Loss of the family gathering area.* Older children who are disrespectful to you or any other family member might lose the privilege of being in the room where you gather most as a family (usually for a few hours or the rest of the day, depending on the crime). If rudeness continues, you could establish a stricter criterion: "If you can't treat your family respectfully, then you may not see your friends."

- *Loss of phone privileges.* Any child who uses disrespectful language on the telephone—including failing to answer the phone in a courteous manner—loses phone privileges for a set period.

- *Grounding.* When disrespectful behavior becomes unruly, vulgar, or downright uncivil, then it's time to take the next step and ground your teen. Grounding means he must stay on the house premises for a specified length of time—generally one to three days—and lose all social privileges and the use of the car. If the offense is particularly egregious, some parents also pull some or all home entertainment privileges—TV, video games, and phone. The reason is simple: unless the behavior stops, it will continue to spiral out of control. This is especially true with preadolescents, so stop the behavior on the spot and simply don't allow yourself or other adults living in your home to be treated disrespectfully.

Step 4. Teach New Behaviors to Replace Inappropriate Ones If you notice that your child is continuing to repeat the same disrespectful behavior, then it may be time to teach him a new, more acceptable behavior. This is one step we frequently overlook. Very often the reason kids continue their rude behavior is that no one took time to show them a different way to behave. Remember that children learn new behaviors through repetition, so practice the new technique again and again until your child masters the more respectful skill. Changing a behavior generally takes a minimum of three weeks, so consistently stick to teaching the new behavior until you see a change. And do remember that the best time to teach any new behavior is when you and your child are calm and relaxed—*not during the conflict.* Here are a few ideas for replacing disrespectful behaviors:

- *Use emotion words.* Help your child develop an emotional vocabulary so that he can express his frustrations more appropriately: "You sound angry. When you feel like that just say, 'I'm angry' instead of grunting. That way you won't get in trouble for sounding rude."

- *Say the problem.* Help your child put into words what is upsetting her: "I know you're upset, but that's not a polite way of letting me know. Tell me what's bothering you in words."

- *Role-play the new behavior.* Show the child the new behavior by modeling it: "When I'm talking, you shrug your shoulders and make an obscene gesture with your fingers. I'm sure you don't think I can see it, but I can. Watch me when I talk to you like that. See, it doesn't look respectful. Now watch how I keep my shoulders straight and face you when I talk. That's more respectful."

- *Find another word.* Help the child find a more appropriate behavior or word to replace the inappropriate one. "That's a swear word, and it's disrespectful. Let's think of another more appropriate word to use when you're mad so that people won't think you're rude."

- *Practice the new voice.* Show your child what a more acceptable voice sounds like. "That voice is whining and sounds rude. Listen to how a nice voice sounds when I'm asking for something, then you make your voice sound like mine."

Step 5. Encourage Respectful Behavior One of the simplest ways to increase the frequency of a behavior is to reinforce it when we see our child doing it right. Studies have shown, however, that the majority of the time we do the opposite: instead of "catching" our kids being respectful, we point out when they're acting incorrectly. So any time you see or hear your child practicing respectful behaviors, acknowledge them and express your pleasure. Here are a few examples:

Building Moral Intelligence

MORAL INTELLIGENCE BUILDER
Point Out Disrespectful Behaviors to Kids

One way to help children avoid making disrespectful comments is to create a signal that is agreed on by all involved. Then whenever you or anyone else notices that a rude, discourteous comment has been issued, the signal is sent to the offender. If you consistently use the technique, it can be amazingly effective in minimizing disrespect—especially with kids who have a habit of making rude comments and may not recognize how often they are saying them. A word of caution: tell children to send only the signal to the offender. They may not comment on the offender's behavior, which could result in a conflict. Here are a few unique signals families and schools are using:

- *Code word.* Many parents and teachers tell me the easiest signal they've tried is a previously agreed-on code word such as *put-down, zinger, killer comment,* or *heart shrinker.* As soon as the child makes a disrespectful comment, whoever hears it says the code word to the offender.
- *Family signal.* To stop her child's sarcastic comments, a mom from Wichita told me that whenever he makes one when they are in public, she pulls on her ear. Only she and her son are aware of the signal, but it instantly cues him that he's said something disrespectful and reminds him to stop.
- *Thumbs down.* Jefferson Elementary School in Hays, Kansas, uses a thumbs-down hand signal, and every staff member, parent, and student at the school is aware of it. Gary LeCount, the principal, reported that the teachers were able to minimize discourtesy and disrespect in a very short time because they targeted one behavior and worked together.
- *Noise signal.* A classroom for the blind in Tennessee sends the sound "S-s-s-s" to offenders who use put-downs or make disrespectful comments.
- *Visual signal.* Linda Lantieri and Janet Patti, from the Resolving Conflict Creatively Program, described a class in Anchorage, Alaska, where many deaf children were included in the regular classroom; the class decided to use the American Sign Language sign for *love* as their signal.

- "Danny, I like that respectful tone."
- "Jenny, thank you for listening so politely when I was talking."
- "That's a nice voice, Kelly. Good for you for remembering how to say your words."
- "I know that you were frustrated, but you didn't swear that time. It's hard changing a bad habit, but you're really trying."

Teaching Kids to Disagree Respectfully

Being respectful toward other people doesn't mean you always have to agree with their opinions. We need to let our kids know that it's OK to disagree; the secret is to disagree *respectfully,* and it's a skill you'll need to teach. I use the acronym *FAIR* to help children remember that there are four parts to sticking up for yourself respectfully. Here are the four parts and how to teach them to your child:

> F—*Focus* on the behavior.
> A—*Assert* yourself calmly.
> I—Use an "*I*" message.
> R—*Remain respectful.*

F*ocus on the behavior.* The first step is to tell your child to focus on the *behavior* of the person he's having trouble with, and not how he *feels* about the person. It's often helpful to ask your child to name what the person did that bothered him. ("He cut ahead of me in line," "She grabbed my toy," "He copied the work from my paper," "She made fun of me in front of the other kids.")

A*ssert yourself calmly.* Next, remind your child that her message will always be more respectful if she asserts herself calmly. So tell her to try to keep the anger and frustration she feels out of her voice and posture. Assertive posture includes holding your head high, looking at the person eye to eye, standing with feet slightly apart and arms and hands held loosely by your side. An assertive voice is calm and firm—neither yelling or wimpy.

Use an "I" message. One of the best ways to communicate respectfully is to use an assertive "I" message; you can easily teach the skill to your child. The most important thing is to tell him that instead of starting his message with the word "You," he should begin with "I." The "I" message will help him stay focused on the person's troublesome behavior without putting the recipient down. Your child then simply tells the other person how the behavior made him feel and what the person did that made him feel that way. He may also state how he would like the problem resolved. Here are three examples:

- "I get really upset when you take my stuff. I want you to ask me for permission first."
- "I don't like to be teased. Please stop."
- "I'm not getting a turn playing Nintendo, and it's not fair. You need to take turns."

Remain respectful. The final step is to emphasize to your child that although she should not have to tolerate disrespectful treatment, at the same time she may not act disrespectfully. So name-calling, insults, and sarcasm are not allowed: she must remain respectful when she asserts her complaint. And once she does so, she should either wait for a response from the recipient—who may or may not have another solution—or calmly walk away.

STEP 3: EMPHASIZE GOOD MANNERS AND COURTESY—THEY *DO* COUNT!

Using good manners and acting courteously are two ways we show respect and concern for the rights and feelings of others. There are so many ways to extend respect: offering a chair to a woman if there are no others available, standing to be introduced to an elderly person, asking a friend what she would like to play, listening without interrupting a teacher, waiting for the hostess to sit at the table before eating, holding a door for a stranger, asking a new child about himself, saying thank you to a person to show appreciation. Each gesture of respect strengthens the child's connection with others and helps nurture a bit more civility in his world, as well as boosts his moral behavior.

Respectful, courteous kids also receive some wonderful benefits. Notice how often they're invited to other's homes? Kids (and their parents) just like to be around kids who are nice. Listen to teachers give them accolades! Many studies find that well-mannered children not only are more popular but also do better in school. Courteous children have an edge later in life, too: people in the business world clearly tell us that their first interview choices are those applicants who display good social graces. You can't help but react positively to children who are polite and courteous. Therefore it's critical that we make sure our children are "manner wise" so that they can reap those benefits.

In a world that too often emphasizes incivility, discourtesy, and sometimes just plain crudeness, it is essential that we deliberately tune up our children's social graces. This third step shows you how to help kids gain respect as well as show respect by making good manners a priority in their lives. It's a critical attribute of morally intelligent kids.

Five Steps to Help Kids Learn New Manners

Letitia Baldrige, the author of *More Than Manners!* and a leading expert on etiquette, says that kind manners and good hearts do not develop naturally but instead are the result of considerable effort, patience, and quality time extended by adults with their children. So what's the best way to help your child become more courteous and better mannered? The answer is to deliberately teach manners your child doesn't already know. And there are five important steps to teaching kids *any* new courteous behavior:

1. Identify your child's "manner needs." Look over the list of eighty-five important manners kids should learn that appears in the Moral

Intelligence Builder on page 152 and choose a few manners your child now lacks that, if she were to learn them, would boost her reputation as well mannered and courteous. Then select one to teach.

Samantha's mother looked over the list of manners and then thought about her daughter. The last time guests came to the house, she noticed that her seven-year-old daughter stood back and didn't seem to know quite what to say. Her mother decided that teaching Samantha a few basic conversation manners would be a good place to start.

2. Model the new courtesy skill to your child. Find a private time to demonstrate the manner to your child. There's no better teaching method than having your child see someone do what you want her to learn. Talk with her about why the skill is important and be sure to explain when she should use it.

MORAL INTELLIGENCE BUILDER

Eighty-Five Important Manners Kids Should Learn

Manners are learned throughout childhood; at each age, children must acquire new skills for different occasions. Here's a list of what most etiquette experts say are some of the most important manners to teach children. Check off any your child already uses. Those that remain are ones you can help your child learn.

Essential Polite Words

- ☐ Please.
- ☐ Thank you.
- ☐ Excuse me.
- ☐ I'm sorry.
- ☐ May I?
- ☐ Pardon me.
- ☐ You're welcome.

Meeting and Greeting Manners

- ☐ Smiles and looks person in the eye.
- ☐ Shakes hands.
- ☐ Says hello.
- ☐ Introduces self.
- ☐ Introduces other person.

Conversation Manners

- ☐ Starts a conversation.
- ☐ Listens without interrupting.
- ☐ Looks at the eyes of the speaker.
- ☐ Uses a pleasant tone of voice.
- ☐ Appears interested in the speaker.
- ☐ Knows how to maintain a conversation.
- ☐ Knows how to end a conversation.

Table Manners

- ☐ Comes to the table on time.
- ☐ Knows how to correctly set a table.
- ☐ Sits up straight.
- ☐ Places napkin on her lap.
- ☐ Takes his hat off.
- ☐ Makes only positive comments about food.
- ☐ Waits for the hostess to sit before serving or eating.
- ☐ Puts modest portions of food on his plate.
- ☐ Eats food only on his own plate.
- ☐ Eats soup without slurping.
- ☐ Knows proper way to cut meat.
- ☐ Asks, "Please pass the . . ."
- ☐ Doesn't grab serving dishes or reach over someone for food.
- ☐ Knows how to use utensils correctly.
- ☐ Keeps his elbows off the table.
- ☐ Chews with her mouth closed.
- ☐ Doesn't talk with food in his mouth.
- ☐ Places knife and fork sideways on plate when finished.
- ☐ Asks to be excused before leaving table.
- ☐ Offers to help the hostess.
- ☐ Thanks the hostess before leaving.

Hospitality Manners

- [ ] Greets guest at the door.
- [ ] Offers guest something to eat.
- [ ] Stays with the guest.
- [ ] Asks guest what he'd like to do.
- [ ] Shares with the guest.
- [ ] Walks guest to the door and says good-bye.

Anywhere and Anytime

- [ ] Covers mouth when she coughs.
- [ ] Refrains from swearing.
- [ ] Refrains from belching.
- [ ] Refrains from gossiping.
- [ ] Holds a door for a woman or elderly person.

Visiting Manners

- [ ] Greets host's parents.
- [ ] Picks up after himself.
- [ ] If spending the night, keeps room straight and makes bed.
- [ ] Offers to help the parent of the host.
- [ ] Thanks the host and her parents.

Manners Toward Older People

- [ ] Stands up when older person comes into the room.
- [ ] Helps older guests with their coats.
- [ ] Opens the door and holds it open when an older person leaves.
- [ ] Offers his seat if no chair is available.
- [ ] Is considerate of older people's physical needs (hearing, vision, and so on).
- [ ] Holds the car door and helps person into the car if necessary.
- [ ] Is considerate and offers any help.
- [ ] Doesn't address the person's short-comings (wrinkles, hearing loss, cane, and so on).

Sports Manners

- [ ] Plays by the rules.
- [ ] Shares the equipment.
- [ ] Encourages her teammates.
- [ ] Doesn't brag or show off.
- [ ] Doesn't cheer mistakes.
- [ ] Doesn't boo.
- [ ] Doesn't argue with the referee.
- [ ] Congratulates opponents.
- [ ] Doesn't make excuses or complain.
- [ ] Stops when the game is over.
- [ ] Cooperates.

Telephone Manners

- [ ] First greets the person and says name.
- [ ] Politely asks to speak to the person.
- [ ] Answers with a clear and pleasant voice.
- [ ] Asks the caller, "Who's calling please?"
- [ ] Greets the caller by name if she knows him.
- [ ] Politely says, "Please hold on" while she gets the intended speaker.
- [ ] Takes and gives a message.
- [ ] Politely ends a conversation.
- [ ] Turns off cell phone or beeper at movies, concerts, or other public places.
- [ ] If she must use a cell phone at a public place, does so quietly so as not to disturb others.

After dinner, Samantha's mom found a private time to talk with her daughter. "You know you're getting older and will be meeting lots of new people," she said. "One of the best ways to make friends is to let people know you're interested in them. The first thing you do is introduce yourself by saying your name; then you ask the person a question. Watch me. I'll pretend I'm meeting you for the first time: "Hi! I'm Jane. What's your name? Do you live in Cincinnati?"

3. Provide opportunities to practice the skill. Kids learn any skill best through repetition, so give your child lots of opportunities to practice the new skill. You might get the rest of the family involved so that everybody is practicing the same skill together. Some families target a new skill each week. Just make sure everyone is supportive; no teasing is allowed. Rehearsing any new skill is always an important step before your child tries it out in the real world. Besides, as the old saying reminds us, practice makes perfect.

"See how easy it is?" the mother said. "That's how to introduce yourself, and you can use it any time you want to meet someone new. Now you try it, and pretend you want to meet me."

"Hi! I'm Samantha," the daughter began. "What's your name? Do you like to play soccer?"

4. Encourage your child's efforts. New skills take time to learn, and there are usually frequent slips along the way. So continue to encourage your child's efforts and attempts with the skill. Do become a cheerleader and support your child's courtesy attempts by letting her know they are appreciated. And when an inevitable slip does happen, simply say, "Begin again, please"—a nicer, more respectful way of saying, "It's not right, so do it over." One critical point: always offer corrections privately, *never* in front of other kids or adults.

"Samantha," the mother said, "I heard you practicing your introduction skills with the new girl at day care. Good for you! Next time, try looking her in the eye when you speak. It will make her feel you care about her even more."

MORAL INTELLIGENCE BUILDER
Making Creative Thank-You Notes

Writing thank-you cards to others is a habit we should encourage in our children. It's one way they learn to consider other people's feelings rather than just their own. The problem for most parents is getting kids to write them without it turning into a struggle. One trick is to allow kids to create their own way of thanking the person. So here are a few creative thank-you card ideas for kids:

- Pick a flower and press it flat for a few days between wax paper arranged inside a heavy book. Once the flower is pressed, send it inside a heavy piece of folded paper with a note.
- Take a photo of the child wearing or using the gift. The developed four-by-six-inch print makes an instant postcard; the child just writes a brief note on the back and addresses and mails it.
- Make a tape or video just for that person that expresses appreciation.
- Spell out the thank you using M&M's or alphabet cereal glued onto a piece of cardboard.
- Print the thank you using "mirror-image" writing (completely backward). Both the child and the recipient generally have to use a mirror to decipher what the message says.
- Write the thank you on a piece of card stock and then cut it into a few pieces like a jigsaw puzzle.

5. Arrange real-world practice. Your child has seen the new skill and practiced it with you—now she needs to try it out in the real world. And there are endless possibilities: dinner at a restaurant, a visit to someone's home, inviting a child (or teacher!) over, spending the night, going to a birthday party, playing with the soccer team, a walk to the park, or having a party. The goal is always to make sure your child is comfortable using the newly learned skills without your structured guidance. And when she can use the skill, you will know that all your efforts paid off.

"We'll be going to Aunt Mary's house for dinner tomorrow, Samantha," the mother explained. *"Aunt Mary said there will be a few kids there you don't know, so be sure to use your new introduction skills. You're a pro at it now, Samantha!"*

WHAT TO DO ABOUT THE CRISIS OF DISRESPECT

- Treat children respectfully so that they feel respected and are therefore more likely to treat others respectfully.

- Tune up your child's social graces and make courtesy a priority in your home. Eating dinner regularly as a family is one of the easiest ways to teach children table manners, courtesy, and conversation skills.

- Take time to tell and show your kids how to be respectful; *never* assume they have that knowledge.

- Do not tolerate any form of back talk or rudeness. "Nipping in the bud" is always the most successful method of stopping any behavior from becoming a habit. Stop it before it spreads.

- Monitor your child's media consumption closely. Supervise his Internet, movie, video game, and television viewing, allowing only what you feel is appropriate for your child to watch. Be aware of possible crude and vulgar content on recorded music: read and honor the "parental advisory" labels.

- Explain your standards and expectations to the other adults—teachers, day-care staff, baby-sitters, coaches, and relatives—in your child's life. If you work together on enhancing courtesy and respect, you'll *always* be more likely to be successful.

- Make sure your child is surrounded by people—grown-ups as well as kids—who model respectful, courteous behaviors, so that what she is watching is what you really want her to "catch."

THE 5th ESSENTIAL VIRTUE

Kindness

Demonstrating concern about the welfare and feelings of others

Last fall I was on the East Coast helping a small school district implement a character education program. My first meeting was with a district administrator to assess the students' needs, and the discussion has haunted me ever since.

I began by inquiring about the district's high school, but each student issue I addressed—drug use, attendance, gangs, test scores, school violence, racial tensions, and drinking—didn't appear to be problems. Although it was true that the high school was relatively small (about five hundred students), most other high schools had at least one of those issues as a concern, so I continued by asking about the students' emotional needs. Again, the administrator shook his head, saying students were pretty typical of today's high school kids. Rather amazed that the school was so problem-free, I asked a final question: "Have there been any student suicides lately?" The administrator's answer stunned me: "No more than most high schools these days," he replied. "We've had just about one a year for the past few years."

I stared in disbelief: that was an incredibly high rate for any school, but especially for a smaller school. What could possibly be causing so many kids to end their lives? "Are bullying and cliques a problem?" I asked.

157

"No problem," he said. "Though the principal did tell me a parent has been complaining about her son always being picked on. But I don't think it's any big deal."

I pursued it anyway: "How does she say he's picked on?"

During the next minutes I listened aghast as the school official told me the mother's concerns. Apparently a few of the other male students had been taunting the fifteen-year-old for several weeks by calling him some pretty vicious names. The mother reported the incidents to the teachers, but nothing was done. Then, last week the boys took a lawn mower to the hill behind the school and cut the grass to spell out "fag" in huge letters to publicly humiliate him.

"Now the mother said her son won't go to school," the administrator said, shaking his head. "You know, boys will be boys. That mother just has to loosen her strings and let her kid grow up."

I was appalled. How could such obvious harassment be so accepted, and how could one child's emotional distress be so denied? Has meanness become so commonplace that we just ignore it as a fact of life?

Meanness and unkindness are present in epidemic proportions among today's youth. The facts about the rise of children's cruelty are alarming. Although unkindness may not result in visible bruises, studies show it can leave lasting emotional scars and tear away the fabric of moral growth. If we can learn anything from these troubling reports, it is just how destructive cruelty is *and will continue to be* until we commit to fervently applying the best-known cure for halting it: kindness. Nurturing this fifth essential virtue may well be the best way to protect our kids from experiencing the writhing pain of peer harassment and also improve their chances of living in a kinder and more moral world. We haven't a moment to lose.

THE CRISIS OF UNKINDNESS

Kindness is that magnificent ability to show others you are concerned about their welfare and feelings. Acts of kindness are what build civility, humaneness, and morality, and because these acts are based on intentions of doing good rather than harm, kindness is an essential virtue of moral intelligence. Whether our kids achieve kindness is far from guaranteed: research is clear that the traits of compassion and kindness must be inspired, nurtured, and taught, and the sooner we do so the better. The facts about the rise of children's cruelty are alarming: a national study found that the amount of childhood teasing and being mean to others has significantly increased since the mid-1970s. The American Psychological Association declared that bullying is rampant in American schools and may be stoking adolescent anger that can erupt into violence. Whether we want to admit it or not, the steady surge of unkindness is having a dramatic effect on our children's moral well-being. Although there are a number of issues contributing to our kids' moral demise, these four factors are especially toxic in squelching kindness and point to a crisis in its development.

Lack of Modeling by Parents and Other Adults

Researchers agree that one of the best ways children learn moral behaviors is by copying models they deem significant, which is exactly why parents can enhance their kids' moral intelligence. Developmental psychologists have also found one condition that determines the likelihood that modeling will occur: the amount of time spent in the presence of that significant model. There lies the problem: parents are undoubtedly significant in their kids' lives, *but that alone does not guarantee that their children will absorb their values.*

The truth is that we have to be around on a steady basis so our kids have something to absorb. The facts show that many of us are not, and the lack of parental modeling is dramatically impeding children's ability to develop kindness. As noted in other chapters, for a number of reasons—work, parental illness, fatigue, divorce, and commuting, among others—parents today spend 40 percent less time with their kids than parents did thirty years ago. And that means less time for building the virtue of kindness.

Not Enough Encouragement for Kindness

Several years ago, my husband and I traveled to Japan. One night I was in my hotel room flipping TV stations in search of news and saw a commercial I'll never forget. Even though it was in Japanese, I had no trouble understanding the message. It showed a child helping his friend, who had fallen off his bike: the child consoled him, picked up the bike, and made sure his friend wasn't injured; then they contentedly rode off as the word *shinsetsu* flashed on the screen. The word, I later learned, meant kindness. Several Japanese educators explained that kindness is considered a virtue very important for their children to acquire, so one way they encourage it is by showing on TV different ways to be kind.

The learning principle they were using is based on one of the oldest and simplest psychology premises: "The more you see it, the more likely you'll become it." By repeatedly modeling and encouraging kindness in TV ads—and, from what I gathered, at school and home—they increased the likelihood that their children would be kind in real life. I fear that in our own country, kindness is very low on our agenda of qualities we encourage in our kids.

The truth is that American kids are being bombarded with messages that encourage *unkindness,* and they're receiving them in every arena of their lives. *At home and in school:* studies reveal that the average parent makes eighteen critical comments to his child for every one positive comment. I'd venture to say that a similar ratio would be found for teacher comments to students at school. *In the media:* prime-time television, on average, displays five acts of violence per hour; on Saturday morning children's shows alone, more than 90 percent of the programs and more than 80 percent of the characters are involved in violence. Cruel acts are further reinforced in movies, printed news, music, and video games. *Among peers:* a study funded by the Centers for Disease Control found that 80 percent of students in one midwestern middle school admitted that they had bullied classmates during the previous month. The finding supports other reports, including one that found that 75 percent of adolescents had been

Building Moral Intelligence

bullied during their school years. In fact, the National School Safety Center has called bullying "the most enduring and underrated problem in American schools."

Influence of Unkind Peers

There's little doubt that peers do influence—positively as well as negatively—our children's moral development. Because many kids are with peers longer than with their parents each day, that influence can be enormous and becomes even stronger if the adults in their lives are emotionally distant. With no significant adults in their lives to help them form moral convictions, many children turn to their peers as their primary moral teachers. The result can be disastrous to their moral growth if their chosen companions are unkind (because they never received the needed modeling, guidance, or encouragement). The disturbing reality is that there are growing numbers of such peers, which puts more children at risk of receiving lethal lessons.

Even if kids do have strong adult models who are emotionally available, there's another contributing factor: peer cruelty is steadily escalating. That means all kids are being subjected to unkindness, whether they are victims or witnesses of cruelty. The plain truth is that the more children experience unkindness, the less distressed they will be by it and the greater the chance that they will begin to tolerate unkind behaviors.

Desensitization to Unkindness

There is no denying that television, the Internet, radio shows, music, movies, and video games are saturating our kids with violent, cruel images, while newspaper and magazine stories are capitalizing on the sensational and the horrific. This saturation *does* have an impact on our kids' moral development. Research shows that children who have been repeatedly exposed to more violent television programming are less likely to demonstrate kindness by helping younger kids who are in trouble. Madeline Levine, author of *See No Evil,* also points out: "Numerous studies have shown that the more people watch media violence, the less sensitive they become to it."

I witnessed this insensitivity recently while watching the movie *Saving Private Ryan.* Some scenes showing injured and dying soldiers were so excruciating, I was literally writhing. Yet it was when I heard the teens in front of me laughing that I became the most distraught, wondering how they could enjoy watching people die so brutally. Psychologists would say it is because they have seen so much unkindness that they have become desensitized. Witnessing cruelty no longer produces that empathic rush that generates concern for the victim. Instead, these individuals react with indifference and emotional numbness. The steady onslaught of cruel images not only deadens their capacity to feel for others and increases aggressive behaviors but also creates a perception that the world is a mean, cruel, and violent place.

The reasons for this crisis of unkindness are complex, yet one fact is undeniable: this generation of youth has been bombarded with messages laced with meanness and negativity that convey their world as cold, cruel, and selfish. At the same time, the uplifting, compassionate stories showing the positive, caring sides of life are being downplayed in their lives. Therefore it behooves us to recognize these warning signs of moral erosion and do everything we can to inspire this essential fifth virtue in our youth. Until we do, many children's potential for moral intelligence will be in great jeopardy.

WHAT IS KINDNESS?

Kindness means showing concern about the welfare and feelings of others. Kids who have achieved this fifth essential virtue share one characteristic: they are guided by an internal moral compass deep in their hearts that tells them that treating others kindly is just the right thing to do. Their motive is never that they want something in return or that they fear if they aren't kind they'll be punished or will lose social approval. Warmhearted kids are kind simply because they are concerned about the

Signs of Strong Kindness to Share with Kids

There are dozens of ways people display kindness and concern toward others, and the more aware that kids are of specific behaviors of kindness, the more likely they are to incorporate those behaviors into their daily lives. What follows are examples of kindness to discuss and role-play with your child. Consider making this list into a larger chart to hang on the wall as a constant reminder.

What Kind People Say

"Are you OK? You seem lonely."

"Let's pick up the trash. The yard is a mess."

"How can I help?"

"Are you new here? Want to join us?"

"What do you need? What can I do?"

"Don't say that. It hurts her feelings."

"You go first. You seem tired."

"I'm sorry I hurt your feelings."

Comments that make others happy.

Words that encourage and uplift others.

What Kind People Do

Stick up for someone being teased.

Offer to help someone in need.

Show concern when someone is sad.

Refuse to be part of ridiculing others.

Take care of the environment.

Pay attention to others' concerns.

Think about the needs of others.

Practice acts that make people happy.

Show concern when someone is treated unkindly.

---

other person's feelings and needs. And those are the kinds of kids we need more of in our world.

One thing is for sure: stepping back and assuming that our children will become warmhearted and compassionate in a world that's deluging them with pessimistic, unkind messages just won't work. Instead, we must consciously work to replace those negative messages by using only the most effective ways to nurture this fifth virtue. And the best chance we have is for teachers, youth leaders, and parents to work united to stamp out cruelty and enhance the behaviors of compassion, helping, sharing, and kindness. This chapter will show you proven ways to nurture kindness and goodness in children so that they learn to do what's right in a world that is too often cold and cruel.

HOW KIND IS YOUR CHILD?

The statements that follow describe behaviors usually displayed by children who show concern about the welfare of others through their words and actions. To evaluate your child's strengths in this fifth virtue, write the number you think best represents your child's current level on the line following each statement and then add all the scores to get her total score. If your child scores 40 to 50, she's in great shape with this aspect of moral intelligence. If she scores 30 to 40, she could benefit from virtue enhancement. A score of 20 to 30 shows signs of potential problems. A score of 10 to 20 reveals potential danger; consider getting help to increase this essential virtue.

5 = Always 4 = Frequently 3 = Sometimes 2 = Rarely 1 = Never

A Child with a Strong Sense of Kindness	My Child
Says kind comments that "build up" others, without prompting.	_____
Is genuinely concerned when someone is treated unfairly or unkindly.	_____
Sticks up for people who are being picked on or alienated.	_____
Treats animals gently and looks out for those treated unkindly.	_____
Shares, helps, or comforts others without expecting something in return.	_____
Refuses to be a part of insulting, intimidating, or ridiculing others.	_____
Pays attention to the needs of others and acts on those needs.	_____

Gives tender care to someone who needs help or is sad.   _____

Enjoys doing actions for others because it makes them
  happy.   _____

Regularly sees kind and caring behaviors through your
  personal example.   _____

                                        Total Score   _____

THREE STEPS TO BUILDING KINDNESS

Why are some children warmhearted and others cruel? Since the 1970s, extensive research has determined that although children are born with the potential to be kind, the trait must be nurtured if they are to become kind and demonstrate their genuine concern for others. It seems that a child's level of kindness is in large part determined by how much his teachers and parents treated him kindly as well as deliberately taught caring behaviors and instilled in him the importance of treating others kindly.

There are three steps to building kindness. Each step nurtures children's sense of caring, generosity, and concern. The first step is the foundation for developing kindness: helping your child understand the meaning and value of the virtue and how it can make a difference in her world. The second step is helping your child realize the consequences of unkind behaviors so that she'll stop and think before acting in a cruel and mean manner. The last step is encouraging your child to do kind deeds for others—not because she expects something in return but simply because she enjoys spreading happiness.

Here again are the three teachable steps you can use to nurture this essential fifth virtue in your child and build her moral intelligence:

Step 1: Teach the Meaning and Value of Kindness
Step 2: Establish a Zero Tolerance for Unkindness
Step 3: Encourage Kindness and Point Out Its Positive Effect

STEP 1: TEACH THE MEANING
AND VALUE OF KINDNESS

If you could choose only one virtue to nurture in your child, which would it be? Of course there is no right answer, but when I survey parents in my workshops, kindness is nearly always one of their top choices. Their reason is that they feel kindness is the virtue most needed to ensure that their children's world is more caring and peaceful. We all hope our children's future is bright, and here's the good news: kindness is a virtue that can be developed and nurtured. The latest research is very clear: *it is never too early—or too late—to instill the value of kindness.* This first step shows you how to help children understand what kindness is—it all starts with you.

Four Ways to Help Kids Understand Kindness—
It Starts with Us

Just how much influence do we have in nurturing kindness in kids? Here's the latest verdict from researchers: *those parents who are kind and who have taught their children to be kind will most likely have kind children.* When children understand that kindness can make a difference, they will be more likely to incorporate that behavior in their own lives. The best place to start is not with them but with us. If we really want our kids to be caring, we need to make the virtue a priority in our own lives and then reinforce it in our children. The strategies that follow are ones that experts agree are some of the most effective ways to help kids understand kindness:

1. Consciously model kindness. Your child learns a great deal about morality simply by observing your behavior. That's why it's so important to model what you want your child to copy. If you want your child to be kind whenever you are together, *consciously demonstrate kind behavior.* We tend to do kind behaviors so naturally that our children may miss them, so deliberately tune them up. There are so many daily opportunities: watching your friend's child, phoning a friend who is down, picking up

MORAL INTELLIGENCE BUILDER
A Story to Tell Kids About Kindness

Makenzie Snyder was nine years old when she heard a reporter talk about the plight of foster children. What troubled the third grader was learning how foster kids were often transported from placement to placement carrying what few possessions they owned in plastic trash bags. "I felt really sad," she said. Makenzie decided to do what little she could to help make their lives just a little better and told her mom she "wanted to go to a yard sale and get some suitcases." Over the next few weekends, she went to every yard sale in her hometown of Bowie, Maryland, searching for luggage. Then word of her efforts spread. Her Brownie Troop got involved, as did fire department volunteers, neighbors, and friends. Foster children began receiving very special gifts from this special girl. Makenzie packs each bag for each foster child with a stuffed animal and a note that says, "God told me you could use a duffel bag and a cuddly friend, so I send this with love to you." Though Makenzie is just eight years old, her actions clearly show she is a caring, warmhearted child who is touching others. Out of her efforts came the Children-to-Children program, which has distributed more than one thousand suitcases to foster kids around Washington, D.C.

Can you think of people who live around you that could use a little kindness? Think about what they might need, and ask yourself: What can I do to help brighten their world? To really make a difference, you have to plan out what steps to take and then act on those plans. That's how you, too, can make a difference. If you want to help Makenzie spread kindness, contact: Children-to-Children, P.O. Box 3262 Superior Lane, PMB 288, Bowie, MD 20715.

trash, soothing a child, giving directions, asking someone how she is, baking cookies for your family. After performing the kindness, be sure to tell your child how good it made you feel! By seeing kindness in your daily words and deeds and hearing you emphasize how being kind makes you feel good, your child will be much more likely to follow your example. The old saying, Children learn what they live, has a lot of truth to it.

2. Expect and demand kindness. Spell out loudly and clearly your expectation that others must be treated kindly. It sets a standard for your child's expected conduct and also lets her know in no uncertain terms what you value. Nancy Eisenberg, author of *The Caring Child,* found that parents who express their views about hurtful, unkind behavior and then explain why they feel that way tend to have kids who adopt those views. So state your belief to children again and again and again: "Unkindness is wrong, it's hurtful, and it will not be tolerated!"

3. Teach the meaning of kindness. One of the most important steps in teaching kindness is making sure kids know what kindness means, and it's a step too often overlooked. So take time to define the virtue. You might say, "Kindness means you are concerned about other people. Kind people think about another person's feelings and not just their own, they help someone who is in need, and they are kind even when others are not. Kind people never expect anything in return. They just treat other people kindly because they want to help make someone's life better. Kindness makes the world a nicer place, because it makes people happier. And it's a virtue I want you to always use." Consider making and hanging up a poster that lists or depicts kind deeds your family can do for one another. It will serve as a constant reminder of simple ways to make the world a little better.

4. Show what kindness looks like. You can do this activity with your child any time you are together in a place filled with people: a store, the airport, a mall, or the school grounds. Tell her that the object is to look for people who show kindness to others. She is to watch to see what the kind person did to show someone he was concerned or that he cared, and then to observe the reaction of the recipient of the kindness. Many teachers assign students to do a "kindness watch" sometime during the day, then ask them to share their observations with the rest of the class. The teachers tell me that doing the activity always increases their students' kindly behaviors because they have the chance to really see what kind people do and say and the effect the virtue has on others.

A "TIP" for Pointing Out the Impact of Kindness to Kids

Research by psychologists Elizabeth Midlarsky and James Bryan found that explaining to your child the specific way his act of kindness will benefit someone is effective in nurturing kindness. So look for kindly behaviors that naturally occur during the day and use them as great opportunities to discuss how they affected the recipients. The strategy that follows helps kids identify what the kind deed was and how the gesture made a positive difference. It uses the acronym *TIP* to help you remember the three parts:

T—*Tell* who was the kindness recipient and describe his need.
I—*Identify* what kindness was said or done.
P—*Point* out how the kind gesture made a difference for the recipient.

Here are a few examples showing how caregivers enhanced children's awareness of the power of kindness by using the TIP:

Predicament	The Adult Points Out the Kindness
The contents from Bill's backpack spill just as the bus pulls up at day care. Megan helps him put things back.	"Megan, you were kind to Bill when you helped him pick up his backpack. He was upset, and you made him feel better."
Kara sees her brother is upset. A few classmates are insulting him about his "big ears." She tells them, "Stop teasing him."	"Kara, you saw how upset your brother was because those boys were teasing him. You stood up for him and told them to knock it off. Did you see how relieved your brother was? That was so kind."
Marcos sees Jimmy cradling a cat in his arms. When Jimmy tells him the cat has burrs in her fur, Marcos helps his friend remove them.	"Marcos, I saw how concerned Jimmy was about his cat. You were so kind to stop and help him take the burrs out of his cat's fur. Did you notice how thankful your friend was that you were there?"
Isidor sees the kids making fun of Sean because his wheelchair's motor is stuck. Isidor walks past the boys and pushes Sean's chair to class.	"Isidor, those boys were being so mean to Sean. How kind of you to walk right past them and help Sean with his wheelchair. Sean was so upset. His smile showed just much he appreciated your support."

STEP 2: ESTABLISH A ZERO TOLERANCE FOR UNKINDNESS

Some years ago I had the privilege of watching Dr. Sidney Simon, a Harvard professor and author, conduct a stirring workshop with teachers and parents. He wanted to convey the impact unkindness has on children's emotional well-being, and his technique was unforgettable. He began by holding up a large sign with the letters *IALAC*, which he explained stood for "I Am Lovable and Capable." Then he told a poignant story of a young boy who hears nothing but derogatory, ridiculing comments about himself

MORAL INTELLIGENCE BUILDER
The Heart-Shrinkers Story

What follows is my adaptation of Dr. Simon's parable to share with your kids. I tell the story using a huge red paper heart cut from wrapping paper or butcher paper. I print the word *self-esteem* inside the heart to help children grasp the hurtful consequences of unkindness.

Hold up the heart and say, "Your self-esteem is the feelings you have about yourself. Many times those feelings come from what you hear people say about you. Their words can make you feel better about yourself, or they can be hurtful and can shrink your self-esteem. I call these words either heart stretchers or heart shrinkers. Watch what happens to Michael's self-esteem when he hears heart-shrinking words."

Tell the story, crunching part of the heart each time Michael hears an unkind comment, until at the end, the once large heart has shrunk to a very small size—just like Michael's self-esteem.

Michael knows it's a school day, but he's still lying in bed. His mom yells, "Hey, Lazyhead." Crunch. *"Can't you ever get up on time?"* Crunch. *He jumps up to get dressed but can't find his socks; he calls to his mom asking if she's seen them. She shouts, "I told you to put your clothes away."* Crunch. *"You just never listen!"* Crunch. *He runs to the bathroom and bumps into his sister, who screams, "What a jerk!"* Crunch. *"You never look where you're going."* Crunch. *When he reaches the kitchen, he finds a soggy bowl of cereal waiting for him.* Crunch. *His father tells him, "Well, if you'd gotten up on time, your breakfast wouldn't be so soggy."* Crunch. *"But then you can't seem to do anything right, can you?"* Crunch. *He sees his mom shake her head as she looks at his spelling test.* Crunch. *"Look at all these mistakes!"* Crunch. *"Your brother and sister would never get grades like this!"* Crunch. *Michael can barely keep the tears from falling when his brother struts in, takes one look at him and laughs.* Crunch. *"Hey, Dummy."* Crunch. *"When are you going to stop combing your hair like that?"* Crunch. *"Everybody's sure to tell you how stupid you look."* Crunch. *That's when Michael hears the bus driver honk and his sister say, "Well, looks like you're going to miss the bus again!"* Crunch. *"You're not going to be late again, are you?" yells his father.* Crunch. *"Stop crying!"* Crunch. *"You're just acting like a baby."* Crunch. *"Hurry up!"* Crunch. *Michael runs out chasing after the bus, but he is too late. It leaves without him again.* Crunch.

> At the end of the story, I give each child a large red paper heart. I spend a few minutes asking children to think about times people have said heart-shrinking comments to them and invite them to share how they felt. We talk about how often those insults can last a very long time. Then I ask children to think of words they say to people that "stretch their self-esteem and make people feel good about who they are." Children write or draw caring, encouraging, uplifting comments inside their hearts, and then we hang them as a reminder to say more heart-stretching words. You may want to consider doing the same activity with your child.

from his family throughout the day. What made the story so moving was that each time the boy heard an unkind comment, Simon ripped a piece from the sign and tossed it to the ground until finally nothing was left. What was so obvious was how the stream of unkind words had destroyed the boys' feelings of worthiness. I'm still moved thinking about that session.

I've since told a similar story countless times to parents, teachers, and children, and their reaction is always to sit speechless as they watch the pieces of the young boy's self-esteem fall to the floor. (My version appears in the preceding Moral Intelligence Builder.) When I ask children, "How many of you have been hurt by put-downs and unkind words?" almost every hand is in the air. Afterwards parents come to me in tears explaining how much the story reminded them of their own family. Sadly, statistics report that their experiences are all too common.

Studies tell us that on any day in any average American family, a child hears 460 critical statements and only 75 positive acknowledgments. That means a child is hearing more than six times as many negative as positive comments. As mentioned earlier in the chapter, research by the National Parent-Teachers Organization led to a similar finding: daily parent-to-child communication consists of eighteen critical messages to every one acknowledgment. One of the primary reasons the development of kindness may be in crisis is that our children are hearing a preponderance of negative comments—not only from the media and their peers but also from us! This second step offers proven strategies to stamp out negativity and cruelty. It is a critical prerequisite to helping kids become kinder and learn to do what's right.

Four Ways to Reduce Your Child's Unkind Behaviors

Rudy's mom listened in shock as her son made fun of his eight-year-old cousin's appearance. Juan was wearing his new glasses, and Rudy was hassling him with "four-eyes" jokes that were as old as the hills. What Rudy thought was playful teasing was anything but! His jokes were hurtful and belittling. Didn't he see how upset his cousin was? Juan was almost in tears. She couldn't believe her nine-year-old could be so mean and uncaring.

If we want our kids be kind and do what's right, it's imperative that they recognize that unkind words and deeds are hurtful. It's a lesson they must learn if they're to expand their moral understanding of what's right and wrong and to increase their empathy for others. Parents and teachers can play an important role in helping children recognize that unkind actions do have consequences. Research by Nancy Eisenberg, author of *The Caring Child,* finds that parents who give clear messages about the impact hurtful behaviors can have on others tend to raise kinder and more empathic children. So what should you do if your child is unkind? Here are four approaches that experts suggest using to correct unkindness and help the child turn an unkind wrong into a right.

Target the Unkind Behavior—Not the Child   When you see your child being unkind, stop and call his attention to it. Don't fall into the trap of giving a lengthy sermon on the Golden Rule (our lectures generally turn kids off anyway). Instead, take time to name and briefly describe the child's unkind actions. Your message should focus *only* on your child's unkind behavior, not on the child. You want to make sure he clearly understands what unkind behavior you object to and *why you disapprove.* Here are a few examples of how to target unkind behavior:

- "Calling your cousin 'Four Eyes' was unkind. Name-calling is not nice because it puts someone down. That's something I just can't allow."

- "Telling your sister fat jokes and calling her 'fatty' is not kind. You're laughing *at* her, not with her. You may not tease if it hurts the person's feelings."

- "Not asking your friend which show he wanted to watch was uncaring. You're watching only what you want and not considering what he'd like. I expect you to be a more thoughtful host."

Help Your Child Empathize with Her Victim's Feelings   The critical part of disciplining a child who has acted unkindly is helping her understand how her actions affected the other person. This type of discipline also enhances moral intelligence because it helps the child consider the other person's feelings and needs. And experts claim it can be especially effective in enhancing kindness, consideration, and helpfulness. James Windell, author of *Six Steps to an Emotionally Intelligent Teenager,* suggests using a "victim impact statement" to help your child recognize the discomfort or hurt her unkindness caused the recipient. Here are a few questions that help kids reflect on the impact their unkind actions had on their victims' feelings:

- "Can you see how upset Juan is? How did your behavior make him feel?"

- "See, you made her cry. How do you think she feels?"

- "Did you notice how your unkindness made her feel? How would you feel if somebody did that to you?"

Decide on a New Behavior with Which to Replace the Unkind Actions
So far you have pointed out the child's unkind behavior, explained and expressed why it was wrong, and helped him understand how his unkindness affected the victim's feelings. Now ask one critical question: "Next time, what will you do instead?" Too often we may overlook this step

because we assume that the child knows a new way to behave. Don't make that assumption! I've seen many kids become "repeat offenders" simply because no one took time to talk them through what their "replacement behavior" should be. After all, the most effective discipline teaches children how to act right. You might even help the child practice the new behavior. Here's what Rudy's mom could do:

Mom: The next time you see someone with new glasses, remember that he probably feels self-conscious. What will you do that's kinder?

Rudy: I'll tell him they make him look older, or I could say, "I hope your glasses help you see better."

Mom: OK, you have the right idea. Those are kinder. Now pick one idea and pretend I'm the child wearing the glasses. Show me what you will do.

Rudy: Hey, you got new glasses! I hope they help you see better.

Mom: That is much kinder, Rudy. And I expect you always to be kind.

Give Your Child the Opportunity to Make Amends   A final part of your discipline is to help the child learn to take responsibility for her unkind behavior by making amends. Martin Hoffman's research found that parents who call attention to the harm done by the child and encourage her to make reparations can increase their child's consideration and helpfulness. It's very important for the child to learn that once she's been unkind, the action can't be taken back, but that she can ease the other person's discomfort or hurt by apologizing. Because you can't put words in your child's mouth, do involve her in making her own plan.

Mom: You hurt your cousin's feelings, Rudy. You can't take the hurt away, but you can apologize and let Juan know you are sorry. What can you do to make him feel better?

Rudy: Well, maybe I could call him and tell him I'm sorry.

Mom:	That's one idea. What else could you do?
Rudy:	I could write him a note to say I'm sorry or go to his house and apologize. Maybe I could even buy him something nice with my allowance.
Mom:	So which idea will you do?
Rudy:	I think I'll call him tonight and tell him I'm sorry.
Mom:	That's a good plan. Tell me how it goes.

MORAL INTELLIGENCE BUILDER
Ten Reasons Why Kids Are Mean

One thing is certain: all kids are bound to be teased. But why do some children tease more than others or actually seem to enjoy putting others down? Here are a few of the reasons kids are unkind.

1. *Lack of empathy.* He may not fully grasp the emotional impact of his unkindness.
2. *Lack of self-esteem.* She feels unworthy, so she brings the other person down.
3. *Need to retaliate.* He has been picked on and teased, and wants to "get back."
4. *Desire to be included.* As a way of "fitting into" the group, she puts outsiders down.
5. *Lack of problem-solving skills.* Not knowing how to solve conflicts, he resorts to insults or name-calling.
6. *Jealousy.* She envies the other child, so she brings him down to feel better about herself.
7. *How he's treated.* He is treated unkindly, so he mimics the same unkind behaviors.
8. *Desire for power over someone else.* Teasing makes her feel superior.
9. *No expectations requiring kindness.* No one is telling him that unkindness is not allowed.
10. *Poor social skills.* She doesn't know the skills for getting along—cooperating, negotiating, compromising, encouraging, listening—so she resorts to bringing the other child down.

The most effective discipline is instructive: it helps children recognize what they did wrong, learn the consequences of their wrong behavior, *and know how to make it right so they don't repeat the same unkind behavior again.* Our goal should always be to help kids develop an internal moral compass so that they can guide their own behavior *without our instructions and prompting.* The best way to do that is by talking things through to ensure that kids understand the true consequences of unkindness. Although it may take a few minutes, the time is very well spent, because the process is one of the best ways to raise warmhearted kids who know how to do what's right.

Five Ways Schools and Families Are Stamping Out Unkindness

One of the first steps to ending unkindness is to establish one clear, non-negotiable rule: unkindness is not tolerated. Many parents and teachers write the rule and post it as a reminder. I've visited many schools and knew instantly they were stamping out unkindness because the rules were posted at their front doors: "Put-downs are not permitted" and "Unkindness is not allowed." Here are five other ways schools and families are spelling out their expectation that there must be no unkind, cruel behavior.

1. Make "no put-down" posters. Students at Ralph Sheppard Elementary School in Vancouver had a unique homework assignment recently: they were to create posters using words, symbols, or drawings illustrating that unkindness was not tolerated on campus. The posters were then displayed on every available outdoor wall space. Everywhere you looked was the same critical message: "This Is a No Put-Down Zone." The effect was potent!

2. Create a "no put-down" pledge. Many families, clubs, and classrooms are so adamant about thwarting unkindness that they ask members to take a kindness vow. The pledge is usually created first by asking everyone for suggestions, then taking a vote for the best guidelines. The winning pledge is written on a piece of paper, signed by all members, and posted as a concrete reminder. A Boston family told me they reduced yelling by reciting to one another: "We only speak to one another in calm, kind voices." Barbara Inman, a teacher in Mercer Island, Washington, starts each day by having her students recite, "Today I will try to do my best, look for the good in others, and treat everyone the way I'd like to be treated." Bay View School in California even created a kindness school motto that they post on campus: "Bay View: A Place Where Everyone Cares."

3. Hold a put-down burial. Chick Moorman, a national educational consultant based in Michigan, told me that one of the most powerful activities he's ever observed was a classroom "put-down funeral." The teacher began the ceremony by asking students to write as many unkind words or deeds as they could think of on slips of paper. The put-downs were placed in a shoe box, and the students then marched solemnly to the playground, where the box was buried. The symbolic gesture clearly conveyed to the class, "Those unkindnesses are buried and are never to be used again. They are dead." Many parents, youth leaders, and teachers have shared with me that they, too, have conducted put-down funerals, and it always has a dramatic impact on children.

4. Make a turnaround rule. One way to help children learn to say more kind comments is by establishing a rule of "One unkindness equals one kindness." Whenever a child says an unkind comment, she must turn it around and say something kind and caring to the recipient. Here's how it works: suppose I hear my child say a put-down, such as "Kevin is so stupid." I say, "That was a put-down. I need a 'put-up,' kind statement now, please." I then expect her to say a more caring, positive statement in its place. She might say, "Well, he's a great soccer player." A word of caution: the turnaround rule is wonderful, but it works *only* if children know what kind comments are *and only if it is consistently enforced.* For some kids, writing the kind comment is far more comfortable than saying it. That's OK: it's a first step toward becoming more caring.

5. Penalize put-downs. One family I know has a special technique that squelches unkindness. The family keeps a large jar in their bookcase. The house rule is, "Any family member who says a put-down, swears, or is unkind must put twenty-five cents of his or her money in the jar for each unkind offense—and parents are included! If you're short of money you must 'work it off.'" A list of twenty-five-cent chores is always posted on the refrigerator. When the jar fills up, the family brings it to their favorite charity. The parents swear their family is far less negative and much more positive.

Six Ways to Help Kids Counter Unkind Treatment, Taunting, and Prejudicial Slurs

My son is only seven, but he's been coming home upset every day. He says a boy named Sean keeps calling him names and making fun of him because he has an accent. Now the rest of the kids won't play with him because they are

MORAL INTELLIGENCE BUILDER
The Problem of Bullies

The National Threat Assessment Center of the Secret Service conducted the most comprehensive study of school violence and shootings to date; and of the forty cases studied, the center found that the *only commonality of violence-prone students was that they had been harassed by peers.* If we can learn anything from these tragedies, it is that we cannot overlook just how emotionally and morally destructive peer cruelty is to children and that we must clearly emphasize that unfair treatment is never permissible. Unkindness is striking our kids at alarming rates:

- A study by the National Association of School Psychologists reports that one child in seven—as many as five million elementary and secondary students in the United States—is a bully or the target of a bully.
- In some cases, the same child is a bully one day and a victim the next.
- In a nationwide survey, 43 percent of children said they were afraid to go to the bathroom for fear of being harassed.
- The National Education Association reports that every day, 160,000 children skip school because they fear being attacked or intimidated by other students.

afraid Sean will start picking on them, too. My son is miserable and doesn't want to go to school. What can I do to help him?

Some of the toughest problems parents must deal with happen right on the school playground, where unkind kids abound. Although we can't prevent the pain insults can cause, we can lessen our kids' chances of becoming victims. The best thing to do is teach our kids how to deal with their tormentors. Here are six strategies you can teach your child to help her stick up for herself. Remember, what may work with one child may not with another, so it's best to discuss a range of options, choose the one or two your child feels most comfortable doing, then practice them together over and over until she feels confident enough to use them in real life. Doing so will show her there are ways to resolve conflicts fairly without losing face or resorting to violence. Most important, she'll learn that no one should have to be treated unkindly.

1. Assert yourself. Teach your child to face his tormentor by using a confident posture: hold your head high, stand tall, and look the person straight in the eye. Your child should name the unfair behavior and tell the aggressor in a firm, calm voice to stop: "That's teasing—stop it," or "Go away." Sometimes the best response is just to say, "Cut it out!" Keep in mind that how kids deliver their lines is usually far more important than what they say, so help your child practice using assertive posture.

2. Ignore it. Bullies love to know that their teasing has upset their victims, so help your child find a way to not let her tormentor get to her. I asked a group of eleven-year-olds how they handle unfair teasing, and they unanimously said the worst thing a kid can do is let the teaser know the teasing bothers her. Here are their suggestions on how to ignore teasers: pretend they're invisible, walk away quickly without looking at them, quickly look at something else and laugh, look like it doesn't bother you, stay quiet, and look completely uninterested. Ignoring a teaser isn't easy: it takes lots of practice and encouragement from parents for kids to learn this skill.

3. Question the insult. Ann Bishop, who leads violence prevention programs, tells her students to respond to an insult with a nondefensive question: "Why would you say that?" or "Why would you want to tell me I am dumb [or fat or whatever] and hurt my feelings?"

4. Use "I want." Communication experts suggest teaching your child to address the tormentor, beginning with "I want" and saying firmly what she wants changed: "I want you to leave me alone" or "I want you to stop teasing me." The trick is to say the message firmly and forcefully so that it doesn't sound wimpy.

5. Agree with the teaser. Consider helping your child create a statement agreeing with her teaser. Teaser: "You're dumb." Child: "Yeah, but I'm good at it." Teaser: "Hey, Four Eyes." Child: "You're right, my eyesight is poor."

6. Make fun of the teasing. Fred Frankel, author of *Good Friends Are Hard to Find,* suggests that victims answer every tease with a reply *but not tease back.* The teasing often stops, Frankel says, because the child lets the tormentor know he's not going to let the teasing get to him (even if it does). Suppose the teaser says, "You're stupid." The child says a rehearsed comeback, such as, "Really?" "So?" "You don't say," "And your point is?" or "Thanks for telling me."

Sure, all kids will be teased, taunted, and treated unkindly at one time or other. But when it comes to bullying, fun teasing is not what is at stake. A bully's sole intent is to hurt his victim, and the harm can take the form of physical, verbal, emotional, or sexual abuse. One of the best ways to squelch harassment is to arm your child with skills so that he has the tools to stick up for himself and others when treated cruelly. Of course, no child should ever have to deal with ongoing teasing, meanness, and harassment. It's up to adults and kids alike to take an active stand against bullying, teasing, and prejudicial slurs and to stress that unjust treatment, intolerant behaviors, and cruelty are *always* unacceptable. It's a critical step to building a more humane world for our kids.

STEP 3: ENCOURAGE KINDNESS AND POINT OUT ITS POSITIVE EFFECT

I was visiting a school in Indianapolis and saw a hall bulletin board I'll never forget. It actually gave me goose bumps—believe me, this was a first! The board was covered from floor to ceiling with student-made paper hearts, and the caption over them read, "Changing the World One Heart at a Time." The hearts were lovely, but how the board came about was what made it so moving.

The principal told me the board had been empty—until Ryan, a fourth grader, walked by it on his way home one day. Ryan rarely spoke, and, unbeknownst to anyone, his home was in turmoil. His father was an alcoholic who frequently beat up Ryan's mom while the fourth grader hid in his closet. Fearing his dad would severely injure his mom if he told anyone, he played it safe by emotionally distancing himself from his teachers and classmates and remaining silent.

That afternoon, though, another classmate saw Ryan eating by himself and recognized something everyone else had missed: Ryan looked lonely. So Ned, ignoring his friends' admonishments, asked Ryan if he could sit with him. Ryan later told the principal that he was so amazed that somebody wanted to eat with him, he couldn't stop thinking about it the rest of the day. He wanted to find a way to thank Ned for his kindness. It was still on his mind as he passed the bulletin board. He picked a paper off the floor, quickly tore it into a heart shape, then jotted a note: "Ned, thanks for having lunch with me today. It made me happy. Ryan," and pinned it to the board.

The next day, another student read the note and, copying Ryan's gesture, tore a paper heart and wrote a note of appreciation to another classmate. Then another student repeated the gesture, and another, and by the time I got to the school, over four hundred student-made hearts filled the board, and the hall as well. And it was all started by one child. I stood there soaking up these children's gestures of kindness and then looked back at the heading, "Changing the World One Heart at a Time." It was the perfect caption to describe what I saw. I also realized that it was the exact message more children need to understand: they really can make a difference, one kindness at a time. We are the ones who must make sure children are aware of that power.

The more children practice doing kind behaviors, the better they will feel about themselves and the better others will feel about them. Doing kind deeds is simply one of the best ways for children to enhance their self-esteem. As your child continues to do kind deeds for others, she will find she can't get enough of it: she will start going out of her way to perform more kind acts.

As you begin nurturing this virtue, it is very important to make sure you encourage your child to extend kindness, otherwise she may never recognize how good she can feel giving to others. This step offers ways to enhance children's kindness toward others. It will help them learn one of life's greatest lessons: genuine kindness can make a difference in the world.

Helping Children Recognize That Kindness Can Make a Difference

When my children were little, we played a game called the Silent Fuzzy Pass. Fuzzy was a bright orange, ragged old stuffed animal that I suppose was a bear (though it's debatable). Each night, Fuzzy "mysteriously appeared" on one of my sons' pillows because the receiving child had been especially caring that day—and trying to sneak it there was always challenging. I only needed to put Fuzzy out once for the game to be effective. The very next day—and the next few weeks—the boys were on a "kindness alert," watching for a brother to say or do something nice so that they could later try to guess who Fuzzy would visit that night. All day long they would run to me with "kindness reports": "Zach was really nice. He shared his toys with me." "Jason was kind. He let me choose the game we played." The only rule was that the boys had to explain why they felt the deed was kind. Later that night they would run to their pillows to see who Fuzzy had visited. The nonrecipients would tell the honored brother why Fuzzy probably chose him by reciting the kind deeds they remembered

MORAL INTELLIGENCE BUILDER
Helping Kids Think About the Power of Giving

Dr. Ervin Staub, a world-renowned researcher from the University of Massachusetts, has extensively studied the development of empathy. His studies found that children who are given the opportunity to help others tend to become more helpful in their everyday lives. *This is especially true if the effect of their kind actions on the people they helped was specifically pointed out to them.*

To help your child understand that kindness can make a difference, take a few minutes to ask these important empathy-building questions after she performs any kind actions. They will help her recognize the impact her kindness can have on others as well as on herself.

- What did the person do when you were kind?
- How do you think he felt?
- How would you feel if you were the person?
- How did you feel when you being kind to him?
- How did you feel when you saw his reaction to your gesture?

him doing earlier. Then the discussion would turn to their telling the brother how much they liked receiving his kind gestures, and the smile on the listener's face was always priceless.

I still don't remember how our "Fuzzy visits" got started. It probably was one of those spontaneous parenting moments when my kids' "kindness level" needed readjusting, and the idea just came. But it was amazing how such a simple little strategy could be so effective in boosting the virtue in my family. It sure taught me a few things: I learned that by really targeting kindness for a few weeks at home, my sons focused more on the behavior, and doing so helped them acquire a repertoire of kind deeds. I also learned the importance of letting my children know that their kind deeds positively affected others. Their kind gestures blossomed in our home—and it was so simple! I've used these virtue-building lessons with my kids as well as students ever since.

Three Ideas for Helping Kids Practice Doing Kind Deeds

Studies firmly support the theory that by practicing small acts of kindness, people are often guided to perform more widespread acts of compassion *even though that may not have been their original intention.* Drs. Samuel and Pearl Oliner discovered this phenomenon in their famous landmark study in Europe involving the rescuers of Jews from the Nazi persecution. In their interviews with the rescuers, a significant number said they had first planned to give only limited help, but their commitment grew once they became involved.

The same phenomenon will take place with children once they recognize that their acts of kindness are appreciated. The more opportunities children have to experience what it feels like to be the giver of kindness, the more likely they will incorporate the virtue as part of their character. We need to make sure our children have those opportunities to extend kindness. What follows are a few ideas parents, teachers, and club leaders have used that encourage kids to practice doing kind deeds.

1. Create a kindheart centerpiece. A family from Toledo shared this heart centerpiece activity with me; it not only makes a charming decoration but also nurtures kindness. Gather your family together and brainstorm a list of kind deeds kids can do for just about anybody. Set one criterion: the deeds must all come "straight from the heart" and can't be something you purchase. Here are a few suggestions other kids have come up with: say hello, ask how they are, offer to help, share something, give a compliment, invite them to play, give a pat on the back, give praise, give a high five, let them choose first.

Next, help your kids cut out fifteen to twenty-five colored paper heart shapes about three inches wide. On each heart, write a different kind deed. Then have kids decorate the hearts with whatever art supplies you

Building Moral Intelligence

have handy—glitter, stickers, marking pens, doilies, paper scraps. Tape a pipe cleaner onto the back of each, an inch or two up the center, leaving the rest sticking out at the bottom like a lollipop. Now place the "heart flowers" into any vase. Every morning, invite each family member to pull a heart shape from the centerpiece. Encourage him to do the kind deed for people sometime that day. Each night at dinner, have everyone take turns describing his kindness-giving experience. Be sure to point out that people react differently to kindness and that not everyone may seem appreciative, but kind deeds are always the right thing to do.

2. Assign secret kindness pals. This idea is a great way to help children learn that giving can be just as fun as receiving. Start by writing each child's name on a paper slip; put them all a basket, bag, or other container. Each participating child then takes a turn pulling a slip; the pulled name becomes the child's secret kindness pal. Explain that her task for the next week—a few days for younger kids—is to do a *secret* act of kindness toward her pal each day. Emphasize that the pal should not "see" the child performing the deed—that's what makes it secret and what makes the game so intriguing. Some of the secret deeds kids come up with are just plain wonderful. I've had students bake cookies, draw pictures, write a song, pick a flower bouquet, and string a necklace. My own kids secretly cleaned a brother's room (a true first!), did laundry, and even ironed a shirt (though this was definitely a time when the thought was what really counted, *not* what the shirt looked like later).

My favorite example came from a Girl Scout troop in New York. Each girl's secret buddy was a cancer patient in a pediatric ward. Each day for a month, the girls did secret kindly deeds for the children, such as leaving e-mail messages for them on the hospital computers, bringing toys, making colorful posters to wish them a happy day, baking cookies, and even making tapes of their favorite music to give. The patients adored the gestures, but the girls got even more enjoyment from doing the secret caring deeds.

When I did this activity with students, I always allowed a few minutes before dismissal to ask, "Has anybody done something nice for you? What was it? How did it make you feel? Who do you think your secret pal was today?" The discussion always generated ideas for more secret kind gestures and also clearly let the senders know that their gestures were appreciated. Warning: the key to the activity's success is keeping the secret pal secret—which is almost impossible for some kids—so try to keep things lighthearted even if the secrecy rule isn't strictly adhered to. Feel free to give younger kids hints for ideas they might try.

3. Make a giving tree. One of the cutest ideas I've seen for helping kids practice kindness was done by a Boys and Girls Club in Atlanta during the holiday season. The leaders first read *The Giving Tree*, by Shel Silverstein, a wonderful parable about a tree and a boy who grow old together and finally recognize that the greatest gift is giving of yourself. Next they stood a large leafless tree branch in a pot and placed it in the middle of the room, where it looked pretty sad and lonely. The leaders then asked the kids to think of kind gestures they could do for someone who looked sad or lonely. Each child's idea was written on a six-inch leaf shape precut from colored paper, then hung to the branch with a paper clip. In a short time, their Giving Tree was covered with kind ideas, such as give a hug, smile, call her at home, ask her to play, sing a song, say a kind word, share something, ask what you can do, draw a picture. The leaders finally said, "Each day during the week when you come to the club, go to the Giving Tree, find an idea you could do for someone to make his day brighter, and then do it. It will make not only his day better, but also yours."

Parents, scout leaders, and teachers have told me that they also made Giving Trees to help promote kindness with children. All you need is a small branch, plaster of paris, construction paper, scissors, paper clips, and a can. In fact, a fun family outing is taking a walk together just to find "the perfect branch." My girlfriend Cindy Morse kept her tree for years by her kitchen table. Every holiday, her children decorated the tree: paper bunnies for Easter, Kleenex ghosts for Halloween, American flags for the Fourth of July, and hearts with kind deeds for Valentine's Day. It's a wonderful family tradition you might want to begin.

MORAL INTELLIGENCE BUILDER
What the Research Says About Parental Influence

One fascinating study showing how parents can influence the development of kindness was conducted by Samuel and Pearl Oliner, authors of the book *The Altruistic Personality*. To discover why some people would put themselves at great personal risk while so many others did not, the Oliners interviewed Christians living in Europe during World War II who either did or did not help Jews escape from the Nazis. They found several important distinctions between the upbringing of rescuers and that of nonrescuers, which are important clues to understanding how to nurture kindness and goodness in our children.

- The rescuers' parents strongly emphasized kindness and expected their children to apply the value to all people.
- The rescuers' parents administered little physical punishment in disciplining their children, using moral reasoning instead.
- The rescuers' parents tended to have closer relationships to their children than did the bystanders' parents and were felt to be warmer and more supportive.
- The rescuers' parents modeled caring behavior in their interaction with people outside the family.

WHAT TO DO ABOUT THE CRISIS OF UNKINDNESS

- Monitor your child's media selections—television, music, video games, and the Internet—and watch what is reflected in his clothing, language, and behaviors. Take an active stand against vulgarity, cruelty, and violence.

- Make sure you are a positive, affirming role model and surround your child with people of high character.

- Take an active stand against cruelty and just plain *do not allow it.* Expect and demand that children treat all living beings in a moral and caring manner. It's the best way to make the world a better place.

- The best moments to teach kindness are usually not planned—they just happen. Capitalize on those moments to help your child understand the power kindness can have. Children are more likely to be kind if they understand why kindness is important and how it affects others.

- Take time to tell and show kids how to be kind—*never* assume they have that knowledge.

- Kids don't learn how to be kind from reading about it in a textbook but from doing kind deeds. Encourage your child to lend a hand to make a difference in his world, and always help him recognize the positive effect the gesture had on the recipient.

- Look for ways for your child to do kindly deeds, not just in your home but also in your community. For example: taking extra toys to a children's ward in a hospital, working at a soup kitchen, planting flowers at a shelter, or reading to the elderly. The more your child experiences the miracles of kindness when young, the greater the likelihood that she will make kindness a habit for life.

Building Moral Intelligence

Tolerance

Respecting the dignity and rights of all persons, even those whose beliefs and behaviors differ from our own

In December 1999, the small seacoast community of Duxbury, Massachusetts, was shocked when one Jewish family received a message of hate for the holidays. "This is what happens when you don't decorate for Christmas," the note lettered in red and green read. Police say it was written by two fifteen-year-old girls who shot paintballs at the family's home and threw rocks that shattered a glass door. Within weeks, five other major incidents of anti-Semitism were reported in New England—all involving teenagers. The occurrences troubled experts because the characteristics of the perpetrators defied the traditional hate crime offenders: they were younger than most, and they were female.

On March 24, 2000, a thirteen-year-old Asian student from James Workman Middle School in Cathedral City, California, pleaded guilty to creating a website with a "death list" of twenty-nine fellow students. The website, titled "People to Kill," included a page with a quiz in which viewers could pick the five most hated students by answering the question, "Who is the most hated eighth grader at James Workman Middle School?" The boy told police that he had placed his eighth-grade classmates' names on the page because of their economic status and because they had teased him about his ethnicity.

On March 4, 2000, police found Derik Lehman's hate-filled diary in which he allegedly tried to recruit classmates to help him kill fellow students who had ridiculed him. The Royal Palm Beach High School junior filled a composition notebook with swastika drawings and a school map detailing where the executions could take place. Lehman wrote, "My hate is unconditional. I look up to people like Hitler and grin at Eric Harris and Dylan Klebold's acts of murder and suicide." (Harris and Klebold were the two perpetrators of the 1999 Columbine High School massacre in Colorado, who killed one teacher and twelve students, wounded twenty-three students, and then killed themselves.)

Intolerance can be demonstrated in many ways—verbally, physically, or in combination—but in every case the perpetrator displays coldhearted disrespect for his victims, targeting their race, ethnicity, age, religion, disability, beliefs, gender, appearance, behavior, or sexual orientation. Whatever method the perpetrator uses, acts of intolerance always cause the victim pain and are therefore always immoral. Figures show that our youth are displaying immoral, intolerant actions at alarming rates—*and at younger and younger ages.* Researchers say that most hate crimes are committed by youth younger than nineteen. If our kids are to have any chance of living harmoniously in this multiethnic twenty-first century, it is critical that we nurture this sixth essential virtue *and start doing so when our kids are very young.*

THE CRISIS IN THE DEVELOPMENT OF TOLERANCE

Tolerance is a powerful moral virtue that helps curtail hatred, violence, and bigotry while at the same time influencing us to treat others with kindness, respect, and understanding. Tolerance does not require that we

Building Moral Intelligence

suspend moral judgment; it does require that we *respect differences.* This sixth virtue is what helps our children recognize that all persons deserve to be treated with love, justice, and respect, even if we happen to disagree with some of their beliefs or behaviors. It is a crucial component of moral intelligence that we must instill in our children.

Thomas Lickona, author of *Raising Good Children,* explains that tolerance as an ethical virtue has two aspects. The first is *respect:* for the basic human dignity and unalienable human rights of all persons, including their freedom of conscience to make moral choices as long as they don't infringe on the rights of others. Though our conscience may lead us to object to the moral choices other people make and even to attempt to persuade them they are mistaken in their beliefs or behavior, the virtue of tolerance keeps us from trying to force our views on others or unjustly restrict their liberty. Tolerance enables us to agree to disagree about even the most controversial of issues; it enables us to live with our deepest differences even as we continue to debate them.

The second aspect of tolerance is appreciation of the richness of human diversity, of the many positive qualities and contributions of people from all backgrounds, races, religions, countries, and cultures. We want our children—at home, in school, and in society—to be able to learn about what is interesting, useful, and enriching about other ways of thinking and living and benefit from such exposure. At the very least, we want our children to understand the great diversity of the human race and of each and every human family. Each person is unique. Tolerance in this sense is trying to find the good in all people.

Children are not born hateful: prejudices, biases, and stereotypes are learned or arise in the absence of adequate socialization. And there lies the crisis: in recent years, a number of powerful influences that breed intolerance have infiltrated our children's culture and are countering their development of tolerance. Of the myriad causes of intolerance and lack of respect for human differences, the following six factors are especially toxic.

Lack of Moral Monitoring

Charles Figley, a professor at Florida State University, echoes the sentiment of many experts: "Every child needs one person he or she can look up to, interact with and be monitored by." Many of today's children are growing up without moral monitoring. The reasons are many: the extended family has diminished, divorce affects half of all American families, financial pressures have forced both parents into an overtime workplace culture, and a hectic living pace leaves many parents exhausted and emotionally unavailable. Without significant adults in their lives, kids must interpret for themselves the mixed moral messages that are flooding them at record levels. James Comer, a professor of child psychiatry at the Yale Child Study Center, points out that never before in human history has there been so much information going directly, unfiltered by adult caregivers, to children. Never has there been as much readily available data countering tolerance.

Decline of Meaningful Community Support

Over the last few decades, many community support systems have crumbled, leaving large numbers of youth with few or no meaningful sources of human connection. The following are just a few reasons that kids' sense of belonging is dwindling: America is the most mobile society in the world, which means that many kids don't even know who lives next door to them, not to mention that they are unable to develop neighborhood connections. The extended family has deteriorated; except where they are the primary caregivers, grandparents and relatives play a less significant role in helping parents parent. Meanwhile, parental availability has dwindled, leaving many kids home alone after school. Schools—particularly high schools—are larger and more depersonalized. With ever-increasing class loads, many teachers don't have the time to develop much-needed relationships with students. Many community programs, such as park and recreation programs and community centers, have lost funding, so kids often must fend for themselves after school or return to empty homes.

William Damon, director of Stanford University's Center on Adolescence, points out, "Without the connectedness of a real community," there are "no checks on the cynicism." Damon adds, "The culture is much more toxic today. And the lack of community structure pushes kids towards hate." Thomas (T. J.) Leyden, former recruiter for the white supremacist and neo-Nazi movements who now helps police and human rights organizations, tells us why. Leyden explains that a key recruiting tactic hate groups use is to look for alienated boys around junior high age, because their desire to belong is so strong, their values still so malleable. "Age twelve is where they start," he says. "They go to junior highs, arcades, parks, anywhere where there are kids. They look for young, angry kids who need a family." Hate groups succeed in their recruitment efforts because they work hard to make these boys feel cared about and to offer a group they can belong to.

Accessibility of Internet Hate Sites

On any given day in this country, 40 percent of our fourteen million American teenagers surf the Internet, and they have access to intolerance at its worst. Researchers at the Simon Wiesenthal Center in Los Angeles, who regularly search the Web for hateful content, say there currently are over fourteen hundred racist, white supremacist, anti-Semitic, and other hate sites online, including such groups as the neo-Nazis and the Ku Klux Klan. Data reveal that our kids are logging onto these hateful sites in growing numbers. A recent poll conducted by *Time* magazine and CNN found that 25 percent of the teens surveyed admitted visiting Internet sites that have information about hate groups, and 62 percent of those polled said their parents know little or nothing about their visits. For kids who haven't developed solid moral values, these sites offer tempting new belief structures.

Racially Charged Video Entertainment Aimed at Youth

Today's youth are offered a wide array of entertainment outlets that encourage intolerance. Perhaps the favorite is video games. One of the most popular video games among youth these days is *Doom*. If you're not aware of this one, get ready: the game now comes in a new racist version with a plug-in that changes the victims' skin color. Now available on Ku Klux Klan websites is perhaps the most repugnant game of all, *Hang Leroy,* in which white supremacists can stage lynchings. Although your child may not own these games, keep in mind that chances are high that his peers do, and even if they don't, kids love to talk about such emotionally charged information.

Hate Music

As if websites and video games aren't enough for nurturing intolerance, kids can also choose from hundreds of music CDs that feature some of the most vile, hateful, and racist lyrics you could ever imagine. Currently more than fifty thousand "white power" rock CDs are sold every year in America that call for murdering black people or creating a whites-only revolution. One of the more popular recent numbers is called "Aryan Love Song." There are also hundreds of CDs by black and Latino hip-hop musicians with their kill-the-white messages to choose from. Considering that between the junior high to senior high school years, the average teenager listens to countless hours of rock music, there is more than ample time to plant the seeds of intolerance.

Prejudice and Stereotypes Displayed on Television

Many feel that one of the biggest culprits perpetuating discrimination, prejudice, and racism is television. Diane Levin, author of *Remote Control Childhood?* proposes that much of commercial television reinforces exaggerated or extremely narrow representations of people and gives kids distorted opinions about the world. For example: white actors continue to appear in the bulk of the major roles, whereas people of color appear in less than 11 percent of prime-time shows and 3 percent of children's programs. In addition, a disproportionate number of women, African American, Native American, and Latino characters are portrayed as poor and unsuccessful, whereas white characters are generally cast as richer and more successful. The danger is that by repeatedly viewing such images, kids may unconsciously develop the biased view that white people are more important than others.

Because today's youth spend more time in front of TV sets than in classrooms, the lessons of intolerance they view are lethal, and the effects of those lessons should *never* be considered trivial. Madeline Levine, author of *See No Evil,* points out, "If you are elderly, it is not trivial that the media insist on reducing you to a dotty simpleton. If you are an African American, it is not trivial that the media vacillate between worshiping you as a sports hero, laughing at you as a buffoon, or reviling you as a thug. If you are a woman, it is not trivial that every female newscaster must be ten or twenty years younger than her male counterpart. If you are a parent who tries to convey the values of hard work and good education to your children, it is not trivial that Beavis and Butt-Head have become the supermodels of teenage sloth and indifference."

These six factors all point to a crisis in the development of tolerance. Certainly no one factor causes kids to adopt intolerant attitudes, but when so many influences are so deeply embedded in our culture, it behooves us to fervently nurture and advocate tolerance in our youth. Until we do so, many children's moral intelligence will be greatly shortchanged, and we'll all be left wondering which really is the greater moral influence for kids: their parents, or a culture that too often breeds intolerance.

WHAT IS TOLERANCE?

Two years ago, I was invited to conduct a series of parent workshops in the Stockton Unified School District. The area was heavily populated with Vietnamese and Cambodian immigrants and had been the site several years earlier of a horrendous school shooting where a deranged white man dressed in battle fatigues opened fire with a semiautomatic weapon on the playground at Cleveland Elementary. Within minutes, five children—all sons and daughters of refugees from South East Asia—had been slaughtered, and twenty-nine children and adults were wounded. Suspicion was high that the racial composition of the student body might have been part of what motivated the killer, who turned out to be a former Cleveland Elementary student.

Racial tensions in the community became hot, and the school district had been working hard to restore harmony. A banner across one school door enunciated the community's view: "Racists are ugly—let's stop them."

The neighboring district I was working in that night made a commitment to parent education, and over the next year I was contracted to do several sessions addressing positive discipline, enhancement of self-esteem, and anger management. The first minutes of the opening session proved to be one of my most interesting speaking experiences.

As I spoke to the 350 parents that night, my words were simultaneously translated into the seven different languages of the audience: Cambodian, Chinese, Vietnamese, Hmong, Laotian, Hindu, and Spanish. It was so obvious just how culturally diverse America has become. It was also quite clear that for our kids to live harmoniously in this multiethnic world, they must learn to accept each other's differences. For them to do so, we must ensure that tolerance is well nurtured from a very early age, before the seeds of intolerance can be planted.

Tolerance is the essential moral virtue that helps kids respect each other as persons regardless of differences, be they of race, gender, appearance, culture, beliefs, abilities, sexual orientation, or abilities. Tolerant children have the ability to maintain this respect even if they disagree with someone's perspectives and beliefs. Because they have that capacity, these kids are less tolerant of cruelty, bigotry, and racism. So it is not surprising that these children grow to become adults who find ways to make our world a more humane place. Increasing children's tolerance is what will help them reject prejudice, biases, stereotypes, and hatred and learn to respect people more for their character and attitudes than for their differences. This chapter shows you how to foster this sixth essential moral virtue in your child, significantly increasing his moral intelligence.

HOW TOLERANT IS YOUR CHILD?

The statements that follow describe behaviors usually displayed by children with a healthy sense of tolerance. To evaluate your child's strengths in this sixth virtue, write the number you think best represents your child's current level on the line following each statement and then add all the scores to get his total score. If your child scores 40 to 50, he's in great shape with this aspect of moral intelligence. If he scores 30 to 40, he could benefit from virtue enhancement. A score of 20 to 30 shows signs of potential problems. A score of 10 to 20 reveals potential danger; consider getting help to increase this essential virtue.

5 = Always 4 = Frequently 3 = Sometimes 2 = Rarely 1 = Never

A Child with Healthy Tolerance	My Child
Displays tolerance toward others regardless of age, culture, religion, or gender.	_____
Shows respect toward adults and authority figures.	_____
Is open to knowing people with different backgrounds and beliefs than hers.	_____
Voices displeasure and concern when someone is insulted or put down.	_____
Sticks up for the "underdog"; doesn't allow unfairness or intolerance.	_____
Refrains from making comments or jokes that put another group or person down.	_____
Has pride in his culture and heritage.	_____
Is friendly and open to people regardless of their race, religion, sexual orientation, beliefs, appearance, age, gender, disabilities, or culture.	_____
Focuses on the positive traits of others instead of on their differences.	_____
Refrains from judging, categorizing, or stereotyping others.	_____
Total Score	_____

THREE STEPS TO BUILDING TOLERANCE

Tolerance, a key virtue for helping our kids get along in a diverse world, is a trait that is learned and can be taught. There are three steps to building this essential moral virtue in your child. Because the foundation for tolerance is built in the home, the first teaching step shows you some of the most effective strategies for modeling and nurturing the virtue in your child when she is still young. Because learning to get along with people who are different from them will be a big part of our children's lives, the second step provides ways to help your child accept, respect, and celebrate the diverse talents, cultures, and contributions of others. The last step teaches her ways to counter conventional stereotypes before they turn into hateful prejudices that could haunt her views forever. These three steps will increase the tolerance your child will need to face our multiethnic, diverse world and live harmoniously.

Here again are the three teachable steps you can use to build tolerance in your child and boost her moral intelligence:

Step 1: Model and Nurture Tolerance
Step 2: Instill an Appreciation for Diversity
Step 3: Counter Stereotypes and Never Tolerate Prejudice

STEP 1: MODEL AND NURTURE TOLERANCE

I was in the Portland, Oregon, airport last year and witnessed one of the most powerful yet simple lessons of tolerance I've ever seen. Around two dozen preschool children and their teachers on an airport field trip were walking hand in hand and wearing T-shirts that read "Children Are Not Born Racist." It was quite an image. Other passengers were struck as I was, and many stopped to stare. One man standing near me said to no one in particular, "If only parents could understand that one message—maybe we could get along." How right he was! The lesson conveyed on those shirts is what all research confirms: we are not born with intolerant beliefs—we learn them as children from the environments in which we live. So if we really are concerned about ending racism, bigotry, intolerance, and hate, we must consciously model and nurture tolerance in our homes and schools when our kids are very young. It's the best chance we have to help children grow to appreciate and respect others who are different from themselves. This first step shows you strategies so that you can begin.

Six Practices That Help Raise Tolerant Kids

A favorite Native American saying is, "Your actions speak so loudly, I cannot hear what you say." These words are terribly important when we think about the most effective ways to nurture tolerance in our kids. Research finds that our direct teaching about respecting others has much more impact on our kids when our actions are consistent with our words. That's because moral behaviors are *caught* as well as *taught*—that's why we must both practice what we preach and preach what we practice. Here are six practices that are effective ways of conveying to your child how strongly you believe that all people—regardless of race, gender, religion, age, ability, sexual orientation, economic background, appearance, or culture—should be treated with respect for their dignity as persons.

1. Confront your own prejudices. The first step to helping kids become more tolerant is to look in the mirror and examine your own prejudices. None of us are completely free of some prejudice or stereotypical beliefs. Most of these conscious or unconscious beliefs are deeply entrenched. We grew up with them and learned them in our own family of origin, and they're still residing within us. The problem is that prejudices and stereotypes can be so deeply seated that we may not even be aware they are there. But our kids sure are! Chances are that you are communicating those attitudes (usually quite unintentionally) to your child.

I honestly don't recall my parents passing on prejudices; but one of my relatives did, and his opinion was loudly voiced: the homeless are lazy, and they use any money donations to buy alcohol. Because his stereotype was repeated so often, it remained in the back of my mind. I discovered I was unconsciously passing it on to my sons years later. On rare occasions when we would pass a homeless individual, I would admonish my kids not to give out money; after all, "it would never be put to good use." When my sons were teenagers, they were the ones to dispel my prejudice, and it started when they befriended a homeless man who stood outside our church every Sunday. Each week I'd watch them say hello and give him their loose change or a dollar before they went inside. During winter they brought him extra blankets and warm clothes from their closets. Their routine continued, and then one Sunday, to my amazement—and I'm sure to theirs as well—the man accompanied them inside to the service. I'll never forget how, when the collection basket for the poor was passed, he took the change my sons had just given him and put it in the basket. My sons smiled rather sheepishly at me, as if to say, "Told you so." I realized then just how strongly that prejudice had remained with me all those years—until my kids erased it.

The surest way our children learn intolerance is through our example: make sure you aren't a lethal contributor of prejudices. You might begin by reflecting on your own childhood upbringing: What were some of your parents' prejudices? Do any of those remain with you today? Take time to reflect on how you might be projecting those old, outdated ideas to your child. Then make a conscious attempt to temper them so that they don't become your child's prejudices. Sometimes you might not even know you are tainting your children's moral views.

2. Commit yourself to raising a tolerant child. Parents who take time to think through how they want their kids to turn out usually succeed simply because they planned their parenting efforts. If you really want your child to appreciate and respect diversity, then you must adopt a conviction early on to raise him to do so. Once your child knows your expectations, he will be more likely to embrace your principles.

3. Refuse to allow discriminatory comments in your presence. Your child may make prejudicial comments or repeat discriminatory jokes—for example, "Those guys are a bunch of fags," "Hey, did you hear the one about the Polack who . . . ?" "Those Chinese kids are all such brainy nerds, they'll all get into college before me," or "Of course he'll make the basketball team. All those black players have an unfair advantage!" How you respond to these statements sends a clear message to your child about your values. When you hear such comments, emphasize your discomfort and verbalize your displeasure: "That's disrespectful, and I won't allow such things to be said in my house," or "That's a biased comment, and I don't want to hear it." Your child needs to hear your discomfort so that she knows you really walk your talk. It also models a response she should imitate if prejudicial comments are made in her presence.

4. Provide positive images of all ethnic groups. From the time your child is very young, expose him to positive images—including toys, music, literature, videos, public role models, and examples from TV or newspaper reports—that represent a variety of ethnic groups. The more your child sees how you embrace diversity, the more prone he'll be to follow your standards.

5. Encourage involvement with a wide range of diversities. Encourage your child, no matter how young, to have contact with individuals of different races, religions, cultures, genders, abilities, and beliefs. Involve your child in programs—whether they are in school, after school, or even at a summer camp—that foster diversity. Make sure you display openness to people who represent a range of diversities so that your child imitates how you respect differences.

MORAL INTELLIGENCE BUILDER
Hidden but Dangerous Adult Prejudice and Stereotyping

Stereotypes and prejudices often become so much of our culture and so entrenched in our jokes and casual comments that we may be unintentionally passing them on to our kids. Such stereotypes can address gender, race, age, lifestyles, beliefs, appearance, abilities, religion, and culture and are always sweeping generalities with no factual base. Here are a few beliefs to watch out for; we may think they are harmless, but they can be quite hurtful:

All blacks have rhythm.

The homeless could get jobs if they tried.

Teenagers only care about themselves.

Girls are poor at math.

The Chinese are sneaky.

Blondes are dumb.

Stepmoms are nags.

Asian kids are all great students.

Cheerleaders are "easy."

No politician can be trusted.

All Jews are rich.

Italians are all in the Mafia.

The Irish are all drunks.

Police officers are racist.

Latinos make great lovers.

Boys who don't play sports are wimpy.

The elderly are all senile.

The Polish are dumb.

Native Americans are quick tempered.

Football players are stupid.

6. Live your life as an example of tolerance. The best way for your child to learn tolerance is for him to watch and listen to your daily example. So ask yourself each day, If my child had only my behavior to copy, would he be witnessing an example of what I want him to emulate? Make sure you are walking your talk.

Where to Begin: Four Ways to Help Kids Develop a Sense of Personal Identity

A common practice I've noticed in my consulting work is for high schools to implement diversity training programs as a means of reducing racial tensions among their students. Although I fully agree with the philosophy behind such programs, my concern is that they are starting so late to plant the seeds of tolerance. Children can acquire prejudices and stereotypes when they're very young, so the greatest chance we have in helping our kids become more tolerant is to instill in them the habits of this essential virtue early—*and the earlier the better.* Although it's certainly never too late to begin, the sooner we start, the better the chance we have of preventing insidious, intolerant attitudes from taking hold.

How do we begin to inspire tolerance in our kids? An important point to remember is this: before a child can learn to appreciate and tolerate others, he has to appreciate himself. Clyde W. Ford, author of *We Can All Get Along,* explains: "Children will not learn to accept and tolerate differences in others if they have not experienced acceptance and tolerance for their differences." So an important beginning step to fostering tolerance is to help your child understand how you and your family respect the special qualities of each member. The following activities help your child recognize his unique identity and the special qualities he offers to his family as well as to society. Although these activities are primarily designed for younger children, the concepts are important for kids at any age.

Play the "Who Am I?" Game　Gather your family together and discuss how each person present has special qualities that make her unique. Then teach them how to play a game that will help you recognize those qualities, called Who Am I? Explain that each person takes turns saying one true and positive statement about herself, starting with "I am . . . " Family members may help by supplying information about each other. The game continues for several rounds until members run out of "I am" statements. Here are a few ideas: "I am a goalie, I am Jewish, I am kind, I am a middle child, I am dark-haired, I am a brother, I am sensitive, I am brown-eyed, I am creative." To help your child internalize her positive images, remind her of the traits a few times during the week at moments that arise naturally: "I love your paintings. You really are creative," or "I admire how kind and sensitive you are. Those are the kinds of traits that really matter most in getting along with people."

Make an Identity Place Mat   Help your child cover a twelve-by-eighteen-inch piece of construction paper or tagboard with words or pictures that define her unique qualities and characteristics. Photographs of your child could also be used. If desired, cover the place mat with clear contact paper (available at variety stores) to make it more durable. The place mats can then be used to eat on; they also make great family keepsakes.

Create a People Recipe   Emphasize to your child that many personal characteristics combine to make each person unique and special, just as many ingredients make up a recipe. Ask your child, "What are you made of?" Then help her write down her answers as a recipe on an index card. Ingredients should include physical characteristics, personality traits, ethnic background, and even religious beliefs. Make a card for each member of your family and paste each on a colored piece of paper along with a photograph of the person. You might also include a card for each relative. Binding them all together with string or a one-inch metal ring makes a wonderful "Family Cookbook" to give or save as a special family memory.

Here's a sample of a recipe card that includes the child's cultural heritage, physical characteristics, religion, and a few other attributes:

> ### RECIPE FOR KALIN
>
> 2 teaspoons of Irish
> 1 teaspoon of Catholic
> Stir in 2 huge blue eyes and a dash of smiles.
> Sprinkle with freckles, add a few hugs.
> 1 tablespoon of niceness and a pinch of spunkiness.
> Mix the niceness, then gently add a dash of fun.
> Bake well in the love and care of the Galvin family.
> And there you have the recipe of Kalin, a fabulous, wonderful kid!

Help an Older Child Recognize a Strength Just knowing your child's strengths isn't good enough: you must pass your findings on to your child. The more you can expand your child's awareness of his qualities, the greater the likelihood that he will value his identity. Here are the four keys to unlocking your child's awareness of his special qualities:

- Choose one or two positive qualities you want your child to recognize about herself right away—for example, her optimism, generosity, spirituality, kindness, gentleness, or sensitivity. Make sure the strengths are already present in your child, not ones you *wish* were true about her.

- Now begin to find opportunities to praise the strength frequently. You can start out by giving one strength message a day and gradually work your way up to two to four strength reminders. Usually it takes at least three weeks for a new image to develop, so keep praising your child's strengths for at least twenty-one days.

- Praise your child only when her actions deserve recognition and when you mean it. Children are great at distinguishing the genuine from the insincere.

- Point out examples of how your child displays the strengths. Be specific in your praise so that your child knows exactly what she did to deserve recognition. Here are a few examples: "You're very open-minded; you always seem to listen to everyone's ideas before you form an opinion." "You are so caring. I noticed how you stopped to ask that woman if she needed help with her groceries." "You always seem to have something upbeat and positive to say about people. It brightens everyone's day."

MORAL INTELLIGENCE BUILDER
A Story to Tell Kids About Tolerance

Samantha Reed Smith, a fourth grader from Manchester, Maine, did more for building tolerance than most people do in their entire lives. Her quest began when she read about the growing arms race between the Soviet Union and the United States and became so worried about nuclear war that she decided to write a letter to Yuri V. Andropov, the Soviet leader at that time. Although only ten, Samantha expressed the concerns of many adults: "God made the world for us to live together in peace and not to fight." Touched, Andropov invited her to visit his country to see for herself that "in the Soviet Union everyone is for peace and friendship among peoples."

On July 7, 1983, Samantha and her parents went to the Soviet Union. Reports of her peace crusade helped change the way two countries felt about one another. For the first time, many Americans and Soviets recognized that they shared the desire for world peace. "If we could be friends by just getting to know each other better," she said, "then what are our countries really arguing about?" By the time of her tragic death in an airline crash, thirteen-year-old Samantha had already made a powerful contribution toward ensuring a more tolerant world.

Samantha Reed Smith was a child who displayed tolerance because she respected and accepted a culture and its beliefs, even though they were different from her own. Whereas many Americans in the 1980s feared the Russian people, Samantha decided to form her own opinions, so she listened openly, asked questions, wrote letters, then reached her own conclusion. Although only in the fourth grade, she already recognized that if people are really going to be able to live peacefully together, they need to form judgments only after learning all the facts. That's the only way to be truly fair. Samantha made a difference in our world.

STEP 2: INSTILL AN APPRECIATION FOR DIVERSITY

At one of my recent workshops, Steffani, a mother from Austin, Texas, shared an experience she had as room mother for her son's fourth grade that she said haunted her. Steffani explained that she was serving cupcakes at their Valentine's Day party when she noticed a student with only a handful of valentines sitting by herself while the other kids continued open-ing their cards. Steffani was concerned because the girl looked so sad and was obviously poor: she had far outgrown her sweater, and her socks had holes in them. Then Steffani recalled hearing from other parents about a new student from India, and she figured this was the child. She became infuriated.

She told us, "This little girl probably didn't know a soul; her parents couldn't afford to buy valentines, let alone probably know what they are; and only a few kids were thoughtful enough to give her any. I finally decid-ed to ask another student why the girl didn't receive any cards, and I couldn't believe what I heard. The boy told me very matter-of-factly that nobody liked her because she was kind of strange and talked funny, her mom wears a dot on her forehead, and she even scared them because she was so different. I just can't imagine kids in this day and age being so intolerant."

To help our children live in a more harmonious world, we must teach them to be respectful of diversity. After all, their world is growing more diverse every day. Whereas some children are responding to change with fear, prejudice, violence, and hate crimes, others are learning to accept and respect differences. The more tolerant your children are, the more open they will be to learning about other people. The more they learn, the less they will be uncomfortable or fearful in any kind of situation, with any kind of person. This second step provides ways to instill in your child an appreciation for diversity in the beliefs, abilities, and backgrounds of others. Teaching your child to become more tolerant is possible, and this section shows you how.

Talking About Tolerance with Kids

Here are some questions to help kids think about the value of being tolerant and respectful of all people's beliefs and differences.

- What is tolerance? Do you think people are born tolerant, or do they become tolerant? Who are some people you know who are tolerant? What makes them tolerant? How do you know if someone is tolerant?
- What kinds of things would an intolerant person do? (Possible behaviors include making fun of people, jumping to conclusions, laughing at someone's disability, gossiping, engaging in name-calling, making jokes about someone's differences, rejecting someone because he looks or acts differently.)
- Why do you think some people make fun of others who look or act differently? Is it right? Why?
- Do you know what it means to be racist? Have you ever experienced racism or witnessed someone else experiencing racism? What happened? How did you feel? Was it wrong or right?
- Suppose a new student comes to school who is of a different ethnic group than your friends. You want to get to know him better. The problem is, your friends don't want to include him because he looks and acts differently. What will you do? What should you do?
- Is it right to exclude people because of their race? What about gender or beliefs? Should private clubs be allowed to exclude people from membership because of their gender or beliefs?

Six Ways to Develop Your Child's Pride in His Culture

The starting place to help children understand diversity is for them to look at their own ancestry. The family is where children not only experience a sense of belonging but also acquire their primary language, their knowledge of their ethnicity, their spiritual or religious beliefs, and their values. It is through this membership that kids define their identity and develop pride in their cultural heritage. Learning about their family background helps children connect with their past and develop an appreciation and respect for not only their own national and ethnic background but also for those of their friends and classmates. As Barbara Mathias and Mary Ann French, authors of *Forty Ways to Raise a Nonracist Child,* explain: "Once your child has a solid sense of self and pride in her own people, it will be easier for her to find joy in the differences of others." So here are six ways to help your child understand his heritage and begin to appreciate just how much the world is a melting pot of different customs and ideas.

1. **Use family photo albums.** Spend time together looking through your family photo albums. They are excellent tools for helping your child discover his cultural heritage as well as for learning about his relatives past and present. You might point out special traits that are shared across gen-

erations as well as identify characteristics your child has in common with other relatives. A family in Rochester created a "Family Hall of Fame" where pictures of relatives from several generations are displayed in their hallway. A mother of four sons in Hartford told me she sets aside vacation time when each child is ten years old so that he can make his own family photo album with her guidance. Each child then has his own personal album to take when he finally leaves home.

2. Create an ancestry map. A great way to help your child gain an awareness of her cultural ancestry (and of geography) is to hang a large world map on your wall and use it to help her find countries, states, and cities that were once, and may still be, home to her relatives. You might pin photographs of family members, print their names, or attach small paper flag replicas next to their country of origin. It can also be a wonderful opportunity to discuss the path your family traveled to get where it is today, and to explain what you know of the reasons for its travels. Mathias and French point out: "If children know where they come from, what obstacles their ancestors have endured and conquered, and what progress they have made over the centuries, they can't help but feel a sense of pride in their people."

3. Keep a family journal. Many families keep a blank book to record their family heritage and keep track of special family memories. Here are a few items to include: a log of visiting relatives, cherished family recipes, photographs of ancestors, a family tree, a family coat of arms, interviews of relatives with descriptions of early family recollections, records of family reunions, a world map depicting the location of family members, and a brief history of your family's ancestry.

4. Create a family recipe book. One of the best—and also one of the simplest—holiday gifts our family created one year was a family recipe book. I first wrote a letter asking every relative to please send a copy of his or her favorite family recipe, a brief description as to why the recipe had such meaning, and a recent photograph of the contributor's immediate family. Wonderful recipes arrived (including ones that had been saved for decades!) from cousins, uncles, aunts, and great-grandparents. My sons and I typed each recipe and description on five-by-eight-inch paper and glued the family's photograph under it. Then we duplicated the pages, had them bound together into booklets at a stationery store, and mailed a copy to each relative. My children now have not only a photo album of their relatives but also a book of wonderful family recipes they can pass on to their own children.

5. Provide children's literature representing your heritage. Many parents start a yearly tradition of giving their child a book about her cultural history for her birthday. This can be especially meaningful for parents with a foreign-born adopted child to help her maintain a sense of cultural identity and belonging with her native country.

6. Hang a flag of your country of origin. Purchase a flag that represents your family's country of origin and hang it proudly. Some families hang their flag to honor special native celebrations; other families put up the flag for family reunions or birthdays. It is a great way to help your child and family develop cultural pride.

MORAL INTELLIGENCE BUILDER
Expose Your Child Early to Multicultural Literature

Jan Arnow, author of *Teaching Peace*, points out that "only 10 percent of the almost five thousand children's books published each year in the United States are multicultural in nature. Of those, fewer than fifty titles annually have been written about Native American and Asian peoples." That is a troubling statistic, because research says that children first become aware of race and gender differences around two years of age, around the time many parents have started nightly bedtime traditions of reading with their kids. Expose your child early to a variety of multicultural literature that features positive images of all cultures and genders. It is one way to increase tolerance as well as reduce or prevent prejudice.

Four Ways to Develop Positive Attitudes About Diversity

One way children sort out their own identities and form ideas about themselves is by figuring out how they are the same as or different from others. Gordon Allport's famous 1950s study of prejudice found that awareness of differences evolves slowly as a natural by-product of children's cognitive and social development, a process that is crucial for positive identity development. It is when our children become developmentally capable of noticing those differences that we must help them form positive attitudes about diversity. Not doing so can plant the seed of intolerance, for kids may interpret differences negatively and reject people who are "not like me." The critical parenting task is to help children at that stage learn to respect differences and develop positive attitudes about diversity.

Marguerite Wright, a black psychologist and renowned researcher on racial awareness, points out that intolerance can also be learned, and often our children's most influential teachers are the very adults they love most. Wright notes that children younger than five really don't see people as members of a particular group of any kind *unless adults draw this to their attention*. She explains: "Children, unless rigorously taught to do otherwise, start out making no distinction among people because of their skin or race. It takes a good while before they are developmentally capable of seeing people primarily in terms of their race, in the way that too many adults do." Wright contends that it is only when adults begin point out "isms"—ageism, culturalism, sexism, "looksism," racism—that young children adopt full-fledged stereotypes that can taint their moral beliefs. It is often *our* remarks, *our* subtle expressions, or *our* gestures regarding those "isms" that plant the seeds of hatred in our young children's minds. It is therefore our responsibility to avoid planting those seeds ourselves and to prevent them from sprouting if planted by anyone else.

Thus it is a combination of learning and development that determines our children's attitudes and behavior from a very early age, and parents can greatly influence that growth. Here are four ways to help your child embrace diversity:

Celebrate Differences Early On   The first step to helping kids develop positive attitudes about diversity is to emphasize from the time they are very young that it is OK to be different. Teachers often begin by having young children make prints of their thumbs and then discussing how, just as no two thumbprints are alike, no two people are alike either. People's differences are one thing that makes the world such a wonderful place. Another possibility is to make a collage together of magazine pictures featuring all different kinds of people and depicting differences in gender, age, race, culture, backgrounds, physical appearance, and even moods.

Expose Your Child to Diversity   Ignorance or lack of information is one of the most common reasons children develop stereotypes. Inexperience, especially if combined with incomplete information, can lead children to have fears or insecurities about others. I learned that lesson through my own son. When he was nine, his teacher arranged for his class to visit a nearby nursing home during the holidays to sing to the patients. I thought it was a wonderful opportunity for kids to learn to serve others, but my son was hesitant. It took me a while to realize that he was uncomfortable because he had not had many experiences with the elderly. But once we talked about what he could expect, his concerns eased. By the time he came home from the actual outing, any fears he had were gone. In fact, he couldn't wait to go visit the seniors again.

To feel uncomfortable with people who are different from us is natural. But by exposing our children to diversity when they are young and talking to them about those differences, we can prevent them from developing fears and stereotypes they can carry into their teens and adulthood.

Give Straightforward, Simple Answers to Questions About Differences
Kids are naturally curious, so you should expect questions about differences. Asking questions is one way for them to sort out how they are different or the same from others as well as to learn to feel comfortable with those differences. Beverly Daniel Tatum, author of *"Why Are All the Black*

Kids Sitting Together in the Cafeteria?" and Other Conversations About Race stresses the importance of answering children's questions simply and honestly even though some issues may seem embarrassing or even taboo. How you respond can either create stereotypes or prevent them from forming. For very young kids, usually a one- or two-sentence answer is enough. Here are a few examples:

Child: Why is Alon's skin so dark? He looks dirty.

Parent: Alon's skin is not dirty. He is clean just like you. Skin comes in lots of different colors: beige, peach, tan, and brown, just like eyes come in different colors. Your skin color is peach, and Alon's skin is brown.

Child: Sally's a girl. She shouldn't be playing football!

Parent: Girls can play the same sports boys do. Some girls like football, and some girls don't. Sally likes to play football, so she should play it.

Child: Why does Ling talk funny?

Parent: Ling may sound funny to you because you can't understand what she is saying. At home she speaks another language, called Chinese, and she is just learning to speak English. There are lots of different languages people speak.

Child: Why is that boy sitting in that chair that moves?

Parent: That chair is called a wheelchair, and it has a motor. The boy's legs don't work the same as yours. The chair is what he uses to get from place to place.

Help Your Child Look for Similarities Encourage your child to look for what he has in common with others instead of how he is different. One fun way to foster tolerance in your child is to play as a family a simple game called Alike and Different. It begins by having family members form pairs. Tell each pair to think of five ways they are alike and five ways they are different. Answers can be written or drawn. "Alike" answers might be, for example, "We are African American, Baptist, dark-haired, brown-eyed, and Williams family members." "Different" answers could be, for example, "I like soccer, she likes tennis; I play saxophone, she plays violin; I am a fourth grader, she is a second grader; I am 4'5", she is 4'2"." In a larger family, have each twosome report their findings back to the family. From then on, any time your child points out how she is different from someone, you might say, "Yes, there are lots of ways you are different from other people. Now let's try to think of ways you are the same."

STEP 3: COUNTER STEREOTYPES
AND NEVER TOLERATE PREJUDICE

Two days after Martin Luther King Jr. was assassinated, a third-grade teacher from Riceville, Iowa, taught a unique lesson about discrimination to her students. The teacher, Jane Elliott, was troubled about racism and wanted to find a way to help her students feel the pain of intolerance. So on the first day, she declared all her brown-eyed students "superior," gave them special privileges, and encouraged them to discriminate against their suddenly "inferior" blue-eyed classmates. The next day, she reversed the roles. What happened astonished both the students and the teacher. On both days, the third graders labeled "inferior" took on the look and behavior of genuinely inferior students, even doing inferior work. And the "superior" students excelled in their work and delighted in discriminating against their "inferior" peers. The lesson proved so powerful in conveying the hurt inevitably associated with discrimination that Mrs. Elliott repeated the exercise with succeeding classes and was always surprised at the positive results. But it wasn't until several years later that she understood the full impact of her lesson.

Fourteen years after her first experiment, eleven of Mrs. Elliott's sixteen third graders returned to Riceville for a class reunion, which was to be filmed for a television documentary. By then the teacher's discrimination experiment had become widely known, and educators and psychologists alike were intrigued with Mrs. Elliott's technique. So her past students were interviewed, and for the first time, they expressed to their teacher how her lesson in discrimination had had an enduring effect on their lives. Each explained that due to their experience, their attitudes had profoundly changed even with regard to the way they were raising their own children.

This teacher taught us all a critical point: it is possible to counter the teaching of hatred by having children experience and understand rejection. Hatred and intolerance can be learned, but so can sensitivity, understanding, empathy, and tolerance. This final step shows ways to teach our children to counter stereotypes before they become full-fledged, lasting prejudices and to recognize that every human being has the right to be treated with respect.

MORAL INTELLIGENCE BUILDER
The Stages of Race Awareness

Clinical psychologist Marguerite Wright, the author of *I'm Chocolate, You're Vanilla,* believes that children develop an awareness of race slowly, in a series of predictable stages. As noted earlier, her research found that unless rigorously taught to do otherwise, children start out making no distinctions among people because of their skin color or race. Wright also believes that racial bigotry is taught, often by the people children look up to most: their parents. The descriptions of the stages here are adapted from Dr. Wright's acclaimed work.

Stage 1: Racial innocence   Age 3

Most children are incapable of accurately identifying their skin color, much less their race. They see people as individuals and not as members of particular racial groups.

Stage 2: Color awareness   Ages 3 to 5

When asked, "What color are you?" children are just as likely to describe the color of their clothes as the color of their skin. They continue to see people without prejudice with regard to skin color or race. Because children are routinely taught racial bigotry, however, they will begin to form negative associations with certain skin colors.

Stage 3: Awakening to social color   Ages 5 to 7

Most children are unable to reliably identify their race, but they can accurately identify their skin color and begin to make relative skin color distinctions. They may begin to adopt skin color prejudices, although they do not fully understand them.

Stage 4: Racial awareness   Ages 8 to 10

Children now accurately identify their race using such terms as *Native American, Chinese, Hispanic,* and *African American.* Unless they are taught not to prejudge people based on their race, children may adopt full-fledged racial stereotypes.

Four Ways to Curtail Prejudice by Teaching Kids to Counter Stereotypes

When my boys were ages six, four, and two, our family moved from the Bay Area to Palm Springs. My husband and I were very excited about living in such an entirely new kind of environment. Before the move, we wanted the boys to be excited also, so we told them of the different desert vegetation and animals they would see and explained how the Cahuilla Indians had settled there years ago. We thought we really had prepared them well for the big relocation, but when moving day arrived, we knew something was up.

As the boys got ready for the long drive, I noticed that the younger ones had packed their bicycle helmets in their backpacks. When I tried to convince them we wouldn't be taking any bike rides soon and that they wouldn't need the helmets, they were adamant that the helmets remain. It took a rather lengthy conversation to finally figure out their very real concern: they were worried about the Indians who lived in Palm Springs. The only knowledge my kids had of Indians was from their favorite video, Peter Pan; *from that they had conjured up an image that was very frightening. They assumed they were going to live in a place ruled by Indians with tomahawks. The helmets would be their protection from the scalpings that would be occurring on a regular basis. By watching Walt Disney's family classic, my kids had formed negative stereotypes about Native Americans that could have haunted them for a long time. I realized then how easily misconceptions can form in kids' minds.*

Studies reveal that by the time children reach school, many have already developed negative conceptions about groups different from their own. Such conceptions are deadly to tolerance, because if they are not countered, they can easily cloud children's views for the rest of their lives. The following are four ways to help curtail prejudices by helping kids recognize and counter stereotypes before they become long-lasting biases.

Point Out Biases and Stereotypes   Our kids' culture is saturated with biases and stereotypical messages, and if these negative values are not countered, our kids can internalize them. Television, film, advertising, music, literature, and jokes are major perpetrators of stereotypes. The best way to squelch biased material is first to familiarize yourself with it, then to explain to your child what a stereotype is, so that he later recognizes them on his own. You might say, "A stereotype is a big sweeping idea we believe about a whole group of people. Usually the belief is wrong because it is not true about every member of the group, so it is very unfair because the person believing the stereotype makes a judgment without getting all the facts." You might discuss a few stereotypes that seem dominant in our culture—for example, that all girls are poor in math, all good basketball players are black, and all blondes are dumb. Asking your child questions that point out biases as they occur is often beneficial in helping him recognize the misrepresentation. Here are a few examples that show how:

Nightly news:	The news always seems to be showing blacks as aggressive and caught doing bad things. Do you think they are reporting the news fairly?
Jokes:	I'm hearing a lot of jokes about blonde girls that always say they are not smart. Do you know blonde girls who are smart? If you were a blonde girl and heard those jokes, how would you feel?
Newspapers:	I've read a number of stories lately about police brutality. Have you read them too? Do you think people might get the impression that all police are unfair and beat up minorities? What do you think?
Film and TV:	So many TV shows seem to show Latinos as disrespectful and poor, while whites are portrayed as wealthier and law abiding. Have you noticed that? Do you think that's a fair image?

Literature:	This is another story in which the stepmother is mean and wicked. Do you think all stepmothers are mean? If kids keep reading stories about stepmoms being mean, what do you think their view of stepmoms will be?

Encourage "Talk Checks" to Squelch Stereotypical Messages   Sara Bullard, author of the book *Teaching Tolerance*, explains that an important part of ending prejudice is helping kids tune in to the way they talk about other people or groups. The trick is to have them listen for any sweeping categorical statements they or another person might make, such as "You always . . . ," "They never . . . ," or "They're all . . . ," because chances are that what follows is a stereotype. So tell your kids that whenever someone in the family makes such a sweeping statement, another family member should gently remind the speaker, "Check that."

Child:	Asian kids always get good grades in school.
Parent:	Check that! Do you think that's true for every Asian child?

Child:	Going to Grandma's is going to be boring. Her friends will probably be there, and they never can hear what you're saying.
Brother:	Hey, check that. You just said that every person who is elderly can't hear. I know a lot of elderly people who hear just fine.

Counter Your Child's Discriminatory Beliefs   What do you do when your child makes a prejudicial comment about a group? The most important thing is not to overreact or be too quick to criticize; doing so will stop his comment *but not his belief.* Your goal is to change his view, and the only way to do that is by listening carefully to your child's words and why he feels that way. In his book *We Can All Get Along*, Clyde W. Ford advises that you do not let the remark slide. Here are two ideas Ford suggests to help counter your child's discriminatory beliefs:

1. Listen carefully without judging your child. When you hear your child make a prejudicial comment, the first step is always the hardest: listen without judging or interrupting your child. You want to gather as many facts as you can to find out why he feels the way he does and what gave rise to his words. That way you can help him change a belief before it turns into a long-lasting prejudice. Suppose your child says, "Kids who don't speak English shouldn't be allowed in our school." You might say, "I want to hear why you said that," or "You sound like you feel very strongly about that. Why is that?" or "Where did you hear that?"

2. Challenge any prejudicial views. When you have all the facts behind your child's statement and are clear as to why your child expressed such views, you need to challenge his prejudicial feelings and point out why they are incorrect. You can do so by providing countering examples, more information, or a different interpretation. It is important for your challenges to be simple, nonjudgmental, and appropriate to your child's level of understanding. For example:

Child:　　Homeless people should get jobs and sleep in their own houses.

Parent:　　There are many reasons homeless people don't work or have houses. Some of them are ill and can't work. Some of them can't find jobs. Houses cost money, and not everyone has enough money to pay for a house or an apartment.

Child:　　Those people should get their eyes fixed so they can see.

Parent:　　Eyes come in all different shapes, and Asian people have eyes that are slanted in shape. Their eyes see just as well as your eyes. So there's no reason for them to get their eyes changed.

Set a Rule: "No Discriminatory Comments"　　Ethnic slurs, jokes, and derogatory remarks seem to be rampant with kids these days. In addition to being painful to the victim, they breed prejudice, hate, and intolerance. Tell your child early and often that making any comment that is insulting to someone or that puts them or the group they belong to down is wrong and cruel, and will not be tolerated. Then reinforce your policy *consistently*:

- "Telling Maria she talks weird is hurtful. She speaks a different language at home and is just learning to speak English. You need to apologize to her."
- "The joke you told Josh is not funny because it made fun of his religion. It's wrong. I can't allow you to hurt other people's feelings."
- "Austin is a Native American, and calling him or anyone else an 'Indian giver' is insulting to his culture. You may not say things that put down other people."

Stopping Hate Starts with Us: We Do Make a Difference

When our second son was in the eighth grade, his social studies teacher, Jo Anne Gill, assigned a project sponsored by the Constitutional Rights Foundation that was also a national competition. Each student was to research an event in history that addressed that year's topic, "Taking a Stand." My son and his partner spent hours in the library and were especially intrigued by a photograph of the 1968 Olympic Games showing two black American sprinters receiving Olympic medals with fists raised in protest. It fit the topic perfectly, and when the boys discovered that John Carlos, one of the pictured athletes, lived in our community, it all seemed too good to be true. So one afternoon, I drove my son and his partner to meet John Carlos, and it turned out to be one of the most unforgettable events of my parenting career.

The boys began their interview cordially enough with questions about the reason for the athletes' protest, and as they began to feel more comfortable, they asked quite pointed questions about racism. I can still remember how patient Mr. Carlos was in trying to describe what it was like to be black and living in Harlem during the 1960s to two thirteen-year-old white kids who didn't have a clue. He was open and frank, and described with powerful personal stories the pain of experiencing bigotry. At one point I experienced one of those rare moments when you actually see your child grasp something quite profound: he was comprehending the effect of intolerance.

At the end of two hours, the boys thanked Mr. Carlos profusely; for the next seven months, they worked nonstop on creating a ten-minute media presentation about the problem of racism in America. It was as though a fire had been lit in these kids, and it was Mr. Carlos's personal explanations that fueled it—and the fire never seemed to go out. Along the way, their project turned from a school assignment into a personal crusade against bigotry. I watched in amazement over the next few months as their team won the school, district, and county competitions, and cheered when they won first place in California. When they won first place in the nation at the University of Maryland, I just cried.

My son and his partner weren't the only ones who learned something about racism. Because of their experience, I learned an incredible lesson myself. Tolerance *can* be taught, and kids' attitudes *can* be positively changed, and I'm firmly convinced that the best way to erase destructive prejudices is through education. We can make a difference in raising more tolerant, non-biased children because we can provide them the kinds of experiences that nurture tolerance and eradicate misrepresentations, teaching kids to respect and celebrate differences. The real question is whether we are willing to make the commitment to teaching tolerance so that a more tolerant world becomes a reality in our children's lifetimes.

WHAT TO DO ABOUT THE
CRISIS OF INTOLERANCE

- The best way to teach kids any virtue is not through our lectures but through our example. So be a living textbook of tolerance for your child and for all other children.

- Help your child discover the positive traits about people and teach him from the time he is very young that no one is better than any other person.

- Refuse to allow discriminatory remarks of any kind in your presence.

- Get in touch with your own prejudices and be willing to change them. Chances are that your child will learn them from you.

- Nurture in your child a sense of pride in her culture, heritage, and identity. She will then be better equipped to face any future abuse about her abilities, appearance, gender, race, or culture. She is also less likely to belittle the appearance, gender, ability, or beliefs of others.

- Children learn to accept and respect different perspectives when they are exposed to different perspectives. So expose your child early to toys, dolls, literature, music, customs, videos, and games that represent a wide range of multicultural groups.

- Encourage your child to participate in social and community activities that promote cross-cultural programs, diversity, resistance to hate groups, and tolerance.

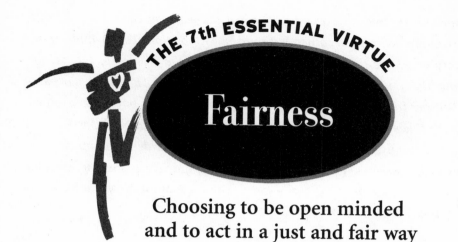

THE 7th ESSENTIAL VIRTUE

Fairness

Choosing to be open minded and to act in a just and fair way

"I will be a junior in a high school in Massachusetts next year and I have this major disappointment. You see, the current valedictorian in my class is a fake, and so are some of the top tier students. I see them cheating, taking easy honors introductory courses and getting A's. I, on the other hand, take the harder honors courses. I will be taking 4 AP exams next year in my junior year. But because I don't cheat I am ranked 13 out of 675. My college goal is to get into MIT. I had dreams in my sleep almost every day of what it would be like to go there. But I don't have a chance of getting in. All those top fake tier students took everything from me. Would anybody be able to support me or help me out? I really need help. I live in a very poor household. I am so mad!" (Posted on the Internet, June 15, 2000, by a sixteen-year-old high school sophomore)

In November 1999, a fifteen-year-old Chicago schoolboy was charged with aggravated battery at his championship hockey game against his long-standing rival. The bell had just sounded, ending the game, and the players were leaving the ice on their way to the dressing rooms when the boy began to charge toward an opponent who had just scored the winning goal. The boys had played hard against each other, but somehow his opponent's fair-and-square victory was more than this boy could tolerate, so he decided to get even by giving into a momentary impulse of savage aggression. He hit the star player full speed from behind with his shoulder, sending the boy hard headfirst into the sideboards. The collision snapped fifteen-year-old Neal Goss's spinal cord and paralyzed him from the chest down. The incident not only left the crowd who witnessed this atrocious display of unfairness in disbelief but also mortified and appalled the entire sports world. (From a story published in USA Today, May 5, 2000)

The truth is that incidents of blatant unfairness among youth are occurring in growing numbers throughout our towns and cities. The trend suggests that many kids have not learned the true meaning of the age-old ethical standard called *fair play*. Instead of playing by the rules, treating competitors justly, and practicing those self-evident truths of integrity, equity, and honesty, these children choose to tip the advantage toward themselves regardless of the moral cost or how their actions could affect others. And the tactics they use are often cruel, violent, clearly immoral, and *always* unfair.

The good news, however, is that fairness can be inspired, nurtured, taught, and learned, and research confirms that we can start when our children are just toddlers. Doing so will improve the moral atmosphere not only on our playing fields and classrooms but also in our families, neighborhoods, workplaces, and society.

THE CRISIS OF UNFAIRNESS

Fairness is what induces us to treat others in a righteous, impartial, and just way, and is therefore an essential virtue for moral intelligence. The problem is that our society is based on such values as competition, individualism, and materialism, which can occasionally contradict the ethical tenets of fairness.

And therein lies the crisis: because these self-centered values are so entrenched in our lives, kids are bound to encounter messages promoting a dog-eat-dog world in which winning is all that matters, greed is an admirable attribute, and success is equated solely with wealth and fame. Certainly there are many factors that impede the attainment of fairness in our kids, but the following four are especially toxic and point to a crisis in its development.

Early Attachment Problems

All children need to be attached to someone who considers them very special and who is committed to providing their ongoing care. When that essential bond between a child and his primary caregiver fails to develop in his earliest years, experts say the result can be catastrophic, because early attachment—or the lack of it—significantly affects the quality of all future relationships. It also has a dramatic impact on the child's moral growth: if the child is unable to relate positively, it is simply unrealistic to think he can learn the behaviors essential to fairness—such as sharing, taking turns, and being open minded.

It's easy to see that many of today's youth will be morally handicapped because of early unfair treatment. Consider these staggering facts: in the late 1990s, data indicated that one-quarter of American infants had been struck by the age of six months and half by the age of one. The Children's Defense Fund estimates that three million children are abused or neglected each year, and three-quarters of the perpetrators are the parents. These kinds of family environments will certainly not help children develop the foundations of fairness. What kids learn instead is to fend for their own emotional and physical survival and not trust the people who harmed them. The result is often the development of lasting attachment disorders. The goal of fairness becomes unthinkable.

Breakdown in Role Models

Example is always the best teacher, and that's why many experts are troubled. Role models who exemplify fairness are becoming scarcer, and there are plenty of graphic displays of unfairness that depict a "win at any cost" mentality. Sports figures seem to be among the biggest offenders. Because they are so often revered by kids, their behavior can be especially unsettling. Pitchers injuring hitters with deliberately aimed pitches, basketball and football players clipping rivals illegally, hockey players blatantly checking opponents, a world heavyweight boxer biting off a chunk of his opponent's ear, an Olympic skater attempting to eliminate a competitor by having the other's leg brutally clubbed—these certainly aren't models who inspire fairness and justice.

Another breakdown in kids' moral development occurs when their role models teach dishonesty. An alarming number of teachers were accused last year of fixing numbers on their students' state tests as well as coaching them with the right answers. Although there are no firm data, educators agree that the problem has escalated over the past years as the pressure to improve test scores has increased. And teachers' cheating recently took a peculiar moral twist at a Maryland elementary school: the heroes were third-grade students who had the courage to question the ethics of their role models and report their teachers' dishonest practices. One can only hope that more kids recognize the immoral actions of the adults in their lives and don't copy their examples.

Another concern is whether parents are adequately modeling fairness. A number of studies confirm that if we want kids to grow up to be fair and just, it's essential that their parents model those traits. Dr. David Rosenhan's ongoing research of highly just and altruistic individuals found a striking commonality in their upbringing: their parents had been actively involved in social justice issues, thus strongly influencing their kids' moral development. The real problem may well be a parenting-time famine: finding enough hours just to complete the daily essentials is challenging enough for parents; doing social justice projects in addition is just plain unrealistic for most. A second problem may be one we tend to overlook: parents simply aren't modeling fairness to their kids to a sufficient extent in their day-to-day living.

Emphasis on Competition

Old-fashioned competition has long been perceived as the catalyst that pushes kids to perform better, but experts on moral growth warn that competition also can impede the development of fairness. The American Psychological Association, for instance, found that pitting students against each other for high grades and test scores drove many to cheat instead of to excel. Researchers also found that those students who took the easy way out by copying classmates' tests or peeking at "cheat sheets" rationalized that doing better than others is far more important than getting the answer fairly and honorably. And our society seems to be emphasizing the spirit of rivalry between kids at younger and younger ages.

One particularly disturbing trend encouraging early competition is the parental obsession with getting kids into top private schools. The result: stiff competition for entry to prestigious preschools. Admissions directors report that competitiveness has never been stronger. In fact, many parents are filling out applications as soon as their children are born. So kids just out of diapers are often already feeling the pressure to perform better than their peers. Data clearly suggest that the craze is not only growing but also spreading from coast to coast.

But kid rivalry is definitely not just in classrooms: youth playing fields also push the "every man for himself" ethic. Considering that over twenty million American kids between five and thirteen participate in organized sports programs, the effect on their moral development can be far reaching. Here's why: these days, the primary emphasis in organized youth sports is certainly not on inspiring fairness or good sportsmanship: it's all about winning. In fact, in many cases the emphasis is on winning at any cost. To achieve that aim, kids once again are being pitted against each other as rivals.

Reduction of Unstructured Play

One of the best ways kids learn fairness habits such as taking turns, sharing, negotiating, compromising, and mutually solving problems is by playing with friends in natural, unstructured settings. But over the past years, the number of those golden unstructured playtime moments in children's lives has dramatically decreased, and this change is affecting our kids' moral development. Many children, for instance, have replaced their playmates with TVs, and considering that the average child under twelve watches almost twenty-two hours per week, that's a huge loss for learning the secrets of playing fairly. These days it seems that many kids prefer the companionship of computer and video games to peer interaction: plugged-in entertainment games have doubled in sales for youth in the past two years. Then there's the fact that an overwhelming number of our kids are simply too busy for play: their heavily structured daily schedules that include tutoring, music lessons, sports, homework, and school simply don't allow kids time to be with their peers. A recent University of Michigan study on how American children spend their free time found that time left over after eating, sleeping, personal care, and attending school, preschool, or day care has decreased from 40 percent to 25 percent of a child's day. So while their academic, music, computer, and athletic abilities improve, their proficiencies in fairness and moral development steadily decline.

These four factors contribute greatly to our national crisis in fairness. But perhaps most lethal to the crisis is that our kids are living in a cutthroat society where the disparity between the haves and the have-nots continues to widen with no end in sight, and the concept of equal opportunity is still a dream for too many. Our greatest challenge may well be finding ways to counter the antiethical tenets of materialism, greed, and every man for himself. Until we do, many children's capacity to treat others in a fair and just way will be greatly limited, as will their moral intelligence quotient that helps them live ethically.

WHAT IS FAIRNESS?

Fairness is the virtue that urges us to be open minded and honest and to act justly. Kids who have developed these traits play by the rules, take turns, share, and listen openly to all sides before judging. Because they do, they live their lives ethically. This seventh virtue is what heightens kids' sensitivity to moral issues: they have the courage to stick up for those

There are many ways people display fairness, and the more aware that kids are of what those actions look and sound like, the more likely they are to incorporate those behaviors into their daily lives. Here are a few examples of fairness to discuss and role-play with your child:

What Fair People Say

"I chose the game, so you go first."

"Let's decide on the rules and shake on them."

"I want to hear both sides of the story first."

"Let's find a way to make things fair."

"Let's take turns: you go first."

"That's not fair. You're not treating him right."

"That belongs to my brother, so we can't use it."

What Fair People Do

Stick up for others who are treated unfairly.

Play by the rules and don't change them midstream.

Keep an open mind and listen to all sides before judging.

Compromise so that everyone gets her fair share.

Take turns and share.

Act fairly at all times, even when unsupervised by adults.

---

treated unfairly and to demand that all people—regardless of race, culture, appearance, gender, economic status, ability, or creed—be regarded equally. And they do so because they know that it is the right and honorable way to act. A child who learns fairness will be much more tolerant, civil, understanding, and caring, and she will grow to be the best kind of citizen, worker, friend, parent, and neighbor we can have.

Today more than ever, as our kids are often exposed to a disturbing array of toxic messages that depict cruelty, hatred, violence, bigotry, injustice, and dishonesty, fairness is an essential virtue to emphasize. Helping our kids learn to treat one another fairly and justly may be the best hope they have of living in a peaceful, moral world. This final chapter offers proven ways to inspire fairness in your child so that he will develop the seventh moral intelligence virtue needed to think, feel, and act right.

Fairness

HOW STRONG IS YOUR CHILD'S SENSE OF FAIRNESS?

The statements that follow describe behaviors usually displayed by children who choose to act in a just and fair way. To evaluate your child's strengths in this seventh virtue, write the number you think best represents your child's current level on the line following each statement and then add all the scores to get her total score. If your child scores 40 to 50, she's in great shape with this aspect of moral intelligence. If she scores 30 to 40, she could benefit from virtue enhancement. A score of 20 to 30 shows signs of potential problems. A score of 10 to 20 reveals potential danger; consider getting help to increase this essential virtue.

5 = Always 4 = Frequently 3 = Sometimes 2 = Rarely 1 = Never

A Child with a Strong Sense of Fairness	My Child
Delights in the opportunity to serve others.	_____
Waits her turn patiently.	_____
Doesn't blame others carelessly.	_____
Is willing to compromise in order to have everyone's needs met.	_____
Is open minded: listens to all sides before forming an opinion.	_____
Displays good sportsmanship—whether she wins or loses.	_____
Willingly shares possessions without enticement or reminders.	_____
Tries to solve problems peacefully and fairly.	_____
Plays by the rules; doesn't change them midstream to her advantage.	_____
Looks out for the rights of others to ensure that they are treated equally and fairly.	_____
Total Score	_____

Building Moral Intelligence

THREE STEPS TO BUILDING FAIRNESS

Fairness is the seventh essential virtue of moral intelligence, and whether it blossoms or lies dormant depends largely on whether or not it's properly nurtured. We can begin to foster the earliest traits of fairness—such as turn taking and sharing—when our kids are just toddlers and as they grow older. There are three steps to building this critical moral trait in your child. Because example is always the best teacher, the first step is one of your most important parenting tasks: showing your child fairness by treating her fairly. The second step helps your child learn the important behaviors of fairness, such as sharing, compromising, listening openly, and solving problems fairly. The last step teaches your child ways to stand up against unfairness and offers ideas to encourage her to do social service projects. Only then will she really be able to recognize that she can make the world a fairer and more just place. These three steps increase the capacities that your child will need to face a world that too often flaunts materialism, an "every man for himself" mentality, and inequality.

Here again are the three important steps you can use to build this essential seventh virtue in your child and boost her moral intelligence:

Step 1: Treat Your Child Fairly
Step 2: Help Your Child Learn to Behave Fairly
Step 3: Teach Your Child Ways to Stand Up Against Unfairness and Injustice

STEP 1: TREAT YOUR CHILD FAIRLY

We tell our kids to be fair and play fair because we know it's important for their making friends as well as for their moral growth. But researchers always point out one critical, often overlooked fact: just telling our kids about fairness will never help them achieve the virtue the way walking our talk does. So if you really want to inspire fairness in your child, you must start by looking inward: examine not your kid's behaviors but your own.

After all, the best way for your child to "catch" fairness is for her to see real examples—and you are your child's first and best model. This first step shows you some of the most effective parenting behaviors that model fairness and justice to your kids. One thing is certain: the earlier we begin inspiring fairness in our kids, the greater the likelihood that fairness will become a moral habit that guides their actions.

Five Adult Behaviors That Boost Fairness in Kids

It should come as little surprise that researchers found that kids who regularly wear seat belts do so because their parents do also. Well, researchers also find learning from example to be the best way for our kids to adopt the behaviors of the essential virtues, including fairness. What follows are five behaviors that researchers find are effective in boosting fairness; adopting them into your repertoire and keeping them tuned up are the best ways for your kids to "catch" them and begin using them in their own everyday habits.

Be a Strong Example of Fairness By observing your decisions and reactions and listening to your casual remarks, your child learns fairness standards. Here are a few questions you can ask yourself about the living lessons he is watching:

- How fairly do you treat him?
- Do you show favoritism?
- Are your expectations for your child's achievement fair and reachable? Are they based on his interests and abilities—or on yours?
- Are the rules you set fair and realistic?
- Do you pay attention to your child's needs and listen openly to his concerns?
- Are you flexible and willing to compromise, or do you rigidly adhere to standards?

- Do you admit your mistakes?
- Do you take sides?
- How do you treat your neighbors, spouse, coworkers, and strangers?
- If someone asked your child if you treat him fairly, how would he respond?

Be sure the behaviors your child is picking up on are ones you want her to copy. A great test is to ask yourself at the end of each day, If my child had only my actions to copy, would she know what fairness looks and sounds like?

Expect and Demand Fairness   Research studies are very clear on one point: kids who treat others fairly have parents who expect them to do so. Therefore, one of the easiest ways to build fairness is to make it a priority in your home—and the sooner you start, the better. Teach your kids that unfairness and cruelty are *never* acceptable, and the moment you see it, stop it: "That's not fair, and I expect you to treat your friends fairly," or "In this home we will always treat one another fairly and act just as we'd like to be treated by others."

Share Your Beliefs About Fairness   Speak regularly to your child about your beliefs and why you feel the way you do. After all, your child will be hearing endless messages that counter your beliefs, so it's essential that he hears about your moral standards. TV shows, movies, newspapers, and literature are filled with issues addressing fairness and justice, so use them to discuss your beliefs with your child. These discussion times are also great opportunities to hear *his* moral views and ascertain his current level of reasoning ability. Here is just a sampling of a few fairness issues in the news lately: the death penalty, DNA testing, genocide, abortion, hate crimes, victims' rights, police brutality, homelessness, unaffordable housing, and random drug testing of high school athletes. Some parents cut out newspaper articles from the morning paper to discuss at dinner that night. They tell me that in no time, their kids start sharing real issues of unfairness that they've encountered during the day.

Listen Fairly and Openly   A common characteristic of individuals who display fairness is that they listen openly without prejudging the speaker. Listening fairly and openly is not only a powerful way to convey that you respect your child's thoughts but also a way to model an essential fairness behavior. The trick for most parents is to avoid interrupting or adding their opinions and instead just to listen—really listen—to their kids. So look for natural opportunities to practice with your child. To let her know you're interested, really focus attentively on her and offer a non-judgmental word or two to encourage her talking, such as "Oh?" "I see," or even "Really?" If you need to bite your tongue so as not to blurt out an opinion (an impulse to which I too often succumb), do so. Offering advice, criticizing, or judging are communication stoppers. The key is to build a relationship with your child so that she knows she can always come to you because you're a fair and receptive listener who values her thoughts.

Set Fair, Realistic Expectations   Every parent wants their children to grow to be the best they can be. Be careful, though: there's a fine line between stretching your child's natural abilities and potential and push-ing him to become what *you* want. Your child may misinterpret such pushing as a message saying "You're not good enough," which diminishes self-esteem, or "You want me to be more like my brother," which exacer-bates sibling rivalry. Here are a few questions to ask yourself to make sure the expectations you are setting are fair and realistic:

- Is my child developmentally ready for the tasks I'm requiring, or am I unfairly pushing him beyond his internal timetable?
- Is what I'm expecting something my child wants, or is it more some-thing I unfairly want for myself?

- Am I setting a fair expectation based on my child's interests and capabilities, or am I unfairly basing the expectation on those of another child?

Comparisons to Be Avoided

I received this message last year: "I'm e-mailing this to you because I don't know where else to turn. I know my dad loves me and wants me to do really well in life, but he's making me feel so bad about myself. All he does is compare me to my brother and tell me I should try to be more like him. If I did I'd get better grades and do better in soccer and probably have more friends. The thing is I can't be like my brother. He's him and I'm me. No matter what I do he'll just always be better. I just don't know how to make my dad love me for just me. The worst thing is I'm starting to hate my brother. I don't mean to. I just do. Can you help me? Jordan."

One of the things children pick up on fastest are our comparisons: "Your brother never got that kind of grade." "Why can't you act more like your sister?" Our kids not only detest these comments but also think they are very unfair—and they're right! All too easily, children can interpret these comparisons as "You think he's better than me" or "You love her more." Even worse, comparisons can break down family relationships and cause long-lasting resentment between siblings. So learn to tune in to comparisons you may be making and avoid using them at any cost. Here are a few ways to avoid the deadliest kinds of comparisons.

1. Refrain from comparing behaviors. Never compare your child's behavior to anyone else's—especially that of siblings! "Why can't you be more like your sister? She's always so neat, and you're such a slob!" "Why aren't you organized like your brother?" Making comparisons can diminish a child's self-worth as well as strain sibling relationships. And your child ends up feeling she has disappointed you because she can never be as good as her sibling.

2. Never compare schoolwork. Kids should compare their schoolwork, test scores, and report cards only to their own previous work—

never to the work of their siblings or friends. Instead of stimulating a child to work harder, comparisons are more likely to fuel resentment. Though we may think we are motivating our kids to try hard by using an example they should strive to copy, in doing so we often unwittingly aggravate rivalry between siblings.

3. Avoid using negative labels. Family nicknames like Shorty, Clumsy, or Klutz can cause unfair ribbings—"Don't worry, he's just the family klutz"—as well as become daily reminders of incompetence. These kinds of labels often stick and become difficult to erase, not only within but also outside your family.

4. Avoid making comparisons based on gender. Basing comparisons among siblings on gender sets up unfair assumptions and promotes stereotypes and biases. "I know you'll want to do more girl kinds of things on the trip, Sally. We can go shopping. Erik will probably want to go to a rugby game or museums with Dad."

5. Avoid praising one child in contrast to another. Complimenting one child's positive actions by contrasting them to those of another child is a deadly form of praise: "I appreciate how you always call to let me know where you are. I can trust you, unlike your brother." This kind of comparison puts down the other child and unfairly puts pressure on the child you praised.

Three Essential Fairness Behaviors to Model to Kids

"His sandwich is touching mine." "I got here first!" "When is it my turn?" "It's mine!" "It's not fair!"

Every parent knows that putting any two kids together for any length of time is bound to produce a few screaming protests, and most of them seem to revolve around the "It's not fair" issue. Although these moments can be the most trying to our patience, they really *are* normal.

The key to survival is teaching kids a few basic rules about fairness, and the real secret is to begin by modeling them yourself. The benefits are significant: not only will life on the home front improve because there are

MORAL INTELLIGENCE BUILDER
How to Avoid Chore Wars and Teach Kids to Help Out

Chores not only help build responsibility but also enhance your child's moral growth—particularly the virtue of fairness—because doing them helps her see herself as a contributing member of a family in which everyone does her fair share. Here are a few tips to avoid the horrid "chore wars" with your child and boost fairness.

- *Model exactly how to do a task.* Go through each chore step by step at least once with your child so that he clearly knows how to do it. Then observe him doing it at least once to make sure he can handle it.
- *Get kids in the habit of helping early.* Even three-year-olds can help around the house by picking up toys, feeding pets, emptying wastebaskets, setting and clearing the table, or watering plants.
- *Give choices.* At a family meeting, brainstorm a list of all the ways kids can help out. Then have each child choose a few. Some experts suggest assigning a child three daily chores (for example, making the bed, putting dishes in the dishwasher, and putting dirty clothes in the hamper) and one weekly chore (such as watering flowers or plants, sorting and folding laundry, stacking magazines and papers, or dusting).
- *Post the chore list.* Make sure everyone is clear about which person is expected to do what and when.
- *Aim for improvement, not perfection.* The effort, not the product, is the most important thing.
- *Don't do any task your child can do for herself.* She needs to see herself as a family contributor.
- *Praise his efforts.* Let your child know how much you appreciate his helping out in your home.

fewer squabbles, but your kids will also be learning a few rules about fair play that they can use the rest of their lives. Here are three important fairness practices to tune up at home.

Spell Out and Model Family Ground Rules for Sharing   Studies show that kids learn behaviors essential to fair play—such as taking turns, sharing, and cooperation—by copying others, and they are much more likely to adopt the new behavior if the person modeling it is important to them. Most morality theorists agree that sharing is one of the most important behaviors to nurture first. Here are examples of how parents have explained and modeled taking turns and sharing to their kids:

Taking turns: Let's make sure to take turns when we play. You go first, then it'll be Sally's turn, then mine.

Sharing: There are kids who don't have any toys, and you have so many. Why not choose a few to share with them, and we can take them to the Salvation Army?

Research shows that kids who share with their peers usually do so because their parents clearly emphasized that they expect them to share. So take time to spell out your sharing ground rules and explain them to your child. One dad passed on his rule: "If it belongs to you and it's in sight, then you must share it." It's also a good idea to emphasize that you may share only items that belong to you; otherwise, permission must be granted from the owner. Without permission, it may not be shared: "I'm sorry, we can't play with that. It belongs to my brother, so it's not something I can share."

Show How to Compromise   Teaching kids to compromise boosts not only fairness but also the skills of conflict resolution and getting along that they use the rest of their lives. Like most skills, the best way to teach the art of compromising is by first modeling it to your kids. Start by describing what it means: "When you compromise it means you're willing to give up a little of what you want, and the other person is too. It's a fair way to solve a problem because everyone is more satisfied: each person can have at least part of what she wants."

You may want to explain a few key points. Your child should understand that each person *always* has the opportunity to present his side, and when he does, he should be listened to. When it is her turn, she should try to explain her case so that the other person really understands her point of view. When it comes to negotiating issues with you, emphasize that although you are willing to compromise on some issues, it never means you have to compromise all the time. In fact, stress right off that some issues are simply not negotiable, and on the top of the list should be anything that goes against your values or concerns her safety. Here is how a parent modeled the skill with her thirteen-year-old daughter:

Parent: Amy, I'm concerned about how much you are on the phone. All your talking is taking up homework time, and your sisters are complaining that they never get a chance to use the phone. You may only use it for thirty minutes each day. That's it!

Child: Come on! That's not fair! I'm older, so I should get to use it longer. Besides, I'm getting good grades.

Parent: I know you're getting good grades, and I'm proud of you for that. But you're on the phone much too long, Amy, and that's not fair to your sisters who want to use it, too.

Child: Can't we work out some kind of a deal? I have all these after-school activities, so I never get to talk to my friends. And I am older. They don't need to talk to friends.

Parent: I'm willing to listen, Amy. The one thing I won't compromise on is that you must finish all your schoolwork before you can use the phone.

Child:	OK, I'll finish all my work first. But I still have to be able to talk longer than only thirty minutes. I never watch TV, so I'd be talking to my friends instead of that.
Parent:	Your sisters are younger and go to bed a half hour earlier than you. How about if you agree to finish all your schoolwork, and then use the phone for thirty minutes. Then if you're not going to watch TV, you can talk an extra thirty minutes once your sisters are in bed. Can we agree on that?
Child:	OK. That seems fair. Thanks, Mom.

Apologize and Say You're Sorry   One of the moral skills we ask of our kids is to say they're sorry for any harm they caused. But, ironically, parents tell me that apologizing to their kids is often difficult for them. Saying you're sorry doesn't mean you're admitting to not being perfect (believe me, our kids have already figured that out) or begging for forgiveness. It's just making a simple and direct statement that expresses remorse and rebuilds your parent-child bond. Parents who apologize are much more likely to have kids willing to say they're sorry to others. Doing so is one way to act justly. Here is how two parents modeled the skill of apologizing to their kids:

Parent:	I'm sorry I wasn't able to keep my promise and go to your game. My boss called a last-minute meeting. I'd so much rather have spent the time with you.
Parent:	I'm sorry I raised my voice and yelled. I didn't mean to hurt your feelings.

Six Principles of Effective Family Meetings to Nurture Fairness

In the 1950s, Rudolph Dreikurs, a psychiatrist, designed the family council model to help families work out problems democratically. Because family schedules are becoming so hectic, the meetings are gaining in popularity these days and are strongly recommended by parenting experts. Many families are also discovering that the meeting format is a great way for kids to practice asserting themselves, making decisions, reaching consensus, hearing different viewpoints, and solving problems, as well as such essential fairness behaviors as sharing, cooperating, and taking turns. The format is also a wonderful way for families to get together at regularly scheduled times and talk about their common problems, concerns, and interests, all in a spirit of fairness. The best part is that the process also helps kids grow morally.

There are many possible topics for your family meetings. You can use them to set television or bedtime hours; plan vacations; announce family activities or menus; settle conflicts; handle repetitive problems or inappropriate behaviors; celebrate positive happenings for individual family members; voice concerns; and establish or revise family rules, curfews, computer times, chores, and allowances. You can begin meetings by announcing any special upcoming family events—such as game times, field trips, test dates, doctor's appointments, parties, or school projects—and clarifying everyone's schedules. Many families set aside a small box for suggestions from members regarding family issues or topics they would like to address at the next meeting. Here are the six most important principles of successful family meetings; modify them to meet your family's needs.

1. Foster fairness. The goal of family meetings is to get your kids involved so that they can practice fairness principles, so it's important to make sure they feel that their ideas count. This is a time to hold back your judgments and encourage your child to speak up. Don't use this time for parental lectures: keep those for private times between you and your child. During family meetings each member's opinion is considered equal, everyone has a right to be heard, and anyone can bring up any sort of problem or concern.

2. Set common courtesy rules. It's important to make the meeting time a place where kids feel safe, so clearly set common courtesy rules for your meetings, and the most important one is that no family member is ever to be insulted or yelled at. Though someone may have a legitimate gripe, it must be expressed in a calm, neutral manner. One of the best ways to do so is with an "I" message (also discussed in the chapter on self-control). Teach the technique to your kids. Explain that by declaring your disapproval starting with the word *I* instead of *You*, any critical, judgmental message is turned into one focusing on the person's actions and not on her self-worth: "I am really upset that you are borrowing my clothes without asking, and I want you to stop." Emphasize also that everyone has a right to be heard, so interruptions are not allowed.

3. Determine decision-making rules. Usually decisions are based on a majority vote, though some experts feel there should be unanimous agreement. Any decisions made in the meeting must be adhered to at least until the following meeting, when they can be changed. Don't project the idea that kids get the final say on every agenda item: you're still the boss. Most parents set a rule that allows their kids to participate in making decisions that the parents already consider negotiable. For example: "Would you prefer going to the lake or the beach for our vacation?" or "Do you want to be assigned the same chores for one week or for two?"

4. Hold regularly scheduled meetings. Most experts suggest holding weekly meetings lasting fifteen minutes for younger kids and slightly longer for older. Post a meeting reminder on your refrigerator or bulletin board and mandate everyone's attendance. Many parents swear that Sunday is best simply because there seem to be fewer commitments that day. Once you have determined the day that works best for your family, schedule the meeting for the same day and time every week.

5. Rotate meeting roles. One way to help kids take an active part in meetings is to assign different roles that can be rotated weekly. Possible roles include that of chairperson (starts and stops meetings and keeps everyone to the agenda), parliamentarian (makes sure rules are followed), meeting planner (posts the meeting date and time), and secretary (keeps meeting notes). Younger kids can use a tape recorder to record the meetings.

6. Create a fun meeting spirit. Experienced parents strongly suggest that you don't hold meetings just to hash out problems; after a while kids will dread coming. Instead, try to keep meetings fun and upbeat. One family from Orlando told me they always start their sessions by having family members take turns complimenting each other for good deeds done during the week. End your meeting on a fun note: serve a dessert; have a family game of cards, Monopoly, volleyball, or touch football; or even rent a great family video to watch together.

STEP 2: HELP YOUR CHILD
LEARN TO BEHAVE FAIRLY

Every parent knows that fairness is a big issue for kids at any age, and it becomes one very early. "That's not fair!" is probably one of the first moral judgments young kids make. Although justice is a difficult concept for children to grasp, it's essential to their moral intelligence. When kids move beyond their often selfish view of fairness as getting what they want and gain an awareness of others' needs and rights, they move up a rung on the moral ladder. Their concern is no longer just that they be treated fairly but that others receive fair treatment as well. These are kids who can really think about fairness issues, who can consider other people's needs in their decisions, and who link their moral thoughts and feelings to their behaviors and thus choose to act justly.

Of course, getting to that moral place is not easy, and it takes time. But a big part of getting our kids started on the path to understanding justice and fair treatment is helping them learn to behave fairly, and that is what this section is about. You will learn ways to help your child acquire some of the most important fairness behaviors as well as a few skills she can use to combat unfair treatment. When she has acquired them, your child will

MORAL INTELLIGENCE BUILDER
The Stages of Fairness and Justice

William Damon, a renowned authority on moral development, thinks that children slowly develop an understanding of fairness in a series of stages, at first believing that fairness means getting what *they* want and gradually acquiring a respect for equal rights and justice. The better you understand these stages and your child's current understanding of the concept of fairness, the better you'll be at helping her reach the next level of reasoning. The following stages are adapted from the works of Dr. Damon and Dr. Thomas Lickona, author of *Raising Good Children*.

Stage 1: "I want to. It's not fair!"　　　　　**Early preschool; ages 1 to 4½**

The child is very self-centered, and her understanding of fairness is self-serving and focused on what will meet her needs. She is generally a very poor loser. *"I'm tired, so I should be first."*

Stage 2: "I better be fair: I'm supposed to."　　　　**Late preschool; ages 4½ to 5½**

The child thinks he should be fair because those in authority tell him he should. He is still quite immature in his thinking about mutual fairness and justice. *"I better give Sam a turn, because if I don't, Dad will be mad."*

Stage 3: "What do I get in return?"　　　　　　　　**Ages 5½ to 8**

The child sees fairness as something that deserves to be returned: you do something for me, and I'll do something for you. Fairness involves rigid, tit-for-tat scorekeeping, and there's an almost passionate belief in equality: *"I'll share it, but what do I get in return?" "He punched me, so I'll punch him back."*

Stage 4: "I don't expect anything for my good deed."　　　　**Ages 8 to 13**

For the first time, the child can think of what others need and extends favors without feeling he deserves to receive something in return. The capacity for true altruism and the beginning of a sense of justice emerge. *"He looked upset, so I let him borrow my Nintendo game."*

Stage 5: Fairness should be universal.　　　　　　　**Ages 12 and older**

The child believes fairness should be extended to all and that it is essential for the good of society for people to cooperate and get along. *"So what if he doesn't speak English? He's a citizen and should be treated fairly."*

not only act more morally but also feel more confident because she knows how to face unfairness fairly.

Three Ways to Foster Sharing in Kids

Leslie arrived early at the day-care center and watched her four-year-old play. She was aghast. In just five minutes, she saw Michael grab his friend's toy, not let the other boy have a turn, and completely monopolize the game the two were playing. She sadly shook her head, realizing that her son would have a tough time starting kindergarten if he didn't learn how to share. But how would she begin to help him learn?

Learning to share is not only necessary for making and keeping friends but also essential to developing the virtue of fairness. Dr. T. Berry Brazelton, professor emeritus of pediatrics at Harvard Medical School, strongly urges us to help our kids learn to share as soon as possible, at least by age two or three. Here are three ways to enhance this essential moral principle in your child:

1. **Create sharing boundaries.** You can never talk about sharing too often with your child, and preparing your child for sharing before a friend comes to play is always a good idea. Fred Frankel, author of *Good Friends Are Hard to Find*, suggests telling your child to put away any toys he does not want to share, before his guest arrives. Frankel stresses that even though this approach sounds odd, he has found that it actually promotes sharing, especially in five- to nine-year-olds. After all, there are certain possessions that are very special to your child, so putting those items away before a guest arrives minimizes potential conflicts. Explain that anything your child leaves out are items he has to share: "Samantha is coming over this afternoon to play. Think about which toys you would like to share with her. And then let's put away the toys that can't be shared."

2. **Encourage sharing behaviors.** The fact is, learning to share can be quite painful for some kids, and that's why your child will probably continue to need gentle reminders that being fair is the right way to act. The

fastest way to increase a behavior is by "catching" your child acting right, so tune in to your child's actions and reinforce her sharing efforts. Always remember to describe what she did so she'll be more likely to repeat the same behavior: "I noticed how you divided the toys so you both had the same amount. That was acting fairly."

3. Emphasize the effect sharing has on others. William Damon explains that the main reasons kids give for sharing are empathic in nature: "It makes the other kids happy," or "When I don't, my friend gets sad and feels like crying." Reinforce your child's sharing attempts by pointing out the impact they had on the other child. For example: "Did you see Kali's smile when you shared your toys? You made her happy." "Joshua really enjoyed coming over because you were such a nice host and shared the equipment." When your child is not fair, ask her to put herself in the other child's place: "How would you feel if John treated you that way and took more toys to play with?"

Nine Things to Do When Your Kids Say "That's Not Fair!"

"I'm at my wit's end," a mother told me. "I try so hard not to play favorites and to treat my kids equally. But no matter what I do, my kids tell me I don't treat them fairly."

Sibling quarrels are among the most exasperating home front issues. Put any two kids together for a length of time, and the three little words you're most likely to hear are "It's not fair!" Don't go crazy trying to make things equal—it's impossible! There are a few things you can do that really will alleviate the bickering *and* in the process help your kids learn to treat each other more fairly. Here are nine strategies to try next time you hear those three little words.

1. Calm everyone down. Intervene when emotions are high, *before* an argument escalates. Use what works best to calm everyone down: running a quick lap outside, doing five jumping jacks, taking three slow deep breaths, lying down for a few minutes, cuddling a teddy bear. If needed, separate the two kids until they can be calm and work things through: "I

MORAL INTELLIGENCE BUILDER
Four Ideas to Help Kids Make Things Fair

Here are a few strategies to teach your child to help make things fair and to reduce conflicts among peers. Just make sure to practice them with your child before she tries them out in real life.

• *Use "Grandma's Rule."* My mother-in-law passed this one on to my kids, and it works like a charm in reducing those annoying "He got the bigger piece" issues. The rule is simple: "If you cut the cake, the other person can decide which piece to take." The rule can apply to lots of things. For example: if you mixed the paint, the other person picks the paint; if you chose the game, the other person gets to go first; if you poured the lemonade, the other person gets to choose her glass first.

• *No "take backs."* Emphasize to your child that once you agree on the rules of a game or agree to a trade with a friend, you may not "take back" (change the rules or take back the object) unless the other person agrees. Teach your child to make an agreement and commit to it by shaking on it. Then the deal is final.

• *Flip a coin.* This one is great when two kids can't decide on rules, who gets to choose what to do, or even who goes first. The child who is to toss the coin asks the other to call heads or tails. If the caller correctly chooses the side that is face up, he wins the toss; if not, then the other child wins and gets to choose.

• *Use a timer.* Teach kids to agree on a set amount of time—usually only a few minutes—for using an item. Oven timers or sand timers are great devices for younger kids to use. Older kids can use the minute hands on their watches. When the time is up, the item is passed to the next child for his turn.

see two angry kids who need to cool down. You go to your room, and you to the other room until you can talk calmly."

2. Clarify feelings. Sometimes all that is needed is for someone to acknowledge the hurt child's feelings. Try it. "You're hurt because you think your brother is being treated more fairly than you are." "You're frustrated because you're not getting a turn at the Nintendo."

3. Let each child tell the story. To help kids feel that they're really being heard, ask each child to take turns speaking to explain what happened. As each speaks, ask everyone to focus on her with their eyes and really listen. No interrupting is allowed, and everyone gets a turn. If you think you don't understand, ask for clarification: "Could you explain that to me again?" When the child is finished, briefly restate her view to show you do understand. You might then ask, "What can you do to solve this problem?"

4. Don't take sides. Stay neutral and make suggestions only when your kids seem stuck. The worst thing to do is take sides. It builds resentment and feelings of favoritism. Besides, it's really not fair.

5. Make the kids part of the solution. Ask those involved what they plan to do to solve "their" problem. Making kids be part of the solution often causes them to stop, think, and quiet down. Do set guidelines for talking it out: no interrupting, no put-downs, and only calm voices are allowed. By taking turns, kids can learn to make their points with words, not blows.

6. Don't let them get up until they solve the problem. One mom told me she sits her two kids at a table and tells them, "I have faith you can solve this. If you need me, I'm in the other room, but don't leave the table until you can work this out fairly." A dad sets an oven timer and says, "Let's see if you can work this through calmly for three minutes. Then I'll return." Another mom sits her preschoolers on the couch and tells them they can't get up until they talk it out.

7. Ask kids to see it from the other side. Kids often get so caught up in feeling they're being treated unfairly that they don't stop to think how the other person might be feeling. So ask, "See it from the other side now. How does Patrick feel?" This also builds empathy.

8. Offer a mediator. If kids can't think of a fair solution, you still don't have to get involved. Suggest that the issue be put on the family meeting agenda. The kids involved can take turns describing the issue at the meeting, and the family might offer a solution or help them remedy their problem.

9. Find out the real cause. When one child keeps crying "unfair," there usually is a deeper issue involved, so find out the real cause of her resentment: Is the other child getting more attention, being manipulative, or bullying? Does he have more toys? Do you take sides? Is the hurt child feeling she is not being listened to or is being taken advantage of? Find out the real issue before it swells into something bigger.

How a Dad Taught His Son to Play Fair

One of the most frustrating parts of parenting is watching your child demonstrate poor sportsmanship. That's exactly what happened to one dad in Salt Lake City, and he passed on to me the unique way he helped his son learn to play more fairly. I'm retelling his story so that you might be able to use a similar approach with your child. After all, we can never talk too much about the importance of being a good sport and a fair player. Here is what this dad did.

Taylor's dad watched his son from the sidelines of the soccer field and sadly shook his head. His son was a great little soccer player, but he was a very poor sport because he didn't play fairly. During the game, Taylor argued about the rules, made excuses for his kicks, hogged the ball, and blamed everyone else for losing. If he kept this up, nobody would want him on any team—regardless of how good a player he was. So that night, Taylor's dad dusted off their old checkerboard and called his son to come join him in a game. For the next hour they played checkers, but the dad's real goal was to help his son learn to play fairly and be a better sport.

They started the game by first reviewing the rules. When Taylor said he understood them, his dad told him they had to stick by them: "Fair players don't argue about the rules. They agree to them at the beginning and don't change them unless everyone agrees to. They also take the game seriously and don't quit. Let's agree to play until one of us wins. Want to shake on it?"

Taylor's dad tossed a coin into the air and had his son call out a side. When Taylor won the toss, his dad told Taylor he could choose the black or red pieces, and because Taylor didn't select the game, he could have the first turn. *The dad also explained how those were two good tips to use with friends so they would see you as a fair player. As they played, Taylor's dad deliberately made a few bad moves. Instead of making excuses he said, "Wow, I wasn't thinking that time," or "You got me there!" And when there was a doubt as to whose turn it was, Taylor's dad suggested they do another coin toss to make things fair; this time Taylor could be the tosser.*

That night, Taylor's father lost his first checker game—on purpose, of course—but he was subtle enough not to let Taylor know. He used the

---

MORAL INTELLIGENCE BUILDER
Seven Rules for Playing Fairly

Here are a few important rules kids need to learn if they are to play fairly and get along. They are adapted from Fred Frankel's book *Good Friends Are Hard to Find.* One of the best times to model them is when you play board games with your kids.

- Find out your friend's interests and choose a game you both can agree on. It makes things fairer.
- Decide on the rules before the game starts and stick by them: no changing rules midstream.
- Use "Grandma's Rule" to determine who will go first: whoever picked the game goes last.
- Play until the game ends; don't quit unless you both agree. For younger kids or children with short attention spans, set an oven timer for a specific play time, and play until the buzzer goes off.
- Be supportive and complimentary to the other players. Try to praise your teammates at least twice before the game ends.
- Never complain about your own playing—or anyone else's. If you can't say anything nice, just don't say anything. Above all: *never, ever boo.*
- Always end the game on a positive note with a handshake or by saying, "Good game" or "Let's do it again." Then offer to help clean up and put the equipment or game away.

Building Moral Intelligence

moment to show his son how to lose gracefully. "Good game, Taylor. Let's play again tomorrow," he said, and shook his son's hand. For the next few nights, Taylor and his dad played checkers. Not only did Taylor's checker game improve, but he also learned an even better game: how to play fairly.

STEP 3: TEACH YOUR CHILD WAYS TO STAND UP AGAINST UNFAIRNESS AND INJUSTICE

When my youngest son was in the eighth grade, he was required to do a year-long historical research project on a topic of his choice. That one assignment proved extraordinary in fostering in him an awareness of social injustice. It all began one Sunday afternoon when Zach and his two teammates started

---

MORAL INTELLIGENCE BUILDER
Talking About Fairness with Kids

Here are some questions to help kids think about the value of being fair.

- What does it mean when somebody is fair? Who are some people you know who are fair? What makes them fair?
- Have you ever been in a situation where you or someone you were with was treated unfairly? What happened? Was the situation resolved? What are ways you can stand up for yourself or another person without making the problem bigger? What things do people say or do that make things worse?
- Do you think the rules at home (at school, in our country) are fair such that everyone is doing his or her share to help? Do some people do more work than others? Is there a way to divide up the work so that it seems fairer to everyone? Is there a chart or sign you could make to spell out everyone's chores?
- Can you think of some people in the world who because of their race, culture, economic status, beliefs, age, abilities, or gender may not be treated fairly? Who are they? Is there anything people can do to make things fairer?

---

browsing through their U.S. history book to find a topic and at one point turned to the section on World War II. Zach's godmother is Japanese American, and he remembered her stories about how her family had been sent to armed camps during the war, but nowhere in his history book was it mentioned. That omission alone seemed to the boys to be an injustice, and it prompted them to choose to study the Japanese American internment camps.

Their first research step turned out to be golden: they wanted to interview internees to find out their views, and in their search located a local resident, Mrs. Cherry Ishimatsu. She met the boys at a local library and that afternoon mesmerized the twelve-year-olds by telling them of her family's three-year emotional ordeal while interned in Jerome, Arkansas. She described the fear of not knowing her fate, the indignity of being allowed only one bag to carry all her possessions, the sorrow of leaving her home and neighbors, and the distress of being imprisoned solely because of her cultural ancestry. She also eloquently conveyed her pride in being an American citizen, stressing to each boy that they must do everything in their power always to uphold the rights guaranteed in our Constitution.

Her personal descriptions were what was missing from all the boys' historical references, and they were what motivated Zach and his partners to pursue their research. Over a period of months, the boys interviewed fifteen more Japanese American internees as well as World War II civilians, veterans, and internment camp employees. At one point, the boys' fathers drove them to Manzanar, one of the abandoned camps, where they camped overnight to get a sense of the strenuous living conditions. As they worked on the project, I repeatedly heard the boys say, "It's not fair," and each encounter strengthened their view that these Japanese Americans had been treated unjustly. They became passionate about proving it to anyone who would listen.

Over that school year, the boys' project grew. It received proclamations from their mayor, a state senator, and their U.S. congresswoman, and won district, state, and national awards from the Constitutional Rights Association. As a parent, though, I think by far the greatest prize my son won was that he grasped the effect injustice can have. It has been four years since that project

MORAL INTELLIGENCE BUILDER
A Story to Tell Kids About Fairness

One night, eleven-year-old Trevor Ferrell was at home watching a news broadcast about homeless people and couldn't believe such an injustice existed. For almost an hour, Trevor pleaded for his mom to take him to downtown Philadelphia so he could see for himself, and she finally gave in. Before jumping into their car, he grabbed a blanket and pillow; he gave it to the first homeless person he saw: an old man lying on a sidewalk grating. The look of disbelief in the man's eyes changed Trevor's life. He couldn't believe the homeless were treated so apathetically by society; it just wasn't fair, he thought, and he decided that somehow he would make a difference.

The very next day, he started asking everyone in his neighborhood for warm clothes, blankets, and food, and the next night he was back in the car with his parents driving him downtown so he could distribute them. Soon Trevor had his parents driving him regularly to make his distributions to the homeless that lived on the streets. Then others began hearing about his efforts, and donations began to pour in. The U.S. Army brought warm clothes, a church gave an extra van to deliver his gifts, friends began helping with deliveries, and strangers sent money.

Trevor has never given up his cause, and through the years others have joined him: the U.S. Army has given hundreds of extra blankets and coats, an abandoned hotel was donated to the campaign to fulfill Trevor's dream of a home for the homeless—and Trevor's Place was born. Each day, Trevor's Place serves dozens of hot meals and provides eighty warm beds for the homeless to sleep in at night. More hard work and donations resulted in Trevor's Next Door, a building next to Trevor's Place that offers a residential living center for women and children and provides social services, day care, and educational programs.

It has been fourteen years since Trevor became aware of the homeless and how unfairly they were treated. Though he was only eleven at the time, he believed that the homeless were not nonentities to view with apathy and that one person, no matter how young, could make a difference. Well, Trevor made that difference by taking a stand against social injustice, and you can too. What can you do to make a difference in your home, your school, your neighborhood, or your city? To find out more about Trevor Ferrell, go to the Trevor's Endeavors home page on the Internet at [http://www.philanthroserve.org/Trevor/TrevorHistory.htm].

was assigned, and I continue to see its impact on my son. I see in him now a young man with not only a more pronounced sense of justice and compassion but also a stronger concern for preserving human rights and understanding both sides of an issue before passing judgment. The experience of working on that project changed his life; it certainly changed mine.

I'm fully convinced there is no more powerful way of boosting kids' moral intelligence than getting them personally involved in an issue regarding injustice, then encouraging them to take a stand. It's a powerful way of affirming to kids that they can make a difference in the world. It's also by far the best way to nurture morality in our kids. After all, it is only by acting on our conscience and heart by doing what we know is right that we are truly moral beings. This third step offers ways to encourage kids to stand up against unfairness and counter social injustice by getting involved in social justice projects.

Seven Tips to Get Kids Started Doing Social Justice Projects

The first time I realized the power of involving kids in social justice projects was when one of my sons was just four. The two of us had gone to see the movie The Bear, *and because it was rated as family oriented, I wasn't prepared for the scene in which a bear is brutally killed. Well, neither was my four-year-old: Zach was devastated, and he sobbed all the way home. At some point during our drive, he exclaimed adamantly that the president of the United States should make a rule against killing bears. Probably to appease him more than anything else, I suggested that he write the president a letter, and as soon as we drove into our driveway, Zach turned into an animal rights activist. He ran inside; grabbed an envelope, paper, and pencil; and asked me to write down his words. Within five minutes, he'd written a letter to the president pleading with him to write a law stopping the "bear killers." He then sealed and stamped the envelope and confidently put it in the mailbox. What I never expected was a response: over the next weeks Zach received dozens of letters from various government officials regarding animal rights, hunting laws, and even a few about bears. And the satisfaction on Zach's face each time he opened a letter was priceless. "See, Mom," he'd tell me, "they know it's wrong, and they're going to do something. I helped the bears." That day my four-year-old taught me just how important it is to help kids know that their actions can make a difference. I also learned a very important lesson: it's never too early to start.*

As is true in most families, each of my children has different interests, skills, and strengths. To have had all of them involved in the same service project wouldn't have been wise. Instead, my husband and I tried to encourage each child to find a project that matched his concerns and talents. My politically oriented son set up campaign headquarters at his high school for his chosen presidential candidate; my son who is great with younger kids taught Bible school to five-year-olds; and my eleventh grader volunteers weekly at the fire department and completed his civil defense training so he can help out in a community emergency. Because our kids chose projects that supported their passions as well as their strengths, they not only enjoyed volunteering but also were committed to their causes.

Often the most difficult part of getting your child to get involved in a social justice project is knowing where to begin. Here are a few ideas passed on from other parents on how to start kids doing projects of their choice.

1. Choose a project based on your child's interests and talents. The first step is to help your child choose something that he is good at and enjoys doing. The Moral Intelligence Builder on page 264 offers social justice projects that pair your child's learning styles and interests with service ideas. Tune in to problems that concern your child and start by looking around your neighborhood. For example: property that needs cleaning up, a park where kids no longer feel safe playing, homeless people living on the streets, shelters that need sprucing up, or elderly people who are lonely. Look for other service projects in the yellow pages under "Social Service Organizations." Keep track of global issues that interest your child, such as Internet hate sites, movie violence, child abuse, drugs, gender inequality, oppression, poverty, human rights, slavery, prison reform, or racial injustice. Help your child analyze the good and bad points of each possibility and then choose the one problem he wants to work on most.

2. Research the topic. Next, help your child find out as much information as she can about the problem. The library is always a good place to start: magazines, newspapers, and the Internet are good sources of information. Ask teachers, kids, neighbors, relatives, coaches, scout leaders, and city officials and write to state officials and government groups. Call organizations familiar with the topic for more ideas. A word of caution: don't be discouraged if the organization is not receptive to actual kid involvement and only encourages your child to collect money and donate possessions. I found that true with all too many. Stress to your child that she doesn't need an organization to make a difference. Any small action is a start.

3. Think of all possible solutions. The next step is to help him brainstorm all the possible ways he could help remedy an unfair situation. Write down all ideas and then help him select the few that he feels most comfortable with and enthusiastic about and that are most realistic. Suppose your child is concerned about the homeless living in the park, and he brainstormed these solutions: build a shelter, get a hotel to house them, put beds in the park, give out blankets, raise money for cots. Now have him choose the ideas he feels are most manageable and that he wants to commit to doing. After a lengthy discussion, he might realize that getting a hotel isn't so realistic (right away, anyway), and he might choose instead to canvass his neighborhood and school for blankets and to advertise in the newspaper.

4. Enlist others in the cause. Many kids enjoy volunteering with others: a friend, your family, Grandma—the more the merrier—so ask your child if she would like to do her project with someone and, if so, find other people who agree with her cause. Some kids like to form clubs, which can include neighborhood kids, classmates, scout or church members, or just friends. The more people in the group, the more energy they have to make a difference.

5. Plan for success. The more your child thinks through his plan, the greater the likelihood he will succeed. So help him organize for success by asking him what resources and people he will need for his cause. For instance, if your child has chosen to volunteer, you might post a large monthly calendar for him to jot down volunteer days and times; a young child can draw a happy face or other symbols. If your child is starting a letter campaign for new legislation, ask, "What do you need to start your campaign?" Then help him list such items as stamps, addresses of officials, computer, printer ink, envelopes, and stationery. If he needs to raise money, encourage him to make flyers to advertise his cause, and suggest places to post them and people to contact. If he needs petitions signed, help him think of good places for signups and come up with ideas about where to borrow folding tables and clipboards. Emphasize that he should always tell you his plans and never go anywhere unfamiliar without an adult.

6. Implement the solutions and evaluate progress. Now encourage your child to carry out her plans. Often getting started is the hardest part for kids, so you might ask, "What is the first thing you need to get started?" Support her efforts so that she carries out her plans. Stress that the best-laid plans never go smoothly, so help your child evaluate her progress and change any areas that need correcting.

7. Celebrate efforts. Whether your child volunteers once a year or once a week, writes one letter or a thousand, support his efforts and affirm that he's helping to make the world a better place.

WHAT TO DO ABOUT THE CRISIS OF UNFAIRNESS

- If you want your child to be fair, *expect* your child to be fair. The easiest way to increase fairness is by reinforcing fair behaviors.

MORAL INTELLIGENCE BUILDER
*Matching Your Child's Interests and Strengths
with Social Justice Projects*

D r. Howard Gardner, of Harvard University, has developed a theory that
every child is born with a unique combination of eight intelligences and
learns best when she uses her strongest intelligences. To help you determine
your child's strengths, read the descriptions of the eight intelligences Gardner has
identified, then try to match your child's talents with special service projects she can
do to help make a difference in our world. Here are some project ideas adapted from
my book *Parents Do Make a Difference*:

1. *Linguistic learners* like to read, write, and tell stories. They learn by hearing and
   seeing words, know unusual amounts of information, have advanced vocabular-
   ies, and memorize facts verbatim.
   Offer to read or write letters for young kids, the elderly, or people with disabilities.
   Start a letter-writing campaign about an issue that concerns you.
   Become a pen pal with an orphan overseas or a patient at a nearby hospital.
   Donate used books to a library, homeless shelter, or classroom.

2. *Bodily/kinesthetic learners* handle their bodies with ease and poise for their age,
   are adept at using their body for sports or artistic expression, and are skilled in
   fine motor tasks.
   Help coach younger children in dancing, gymnastics, a favorite sport, or acting.
   Volunteer for the Special Olympics or help students with disabilities at a local school.
   Make or repair dolls and other toys for needy or sick kids.
   Mend clothes or sew blankets for a shelter.

3. *Intrapersonal learners* have strong self-understanding, are original, enjoy working
   alone to pursue their own interests and goals, and have a strong sense of right and
   wrong.
   "Adopt" someone who could use a friend, such as an elderly person; offer to call
   periodically.
   Teach a special hobby—magic, juggling, art, drumming, calligraphy—to needy
   kids.
   Ask permission to start a food drive at your parents' workplace or in your
   community.

4. *Interpersonal learners* understand people, lead and organize others, have lots of friends, are looked to by others to make decisions and mediate conflicts, and enjoy joining groups.

Start a club and make after-school snacks for homeless kids or soup for a shelter.

Put together a walk-a-thon or read-a-thon and donate the proceeds to a local charity.

Go door-to-door with a parent and friends collecting warm clothes to give to the homeless.

5. *Musical learners* appreciate rhythm, pitch, and melody, and they respond to music. They remember melodies, keep time, may play instruments, and like to sing and hum tunes.

Offer to play an instrument at nursing homes and homeless shelters.

Organize sing-alongs at a shelter or senior citizen center during the holidays.

Tutor needy younger kids in how to play an instrument.

6. *Logical/mathematical learners* understand numbers, patterns, and relationships, and they enjoy science and math. They categorize, ask questions, do experiments, and figure things out.

Tutor math, science, or computers to younger children.

Play chess, checkers, or other thinking games with kids at a shelter or hospital.

Make computer flyers asking for specific donations to a shelter; post them in the community.

7. *Spatial learners* like to draw, design and create things, and imagine things and daydream. They remember what they see, read maps and charts, and work well with colors and pictures.

Beautify any shelter: paint it or hang up hand-painted pictures.

Make homemade holiday greeting cards and deliver them to a hospital.

Do a favorite craft project with the elderly.

8. *Naturalists* like the out-of-doors, are curious, and classify the features of the environment.

Pick a flower bouquet from the garden, tie it with a ribbon, and deliver it to a sick friend.

Plant vegetables and donate the harvest to a soup kitchen or shelter.

Help children at a shelter plant their own garden.

Clean up a park, school ground, or property to make it safe and beautiful.

- Do not tolerate any form of peer unfairness: taunting, name-calling, put-downs, harassment, or plain meanness. Teach your kids that unfairness and cruelty are *never* acceptable.

- Encourage your child when he encounters unfair treatment to stand up for himself and the rights of others. Teach him the skills of assertiveness so he can be confident enough to do so.

- Emphasize acting fairly and good sportsmanship both on and off the field.

- Hold regularly scheduled family meetings. Doing so is one of the best ways for your child both to practice fairness behaviors—sharing, cooperating, taking turns, asserting herself, making decisions, reaching consensus, and hearing different points of view—and to grow morally.

- Children are likely to treat others fairly if they understand why fairness is important and how it affects others. So help your child understand the value of fairness.

- There is no more powerful way to boost kids' moral intelligence than to get them personally involved in an issue of injustice and then encourage them to take a stand; they will learn that they can make a difference in the world. Look for opportunities in your neighborhood or community and get involved together in making the world a better place.

Building Moral Intelligence

Epilogue

Many hundreds of years ago, Confucius said, "The most beautiful sight in the world is a child walking confidently down the road of life after you have shown him the way." I love this saying because it describes so perfectly what our parenting role is really all about. It also reminds us why it's crucial that we build our children's capacity for moral intelligence. Moral IQ is the one ability we seem to be underdeveloping in our kids, yet it's the one they'll need most as they journey into the unpredictable, often cruel, and sometimes violent twenty-first century.

I hope you have found that *Building Moral Intelligence* envisions a world based on compassion, tolerance, respect, and goodness. But I also hope you keep in mind that the vision must begin in a home that provides solid moral examples and expects all family members to adhere to clear moral standards. *You* are always your child's first and most important moral instructor, a role to be taken with immense seriousness. After all, we're given only one chance to do our job well, so we must do it with purpose, conviction, and love.

Keep in mind that your child's moral growth is an ongoing process that will span the course of her lifetime. The moral knowledge, beliefs, and habits you instill in her now will become the foundation she'll use forever. These seven essential virtues are what will ultimately form her character and are the same principles she'll use to direct the course of her life with or without your continuing guidance. They'll serve as her moral compass so that she not only knows right from wrong but also has the deep-seated convictions to stand by her choices, regardless of outside pressures.

Even though we have our children with us only briefly, these tender years are the most pivotal in building moral intelligence. So savor this time with your children and use it wisely, for although they have the potential to achieve moral goodness, it is far from guaranteed that they will: the seven essential virtues must be nurtured, influenced, modeled, and taught.

I wish you and your children well. I know the road may be a bit bumpy and sometimes even rough. But if you stay on course and focused, there will be no better reward: good and decent human beings—the children you raised. And that will be your greatest legacy.

Resources
for Building Moral Intelligence

THE 1ST ESSENTIAL VIRTUE: EMPATHY

For Parents and Teachers

Emotional Intelligence, by Daniel Goleman (New York: Bantam Books, 1995). The classic that stirred our awareness of the need for addressing our children's emotional literacy.

Esteem Builders, by Michele Borba (Torrance, Calif.: Jalmar Press, 1989). Dozens of activities to help kids learn the skills needed for emotional competence and high self-esteem.

The Heart of Parenting: Raising an Emotionally Intelligent Child, by John Gottman (New York: Simon & Schuster, 1997). An excellent guide for helping kids understand and regulate their emotional world.

How to Raise a Child with a High EQ (Emotional Quotient), by Lawrence E. Shapiro (New York: HarperCollins, 1997). A practical guide to helping children master social and emotional skills.

Parents Do Make a Difference: How to Raise Kids with Solid Character, Strong Minds, and Caring Hearts, by Michele Borba (San Francisco: Jossey-Bass, 1999). Literally dozens of practical ways to boost children's empathy and compassion.

Raising Cain: Protecting the Emotional Life of Boys, by Dan Kindlon and Michael Thompson (New York: Ballantine, 1999). Two leading psychologists provide ways to boost emotional literacy.

Teaching Your Child the Language of Social Success, by Marshall P. Duke, Stephen Nowicki Jr., and Elisabeth A. Martin (Atlanta: Peachtree, 1996). Ways to help kids improve their nonverbal skills and thus enhance relationships with others.

For Children Ages Three to Seven

The Bedspread, by Sylvia Fair (New York: Morrow, 1982). Two elderly sisters embroider two very different views of life, clearly depicting that there is no one way that is better.

Fly Away Home, by Eve Bunting (New York: Clarion Books, 1991). A poignant tale of the plight of a homeless boy and his father in their only home: an airport.

Old Henry, by Joan W. Blos (New York: Morrow, 1987). Henry's neighbors don't appreciate the way the eccentric man keeps his yard, so they run him out of the neighborhood, then find themselves missing him.

Silent Lotus, by Jeanne M. Lee (New York: Sunburst, 1994). A young deaf and mute Cambodian girl shows her ability to speak with her hands, body, and feet.

A Special Trade, by Sally Wittman (New York: HarperCollins, 1978). A grandfatherly special friend used to push the baby girl in her stroller. Now he has had a stroke, and the girl pushes him in his wheelchair.

Through Grandpa's Eyes, by Patricia MacLachlan (New York: HarperCollins, 1983). A sensitive tale of a young boy who visits his blind grandfather and learns there is more than just one way of seeing.

For Children Ages Eight to Eleven

The Bear's House, by Marilyn Sachs (New York: Dutton, 1971). A moving account of a lonely girl who must deal with a dysfunctional home environment. Powerful for building empathy.

Blubber, by Judy Blume (New York: Dell, 1974). An overweight girl must learn to deal with ridicule and rejection from her classmates.

Dear Mr. Henshaw, by Beverly Cleary (New York: Morrow, 1983). A Newbery winner about a boy coming to grips with his family's divorce by describing his feelings through a series of letters.

The Hundred Dresses, by Eleanor Estes (Orlando, Fla.: Harcourt Brace, 1972). An impoverished girl is made fun of by her classmates, who mock her for always wearing the same faded blue dress. A powerful story that helps sensitize children to the cruelty of emotional abuse.

The Little Prince, by Antoine de Saint-Exupéry (Orlando, Fla.: Harcourt Brace, 1968). The classic fable of the Little Prince on a search to understand what is truth, who discovers that "it is only with the heart that one sees rightly."

The Stone-Faced Boy, by Paula Fox (New York: Aladdin, 1968). Ridicule and rejection from classmates cause Gus to "turn off" his emotions and become "stone-faced."

For Youth Ages Twelve and Older

Belle Prater's Boy, by Ruth White (New York: Farrar, Straus & Giroux, 1996). Woodrow moves in with his grandfather and bonds with his cousin. The boys learn to face the losses in their lives.

Building Blocks, by Cynthia Voigt (New York: Atheneum, 1985). A twelve-year-old boy wakes up to find himself in the bedroom of a ten-year-old boy who he discovers is to become his father. He literally gets into his father shoes and takes on a whole new understanding of his dad.

A Separate Peace, by John Knowles (New York: Bantam Books, 1994). This classic takes place at an elite boys' boarding school and richly addresses friendship, empathy, betrayal, and tragedy.

Slake's Limbo, by Felice Holman (New York: Dell, 1977). A fifteen-year-old boy hides from his fears by hiding in a cave for 121 days; his experience teaches him just how important human companionship is to survival.

Visiting Miss Pierce, by Pat Derby (New York: Sunburst, 1989). Barry starts to examine his own predicament as an adopted child by befriending an elderly woman and discussing her past.

Videos for Viewing with Children

Bambi (Walt Disney Home Video, 1942). Depicts the harsh realities of nature when Bambi's mother is killed by the hunters. How can you not empathize? A very intense tearjerker—beware!

Dumbo (Walt Disney Home Video, 1941). A lonely little elephant with oversized ears is unmercifully picked on, and it's impossible not to feel for him. Great for discussing others' feelings.

Fly Away Home (Columbia Tristar Home Video, 1996). A young girl whose mother is killed retreats into her own solitary world until she rescues some goose eggs and takes care of the goslings.

Pocahontas (Walt Disney Home Video, 1995). Disney classic that depicts the friendship between a young Indian girl, Pocahontas, and Captain John Smith and how Native Americans and English settlers learned to live side by side.

The Secret Garden (Republic Pictures Home Video, 1987). Frances H. Burnett's classic tale about a sour-faced orphaned girl who is befriended by her invalid cousin. It richly addresses sensitivity and empathy.

Videos for Viewing with Teenagers

Au Revoir, Les Enfants (Orion, 1987). The true story of an eleven-year-old boy attending a Catholic boarding school in Nazi-occupied France, who discovers that three classmates are Jews in hiding from the Nazis. Moving scenes describe the compassion of those who risked their lives to shelter the needy.

The Elephant Man (Paramount Home Video, 1980). The true story of John Merrick, a severely deformed man. The story hits hard the moral lesson that the true beauty of a person lies within.

The Man Without a Face (Warner Home Video, 1993). A disfigured teacher is feared, but a young boy who gets to know him learns that people should be judged by their character, not by their appearance.

Mask (Universal Studios Home Video, 1985). A true story about a severely deformed teenager struggling for self-respect; he earns it by treating others kindly (regardless of how he has been treated).

Watership Down (Warner Home Video, 1996). A full-length animated version of the novel by Richard Adams; told from the point of view of rabbits, it celebrates the best "human values."

THE 2ND ESSENTIAL VIRTUE: CONSCIENCE

For Parents and Teachers

The Book of Virtues: A Treasury of Great Moral Stories, by William J. Bennett (New York: Simon & Schuster, 1993). A glorious treasury of great moral stories to tell kids of every age.

Books That Build Character: A Guide to Teaching Your Child Moral Values Through Stories, by William Kilpatrick and Gregory and Suzanne M. Wolfe (New York: Simon & Schuster, 1994). More than three hundred literature selections that embody strong values and help kids learn right from wrong.

Character Builders: Responsibility and Trustworthiness, by Michele Borba (Torrance, Calif.: Jalmar Press, 2000). A wealth of practical strategies to enhance students' conscience and develop their sense of responsibility.

Educating for Character, by Dr. Thomas Lickona (New York: Bantam Books, 1991). A call for the renewal of moral education in our schools and a precise prescription for how to bring it about.

Golden Rules, by Wayne Dosick (San Francisco: Harper San Francisco, 1995). A readable parent guide featuring ten values parents should teach their kids.

The Good Son, by Michael Gurian (Los Angeles: Tarcher, 1999). A valuable resource on how to shape the moral development of boys. Other books by the author are also recommended: *The Wonder of Boys* and *A Fine Young Man.*

The Moral Child, by William Damon (New York: Free Press, 1988). A classic for parents and teachers on ways to nurture children's natural moral growth.

The Moral Intelligence of Children, by Robert Coles (New York: Random House, 1997). Thorough, research-based ideas on how to raise a moral child. An absolute *must*-read.

Raising Good Children: From Birth Through the Teenage Years, by Dr. Thomas Lickona (New York: Bantam Books, 1983). An invaluable guide to raising decent, caring, and responsible children. A parent-friendly description of the stages of kids' moral growth and practical advice for raising good kids.

Teaching Your Children Values, by Linda and Richard Eyre (New York: Simon & Schuster, 1993). A guide full of practical ways to help kids develop values.

Why Johnny Can't Tell Right from Wrong, by William Kilpatrick (New York: Simon & Schuster, 1993). How to boost kids' moral lives by providing stories, models, and inspiration.

For Children Ages Three to Seven

Aesop's Fables, by Fritz Kredel (New York: Grosset & Dunlap, 1983). These ancient tales are still perfect today because they depict many of the basic moral lessons of life in easily understood terms.

The Children's Book of Virtues, edited by William Bennett (New York: Touchstone, 1996). A rich compilation of moral stories to use for years, beautifully illustrated by Michael Hague.

The Gold Coin, by Alma Flor Ada (New York: Atheneum, 1991). An old woman's generosity touches the heart of a would-be thief. Appropriate for teaching honesty, trustfulness, generosity.

Goldilocks and the Three Bears, by James Marshall (New York: Dial, 1988). A retelling of the classic about a girl who trespasses and makes herself at home without the owners' permission.

Sam, Bangs, and Moonshine, by Evaline Ness (Austin, Tex.: Holt, Reinhart and Winston, 1966). "Mistruths" get out of hand. The main character must deal with her actions and their harmful consequences.

You Can't Sell Your Brother at a Garage Sale! by Beth Brainard and Sheila Behr (New York: Dell, 1991). A practical, fun guide that addresses universal values in a humorous fashion.

For Children Ages Eight to Eleven

The Book of Virtues for Young People: A Treasury of Great Moral Stories, edited by William Bennett (New York: Simon & Schuster, 1997). Moral readings about self-discipline, work, courage, compassion, honesty, loyalty and faith, perseverance, responsibility, and friendship.

D'Aulaire's Book of Greek Myths, by Ingri and Edgar Parin d'Aulaire (New York: Doubleday, 1980). A wonderful collection of Greek myths that should be a moral staple for any child. Despite being immortals, the Greek gods and goddesses still depict all the vices and virtues of humans.

Dear Kalman, by Kalman Gabriel (New York: Morrow, 1999). A twelve-year-old received dozens of letters from some of the world's most interesting people telling him their secrets for successful living.

The Giver, by Lois Lowry (Boston: Houghton Mifflin, 1994). In a world without poverty or inequity, Jonas has an experience that forces him to question essential values we take for granted. Superb!

On My Honor, by Marion Bauer (New York: Clarion Books, 1986). A boy betrays his parents' trust and faces terrible consequences because of his disobedience.

One-Eyed Cat, by Paula Fox (New York: Bradbury, 1984). Disobeying his father, a boy takes a rifle and shoots a stray cat. He feels guilty and takes responsibility for his actions by telling the truth.

Shiloh, by Phyllis Reynolds Naylor (New York: Atheneum, 1991). An eleven-year-old tries to hide a dog from its mean-spirited owner known to mistreat his animals. Great for discussing responsibility and doing what is right.

The Trouble with Tuck, by Theodore Taylor (New York: Avon, 1981). A young girl is told to put her beloved dog to sleep when he becomes blind—which her conscience can't tolerate—so she finds another solution.

For Youth Ages Twelve and Older

April Morning, by Howard Fast (New York: Bantam Books, 1987). In this book set during the American Revolution, a self-absorbed fifteen-year-old witnesses his father's death in the Battle of Lexington and rises in manhood.

Brave New World, by Aldous Huxley (New York: HarperPerennial, 1998). This classic satire causes kids to think about what a world without freedom or responsibility would be like.

The Day They Came to Arrest the Book, by Nat Hentoff (New York: Bantam Books, 1983). A heated debate begins between teachers and high school students over the censorship of *Huckleberry Finn.*

Nineteen Eighty-Four, by George Orwell (New York: Signet, 1950). A timeless classic that sparks powerful discussions about conscience and rights.

The Red Badge of Courage, by Stephen Crane (New York: Vintage, 1990). The horrors of war are seen through the eyes of a young Civil War soldier. He slowly learns to conquer his fear and to follow his conscience and call to duty.

Videos for Viewing with Children

The Adventures of Robin Hood (MGM/UA Home Video, 1939). In the twelfth century, Robin Hood, an exiled nobleman, forms a band to aid the poor and helpless and restore Richard the Lion Heart to his rightful place on the throne. Disney's animated version is available from Buena Vista Home Video, 1983.

Antz (Dreamworks SKG, 1998). An animated film about a colony of ants always doing what they're trained to do, until they learn that sometimes you must buck the system to do what you think is right.

Pinocchio (Buena Vista Home Video, 1940). This timeless Disney production is the story of a rambunctious puppet who longs to be a real boy. His "conscience," Jiminy Cricket, has a full-time job.

The Ten Commandments (Paramount, 1990). Cecil B. De Mille's classic epic about the Ten Commandments, the foundation of Judeo-Christian morality.

You Can Choose: Saying No (Live Wire Video, 1993). Missie Mouse must decide whether to say no to a friend or do something she knows in her heart is wrong. Also in the series is *Doing the Right Thing,* about finding a wallet of money and making the right moral choice.

Videos for Viewing with Teenagers

All the President's Men (Warner Brothers, 1976). The true story of the two *Washington Post* reporters who followed their conscience and would not give up on covering the Watergate break-in.

The Grapes of Wrath (Twentieth Century Fox, 1940). John Steinbeck's saga of an American farm family struggling to survive in the Dust Bowl during the Great Depression. Conscience, compassion, loyalty, and perseverance are represented.

A Man for All Seasons (Columbia Pictures Home Video, 1966). The story of Sir Thomas More and how he gives his life rather than lie about what he believes.

Norma Rae (CBS Fox Video, 1985). Powerful portrayal of a young woman who follows her conscience and in doing so makes a difference. Helps children think about choices they face.

October Sky (Universal, 1999). A true story of a young boy's dreams of becoming a rocket scientist in 1957 and his struggle with his "moral obligation" to remain with his family and town.

On the Waterfront (Columbia Tristar, 1995). Marlon Brando portrays a dockside worker who heroically goes up against his corrupt labor leaders to expose the union's criminal practices.

The Story of Louis Pasteur (MGM/UA, 1936). Battling official censure and public indifference, Pasteur struggles with his conscience to develop the antitoxin that will prevent rabies.

Twelve Angry Men (MGM, 1957). Henry Fonda portrays the voice of conscience as a member of a jury that wants to reach a quick verdict against a young man on trial. The juror's fortitude prevails, and an innocent boy—who would have been falsely accused if it weren't for Fonda—is acquitted.

Websites for Kids

"Adventures from the Book of Virtues" [http://www.pbs.org/adventures/]. Numerous stories and activities based on William Bennett's popular book.

"Covington's Homeless: A Documentary" [http://www.intac.com/~jdeck/covdex2.html]. An award-winning photodocumentary portrays the homeless population of Covington, Kentucky.

"Food for the Hungry: Virtual Learning Center" [http://www.fh.org/]. Describes hunger relief programs worldwide and how to sponsor a child in the Third World.

"Kids Helping Kids" [http://www.geocities.com/Heartland/8677]. Started by a nine-year-old child, this website solicits ideas for helping homeless children.

"Kidz Care Story Center" [http://members.aol.com/kidz4peace/stories/index.htm]. Online picture books in eighteen different languages to teach young kids cultural diversity and compassion.

"Making Hearts Sing" [http://www.wildgear.com/stories/]. Offers a collection of international fables that teach universal moral lessons and traditional values.

Organizations, Websites, and Resources
for Enhancing Moral Development

Center for the 4th and 5th Rs, P.O. Box 2000, Education Department, Cortland, NY 13045. Telephone: (607) 753-2455. Website: http://www.cortland.edu/c4n5rs. The center serves as a resource in character education, provides summer institutes, publishes an online newsletter, provides a detailed twelve-step approach to character education, and has a browsing library.

The Character Counts Coalition, 4640 Admiralty Way, Suite 1001, Marina del Rey, CA 90202. Telephone: (310) 306-1868. Website: http://www.josephsoninstitute.org. A project of the Josephson Institute that represents a national partnership involved in improving the character of America's young people by focusing on the core ethical values the project calls the Six Pillars of Character.

Character Education Partnership, 1500 K Street NW, Suite 501, Washington, DC 20006. Telephone: (800) 988-8081. Website: http://www.character.org. A nonprofit partnership that offers character education resources, publishes an informative newsletter, and hosts an annual conference on character education.

Developmental Studies Center, 2000 Embarcadero Street, Suite 305, Oakland, CA 94606-5300. Telephone: (510) 533-0213. Website: http://www.devstu.org. A nonprofit organization established to develop programs and research to foster children's intellectual, social, and ethical development and to support educators in creating "caring communities." Excellent resources, training, and more are provided.

The Giraffe Project, P.O. Box 759, Langley, WA 98260. Telephone: (360) 221-7989. Website: http://www.giraffe.org/giraffe. E-mail: office@giraffe.org. A curriculum that teaches courageous compassion by using actual stories of caring "Giraffes"—people from 8 to 108 who have stuck their necks out for the common good. Great for service learning and character education for grades K–12.

THE 3RD ESSENTIAL VIRTUE: SELF-CONTROL

For Parents and Teachers

Lost Boys: Why Our Sons Turn Violent and How We Can Save Them, by James Garbarino (New York: Free Press, 1999). A must-read by a national expert: how to identify kids who are at risk, and proven methods to prevent aggressive behavior.

Peaceful Parents, Peaceful Kids: Practical Ways to Create a Calm and Happy Home, by Naomi Drew (New York: Kensington, 2000). If you are going to buy one book on creating a harmonious home, this should be it. Drew is an expert, and her ideas are *practical.*

A Penny Saved, by Neale Godfrey, with Ted Richards (New York: Simon & Schuster, 1995). A parent resource for ideas about chores, allowance, and financial planning.

Raising a Thinking Child, by Myrna B. Shure (New York: Henry Holt, 1994). A resource of ideas for teaching problem solving and feeling identification to children three to seven years of age.

Real Boys, by William Pollack (New York: Henry Holt, 1998). How to help boys develop more self-confidence and the emotional savvy they need to deal with such issues as depression and violence.

Ritalin Is Not the Answer: A Drug-Free, Practical Program for Children Diagnosed with ADD or ADHD, by David Stein (San Francisco: Jossey-Bass, 1999). An excellent resource on ADD and ADHD and techniques for managing behavior without medication.

Tired of Yelling: Teaching Our Children to Resolve Conflict, by Lyndon D. Waugh (Marietta, Ga.: Longstreet Press, 1999). A fifteen-step model to help kids learn to manage anger and handle conflict.

Your Anxious Child: How Parents and Teachers Can Relieve Anxiety in Children, by John S. Dacey and Lisa B. Fiore (San Francisco: Jossey-Bass, 2000). Proven ways to help kids handle stress and cope with difficulties more confidently.

For Children Ages Three to Seven

Bootsie Barker Bites, by Barbara Bottner (New York: Putnam, 1992). Bootsie wants to play games in which she bites—until her friend lets her know her behavior is not appreciated.

Feelings, by Aliki (New York: Morrow/Avon, 1986). A wonderful handbook of emotions, ranging in topics from anger, jealousy, and fear to pride, joy, and love.

Mean Soup, by Betsy Everitt (Orlando, Fla.: Harcourt Brace, 1992). A young boy has a bad day and feels mean until he makes a mean soup with his mother and finds ways to stir his meanness away.

Today I Feel Silly and Other Moods That Make My Day, by Jamie Lee Curtis (New York: HarperCollins, 1998). Twelve emotions are addressed in a delightful rhyme. Included is a cardboard wheel kids can turn to help them identify the basic feelings.

When Sophie Gets Angry—Really, Really Angry, by Molly Bang (New York: Blue Sky Press, 1999). Young Sophie has a very angry day and learns ways to deal with her upset feelings. A great discussion tool to help kids recognize different ways to handle feelings.

For Children Ages Eight to Eleven

Be a Perfect Person in Just Three Days! by Stephen Manes (New York: Bantam-Skylark, 1991). Milo finds a book on "how to be the perfect person," follows the directions, and finally learns the important message: everyone makes mistakes.

Comeback! Four True Stories, by Jim O'Connor (New York: Random House, 1992). Four famous athletes who overcame debilitating conditions through effort, tenacity, and self-control.

Dreams and Drummers, by Doris Buchanan Smith (New York: Crowell, 1978). A straight-A student who wins every contest she enters learns what it's like to finish second and how to deal with it.

Save Queen of Sheba, by Louise Moeri (New York: Turtleback/Demco, 1994). A twelve-year-old traveling alone on the dangerous Oregon Trail with his little sister quickly learns to keep his cool.

The War with Grandpa, by Robert Kimmel Smith (New York: Turtleback/Demco, 1991). Peter must learn to control his anger when Grandpa moves into his room and forces him upstairs.

For Youth Ages Twelve and Older

Driver's Ed, by Caroline Cooney (New York: Dell, 1996). Three teenagers' lives are forever changed when they steal a stop sign from an intersection, and a young mother is killed in an auto accident there because of their impulsive action.

Hatchet, by Gary Paulsen (New York: Puffin, 1987). Twelve-year-old Brian is stranded in the wilderness and is confronted with a multitude of problems. He keeps his cool and solves them all!

Homecoming, by Cynthia Voight (New York: Atheneum, 1981). Abandoned by their mother, four children try to survive as they travel to their grandmother's home.

The Old Man and the Sea, by Ernest Hemingway (New York: Scribner, 1999). The classic of an old Cuban fisherman in a relentless physical and moral battle against a giant marlin.

Trapped, by Roderic Jeffries (New York: HarperCollins, 1972). Two boys are caught in a snowstorm and must overcome their dislike for one another in order to survive.

Zlata's Diary, by Zlata Filipovic (New York: Penguin Books, 1994). An eleven-year-old's diary of growing up in war-torn Sarajevo begins with typical concerns, then records the horrors of war and her plea for peace and respect for life.

Videos for Viewing with Children

Big Changes, Big Choices: Handling Emotions (Live Wire Video, 1994). A set of videos developed for ten- to twelve-year-olds. The sixth volume shows positive ways of expressing feelings. See also *Preventing Conflicts and Violence* (Vol. 7), which helps kids handle anger acceptably.

The Karate Kid (TriStar Home Video, 1984). A teenage boy struggling to find acceptance encounters bullying instead. He discovers that using your fists to handle a problem gets you nothing but injured, so he turns to martial arts and forges an unforgettable relationship with his teacher.

The Marzipan Pig (Family Home Video, 1991). Adapted from the book by Russell Hoban, here are thirty moving minutes that sensitize kids to feelings (especially loneliness and kindness).

Old Yeller (Walt Disney Home Video, 1957). A sensitive tale that addresses issues pioneers faced living in the wilderness and provides opportunities to discuss feelings and choices. *Some scary scenes.*

Ruby Bridges (Buena Vista Home Video, 1998). The true story of the six-year-old African American girl who was ordered by federal judges to attend an all-white school. In doing so Ruby led the cause of racial integration in the school system. Her strength of character is inspiring.

Snow White and the Seven Dwarfs (Walt Disney Home Video, 1938). The wicked queen is so tortured by jealousy that she is willing to risk everything to destroy Snow White. Special emotions to discuss: jealousy, fear, loneliness, happiness, sadness. (This is one of Disney's scariest movies, so beware!)

Tom Sawyer (MGM/UA, 1973). This heartwarming rendition of the American classic is great for discussing the emotions of loneliness, sadness, anger, fear, and happiness.

You Can Choose: Dealing with Feelings (Live Wire Video, 1993). Afraid of the outdoors, Tuggy Turtle hides his fears at a campout, almost ruining his friendship with his buddy.

Videos for Viewing with Teenagers

Chariots of Fire (Warner Home Video, 1981). This spectacular Oscar winner is about two English runners who competed on the 1924 Olympic track team and the different motivations that drove them to compete. One was compelled by hatred of anti-Semitism, the other by the love of God.

Gandhi (TriStar Home Video, 1982). This film about Mahatma Gandhi, magnificently portrayed by Ben Kingsley, chronicles the prejudice he encounters as a young attorney in South Africa, his role as spiritual leader to the people of India, his cause of passive resistance, and his eventual assassination.

Kundun (Touchstone, 1997). A stunning movie depicting the life of the fourteenth Dalai Lama. Great for helping kids understand a bit of Chinese history, the pacifist views of the Dalai Lama, and the increasing difficulties he faces as a nonviolent man in an increasingly violent world.

Paths of Glory (MGM, 1957). Classic antiwar drama set in WWI France, in which a vain officer imposes an unlikely battle strategy—one doomed to fail—on his troops. When it does fail, he demands that three soldiers be selected for execution as cowards. Great for discussing conscience, respect, and self-control.

Places in the Heart (CBS/Fox Video, 1984). This film features Sally Field in an Oscar-winning role as a young widow determined to survive as a cotton farmer during the Depression.

Rudy (Columbia Tristar Home Video, 1992). The true story of a boy whose goal is to play football at Notre Dame despite his mediocre athletic ability and academic record. His self-discipline helps him triumph!

You Can Choose: Resolving Conflicts (Live Wire Video, 1993). The tenth in a series of videos that teaches ways to solve conflicts peacefully and fairly by talking out problems.

Websites for Kids

"Children Now" [http://www.childrennow.org/toughissues/Talk_Open.html]/. This site includes great tips on how to talk to children about such difficult issues as youth violence.

"Conflict Resolution the Peaceful Way" [http://www.stark.k12.oh.us/docs/units/conflict/]. Developed by teachers in Ohio, this site offers conflict resolution activities to use with children.

"Kids for Peace" [http://www.kids4peace.com]. This site provides information to help children become peacemakers, including creative activities and an extensive list of related links.

Organizations Supporting Conflict Resolution

Educators for Social Responsibility, 23 Garden Street, Cambridge, MA 02138. Telephone: (800) 370-2515. Programs and materials about conflict resolution, violence prevention, intergroup relations.

Kids Without Violence Program, P.O. Box 487, 35 Benton Street, Eureka Springs, AR 72632. A clearinghouse of information and workshops on the issue of youth violence.

National Association for Mediation in Education (NAME), 205 Hampshire House, Box 33635, University of Massachusetts, Amherst, MA 01003. Telephone: (413) 545-2462. Promotes the development and implementation of school- and university-based conflict resolution programs.

The National Institute for Dispute Resolution, 1726 M Street NW, Suite 500, Washington, DC 20036. Telephone: (202) 466-4764.

Resolving Conflict Creatively Program (RCCP) National Center, 163 Third Avenue, Suite 103, New York, NY 10003. Telephone: (212) 387-0225. Provides a model for preventing school violence and creating caring learning communities.

THE 4TH ESSENTIAL VIRTUE: RESPECT

For Parents and Teachers

Backtalk: Four Steps to Ending Rude Behavior in Your Kids, by Audrey Ricker and Carolyn Crowder (New York: Fireside, 1998). A commonsense guide to stopping disrespectful behaviors.

Between Parent and Child, by Haim Ginott (New York: Avon, 1972). This classic is rich with helpful ideas showing the difference between respectful and destructive communication.

Character Builders: Respect for Self and Others, by Michele Borba (Torrance, Calif.: Jalmar Press, 2000). A complete program with dozens of practical ideas for teaching students respect.

How to Talk So Kids Will Listen and Listen So Kids Will Talk, by Adele Faber and Elaine Mazlish (New York: Avon, 1982). A guide to communicating more respectfully and effectively with kids.

More Than Manners! Raising Today's Kids to Have Kind Manners and Good Hearts, by Letitia Baldrige (New York: Rawson Associates, 1997). Enhancing kids' decency, kindness, and manners.

P.E.T.: Parent Effectiveness Training, by Thomas Gordon (New York: Signet, 1975). Gordon's book describes a proven method to help enhance the communication between parents and their children.

For Children Ages Three to Seven

But Names Will Never Hurt Me, by Bernard Waber (Boston: Houghton Mifflin, 1976). A story about how the disrespectful actions of name-calling and teasing can hurt.

Elbert's Bad Word, by Audrey Wood (Orlando, Fla.: Harcourt Brace, 1988). Young Albert's use of "bad words" causes all kinds of havoc. A wizard provides a few more appropriate ones.

Grandmother's Chair, by Ann Herbert Scott (New York: Clarion, 1991). Grandmother describes to her granddaughter the past four generations who have used a chair. Great for discussing respect for age.

Manners, by Aliki (New York: Greenwillow, 1990). An assortment of different manners are cleverly illustrated.

My Dog Never Says Please, by Suzanne Williams (New York: Dial, 1997). Ginny has atrocious manners, and her family keeps reminding her. A fanciful story with a great moral!

Perfect Pigs: An Introduction to Manners, by Marc Brown and Stephen Krensky (New York: Little Brown, 1983). A delightful picture book that introduces very basic manners.

For Children Ages Eight to Eleven

Brother Eagle, Sister Sky, by Susan Jeffers (New York: Dial, 1991). A Native American tale about respecting our environment.

The Hundred Penny Box, by Sharon Mathis (Puffin, 1975). Great Aunt Dew has an ongoing tradition in which she houses a penny for each of the hundred years of her life. Illustrates respect for different ages.

The Pushcart War, by Jean Merrill (New York: Dell, 1984). This satire based on a real incident involving the garbage strike in New York City shows how disrespect and negativity began to spread.

Social Smarts: Modern Manners for Today's Kids, by Elizabeth James (New York: Clarion Books, 1996). Offers advice to kids on how to handle all types of social situations.

The Value of Respect: The Story of Abraham Lincoln, by A. Johnson (Danbury Press, 1971). The life of Lincoln is used to teach this core value.

The Whipping Boy, by Sid Fleischman (New York: Troll, 1987). The story of Prince Brat (most aptly named) and Jemmy, an orphan. The tale teaches the power of respect and kindness.

For Youth Ages Twelve and Older

The Bluest Eye, by Toni Morrison (New York: Penguin Books, 1994). A powerful story of a black eleven-year-old who prays for her eyes to turn blue so that she will be as beautiful and valued as all blond, blue-eyed children in America. *For mature teens only:* preview this one first—contains strong language and sexual issues (rape, incest).

How Rude! The Teenagers' Guide to Good Manners, Proper Behavior, and Not Grossing People Out, by Alex J. Packer (Minneapolis: Free Spirit, 1997). Sound advice about manners, conveyed in a humorous way.

A Lesson Before Dying, by Ernest J. Gaines (New York: Vintage Books, 1993). Set in a small Cajun community in the late 1940s, a young black man is unjustly accused of murder and is sentenced to death. A moving tale of respect, dignity, compassion, and unfairness. *For mature teens.*

Netiquette, by Virginia Shea (New York: Albion Publishing, 1994). Highly recommended for today's "online" kids: a guide with dos and don'ts for online manners.

Nothing but the Truth, by Avi (New York: Orchard Books, 1991). A unique novel dealing with issues of respect, freedom, and patriotism and what can happen because of misunderstanding.

The Pigman, by Paul Zindel (New York: Bantam Books, 1983). An unusual friendship between two high school sophomores who are determined to tell the sad, zany story of Mr. Pignati, the Pigman.

The Scarlet Letter, by Nathaniel Hawthorne (New York: Bantam Books, 1981). Set in Puritan New England, this is the story of a young woman who bears an illegitimate child and must wear a scarlet letter *A* on her dress as punishment. *For mature readers.*

Videos for Viewing with Children

Babe (Universal Studios, 1995). An orphaned pig learns his true calling: herding sheep. One line captures the essence of the story: "This is a tale about an unprejudiced heart and how it changed our valley forever."

Beauty and the Beast (Walt Disney Home Video, 1991). Beautiful Belle offers herself to the ugly Beast to save her father's life; she discovers Beast's kind heart and learns not to judge people by their appearance.

Big Changes, Big Choices: Respecting Others (Live Wire Video, 1994). This clearly addresses how everyone is entitled to respect regardless of differences in race, gender, appearance, and beliefs.

Captain Courageous (MGM/UA Home Video, 1937). A touching story of a spoiled affluent boy who thinks the only way to gain friends is to be a bully and buy his way to success at a boarding school. He finally learns that the real way to gain respect is through responsibility and hard work.

Lady and the Tramp (Walt Disney Home Video, 1955). Different as night and day, Lady, the classy spaniel, and Tramp, the downtown mutt, accept their differences and learn to fall in love.

My Fair Lady (Fox Video 1994). An Academy Award–winning classic, great for emphasizing respect, courtesy, and manners (as well as singing along with your kids).

The Point (Family Home Entertainment, 1971). This charming animated musical is the story of a young boy rejected and isolated because his head is round and not pointed like everyone else's.

The Ugly Duckling (Children's Home Video, 1986). Hans Christian Andersen's tale of the lonely ugly duckling who becomes a beautiful swan. It urges us to find genuine qualities in others.

Videos for Viewing with Teenagers

A Bronx Tale (Home Box Office, 1993). A young Italian American boy living in the Bronx witnesses a murder by a mobster who befriends him for not turning him in. Eventually he's forced to choose between the mobster and his father and commit to his moral beliefs. Strong language; violence.

The Miracle Worker (MGM, 1962). The moving story of blind, deaf, and mute Helen Keller and her teacher, Anne Sullivan, whose patience and perseverance enable Helen to communicate with the world. Their respectful relationship is inspiring, and both women are powerful models of solid character.

My Dog Skip (Warner Brothers, 2000). This is the kind of family movie that you wish they'd make more of. A moving, moral tale rich with respect, love, loyalty, courage, and compassion.

Roll of Thunder, Hear My Cry (Live Home Video, 1992). A powerful drama about the struggles of a black family in Mississippi to keep their land and their dignity during the Depression. Based on the novel by Mildred Taylor.

Websites for Kids

"America's Heroes and You" [http://www.webcom.com/~webspin/heroes/sample.html]. Offers sample lessons with questions about specific virtues and historical figures who have exhibited them.

"Kid's Action" [http://www.ran.org/ran/kids_action/index.html]. The Rainforest Action Network offers tips on what kids can do to respect their environment and help preserve natural resources.

"My Hero" [http://myhero.com/]. This site encourages children to read and write about what it means to be a hero and helps kids reflect on what qualities in others they should respect.

"Netiquette Home Page" [http:www.albion.com/netiquette/]. A site for today's kids that features the dos and don'ts of communicating online.

"Recycle City" [http://www.epa.gov/recyclecity]. Games and activities are provided to teach children about the importance of respecting our environment by recycling.

"Yahoo's Netiquette Links" [http://www.yahoo.com]. If you type the word "Netiquette" in the Search box, Yahoo provides a list of links to other sites offering information about online netiquette.

THE 5TH ESSENTIAL VIRTUE: KINDNESS

For Parents and Teachers

The Brighter Side of Human Nature, by Alfie Kohn (New York: Basic Books, 1990). Drawing from hundreds of studies, Kohn makes a powerful case that caring and generosity are just as natural as selfishness and aggression and that they must be developed.

The Caring Child, by Nancy Eisenberg (Cambridge, Mass.: Harvard University Press, 1992). Here is one of the most up-to-date guides to understanding how caring develops.

Raising Compassionate, Courageous Children in a Violent World, by Janice Cohn (Marietta, Ga.: Longstreet Press, 1996). Ways to help children learn the qualities of kindness, courage, and decency.

Teaching Children to Care: Management in the Responsive Classroom, by Ruth Sidney Chaney (Greenfield, Mass.: Northeast Foundation for Children, 1992). An excellent resource for educators on how to create caring learning environments.

For Children Ages Three to Seven

The Brand New Kid, by Katie Couric (New York: Doubleday, 2000). Two little girls show true compassion when a not-so-ordinary boy joins their classroom. A great springboard for discussing the value of kindness and the importance of acceptance.

The First Forest, by John Gile (Rockford, Ill.: John Gile Communications, 1989). A parable reminds us that selfishness is harmful and that harmony flows from grateful appreciation for the gifts we receive.

The Great Gilly Hopkins, by Katherine Paterson (New York: HarperCollins, 1987). A heart-wrenching tale of a foster child who is besieged by unkindness and becomes hardened to rejection.

The Little Brute Family, by Russell Hoban (New York: Troll, 1980). A valuable lesson about how positive, kind attitudes are caught and spread.

A New Coat for Anna, by Harriet Zeifert (New York: Knopf, 1986). Though there's no money to buy Anna a new coat, her mother saves for many months and produces a beautiful gift.

The Quarreling Book, by Charlotte Zolotow (New York: HarperCollins, 1963). A simple book illustrating that how we treat people can have a direct impact on their actions the rest of the day.

Somebody Loves You, Mr. Hatch, by Eileen Spinelli (New York: Bradbury, 1991). A wonderful year-round Valentine to read to children on the impact they have on others.

Wilfrid Gordon McDonald Partridge, by Mem Fox (New York: Kane/Miller, 1985). A young boy learns that his elderly friend is losing her memory and sets out to help her find it.

The Wolf's Chicken Stew, by Keiko Kasza (New York: Putnam, 1987). A hungry wolf learns that making positive overtures can have wonderful consequences.

For Children Ages Eight to Eleven

The Giving Tree, by Shel Silverstein (New York: HarperCollins, 1964). The classic parable for all ages of the gift of giving and the serene acceptance of another's capacity to love in return.

The Indian in the Cupboard, by Lynne Reid Banks (New York: Avon, 1980). A toy Indian given to a young boy comes to life, and because of the Indian the boy learns the value of kindness.

The Pushcart War, by Jean Merrill (New York: Dell, 1984). This satire based on a real incident involving the garbage strike in New York City shows how negativity and unkindness began to spread.

Stone Fox, by John Reynolds Gardiner (New York: HarperCollins, 1980). Ten-year-old Willy enters a dogsled race so that his grandfather's farm might be saved.

The Way to Start a Day, by Byrd Baylor (Old Tappan, N.J.: Macmillan, 1977). Shows examples of ways different cultures celebrate. A catalyst for discussing ways to start days being kind toward others.

For Youth Ages Twelve and Older

The Color of Water, by James McBride (New York: Riverhead Books, 1996). A moving memoir of a young black boy growing up at a time of racial polarization. His compassionate mother, who raises him to have a strong work ethic and a giving heart, is unforgettable. *For advanced readers.*

Great Expectations, by Charles Dickens (New York: Knopf, 1992). The classic of a young orphan boy who mysteriously acquires a great fortune then tries to discover his benefactor.

Little Women, by Louisa May Alcott (New York: Puffin, 1988). A timeless story of four sisters and their wonderful kind regard for one another. It addresses myriad virtues.

Lord of the Flies, by William Golding (New York: Perigee Books, 1959). English schoolboys are stranded on a desert island left to their own devices and stripped of the veneer of "civilization"; they gradually degenerate into cruel, greedy savages without an ounce of kindness.

Of Mice and Men, by John Steinbeck (New York: Penguin, 1993). The friendship between two poignant characters: mentally handicapped, warmhearted Lenny and his protector, George. Heartbreaking moments of a sometimes cruel and selfish world make for ripe moral discussions.

Pay It Forward, by Catherine Ryan Hyde (New York: Simon & Schuster, 2000). What if everyone in the world did a good deed for three people—and what if each of them "paid it forward" by doing a good deed for three more people, and so on, until the world was a different place? That's the lesson twelve-year-old Trevor learns when his teacher makes the assignment.

Tuesdays with Morrie, by Mitch Albom (New York: Doubleday, 1997). The author's Tuesday visits with his dying favorite professor teach him some of the best life lessons: forgiveness, love, compassion, and the importance of family.

Videos for Viewing with Children

Anne of Green Gables (Walt Disney Home Video, 1985). A moving account based on Lucy Maud Montgomery's novel of an orphan living with an old bachelor farmer and his no-nonsense spinster sister and her struggles to cope and find happiness. Her kindness changes the lives of those she touches.

Charlotte's Web (Paramount Home Video, 1972). Based on E. B. White's classic novel; Charlotte, the spider, weaves words of praise in her web, and her kind deed saves Wilbur the pig from slaughter.

Cinderella (Walt Disney Home Video, 1950). Cinderella is a girl of tremendous character: always optimistic, resourceful, and kind—despite the cruelty of her mean stepsisters and stepmother.

The Little Match Girl (Family Home Entertainment, 1991). The Hans Christian Andersen tale of Angela, a homeless little girl who nearly freezes to death but is adopted by a mutt and is finally saved. Great discussion possibilities about homelessness and the need to care.

A Little Princess (Warner Home Video, 1995). Young Sara is sent to a strict boarding school where the headmistress considers her a troublemaker. With courage and kindness, Sara overcomes the hardships and in so doing changes the lives of those around her.

Pollyanna (Disney Home Video, 1960). How can you not love Pollyanna? Her ability to find only the best in people and spread "gladness" to an entire community is a glorious message about kindness.

So Dear to My Heart (Walt Disney Home Video, 1949). A young boy wants to enter his black sheep in the state fair. He learns to believe in himself; he also learns the importance of compassion and persistence.

The Velveteen Rabbit (Rabbit Ears Productions, 1985). The animated classic based on the Margery Williams story of a little boy and a stuffed toy bunny who learn the true meaning of love. It's just wonderful.

Willie Wonka and the Chocolate Factory (Warner Brothers, 1971). A fabulous children's classic that shows that a kind heart really is a finer possession than a sweet tooth.

Winnie the Pooh, Pooh Learning, Helping Others (Walt Disney Home Video, 1994). Winnie shows young kids about helping others.

The Wizard of Oz (MGM, 1939). The classic that everyone loves. Be sure to discuss what the tin man, lion, and scarecrow seek: courage, intellect, and heart. Which do your kids feel is most important in leading a good and decent life?

Videos for Viewing with Teenagers

A Christmas Carol (Home Vision Cinema, 1951). Charles Dickens's classic describes the old unyielding miser, Scrooge, and the horror of seeing his past. The need for kindness is quite apparent and makes for a great discussion about how we live our lives and how others might perceive us.

David Copperfield (MGM, 1935). Charles Dickens's classic of a young boy growing up in an orphanage and the hardship and cruelty he must endure. Rich potential for moral reflection.

The Diary of Anne Frank (Twentieth Century Fox, 1959). A young girl's account of enduring the most horrendous circumstances of hiding in terror from the Nazis. Her indomitable optimistic spirit and ability to find goodness despite evil is an incredible display of character. The book and video are musts.

Edward Scissorhands (Fox, 1990). Edward is a young man created by an eccentric scientist who dies before he can attach hands to his boy creature. He is rescued from a lonely existence with his scissor hands still in place, but he faces trouble fitting in and struggles with being different.

Forrest Gump (Paramount, 1994). This story of an intellectually impaired man whose golden heart transforms the lives of those around him offers a great message that character wins out over intellect.

Life Is Beautiful (Buena Vista Home Video, 1998). A heart-wrenching tale of a bumbling man with irresistible humor, endless love, ingenuity, and a heart of gold. He uses them to instill hope to his wife and to protect his young son in the most deplorable of conditions—a concentration camp. *For older kids.*

Schindler's List (Universal Studios Home Video, 1993). The true story of Oskar Schindler, a German businessman, who bribed the Nazis into allowing him to employ Jews in his Polish factories during WWII and saved over eleven hundred lives. An immense moral message that the kindness of one person can literally change the world. *For mature teens only; rated R for strong language, violence, some sexuality.*

Websites for Kids

"Corporation for National Service" [http://www.cns.gov/]. A national program that promotes youth service opportunities.

"National Youth Leadership Council" [http://www.nylc.org/]. Opportunities for teen leaders to get involved in service projects.

"Youth as Resources" [http://www.yar.org/]. More service possibilities for youth involvement.

"Youth in Action Network" [http://www.mightymedia.com/]. By clicking the icon and using the password "guest," you access lessons about altruism and channels for children to get involved.

"Youth Service America" [http://www.servenet.org/ysanet2/index.html] Another national organization that promotes youth service in the community.

THE 6TH ESSENTIAL VIRTUE: TOLERANCE

For Parents and Teachers

Forty Ways to Raise a Nonracist Child, by Barbara Mathias and Mary Ann French (New York: HarperPerennial, 1996). This simple guide written by a biracial duo helps parents talk openly with their kids about racism and respect for racial differences.

I'm Chocolate, You're Vanilla: Raising Healthy Black and Biracial Children in a Race-Conscious World, by Marguerite Wright (San Francisco: Jossey-Bass, 1998). How to reduce the impact of racism on a child's development—from preschool through adolescence—and in doing so raise more tolerant and emotionally healthy children.

Raising the Rainbow Generation: Teaching Your Children to Be Successful in a Multicultural Society, by Darlene Powell Hopson and Derek S. Hopson (New York: Simon & Schuster, 1993). Designed to help parents teach kids respect and appreciation for all cultural, ethnic, and racial groups.

Teaching Peace: How to Raise Children to Live in Harmony—Without Fear, Without Prejudice, Without Violence, by Jan Arnow (New York: Perigee Books, 1995). Ways to encourage tolerance and respect in kids.

Teaching Tolerance, by Sara Bullard (New York: Doubleday, 1996). Solid research-based suggestions for raising more tolerant, open-minded, and empathic children.

For Children Ages Three to Seven

Amazing Grace, by Mary Hoffman (New York: Dial Books, 1991). A young girl's classmates tell her that because she is black and a girl she can't play the lead in the school play *Peter Pan.* Her family tells her she can do anything she sets her mind to—including playing the part of Peter Pan—and she does!

Angel Child, Dragon Child, by Michele Maria Surat (New York: Scholastic, 1983). A young Vietnamese girl arrives at her new American school and faces taunts by her classmates for her cultural differences.

Aunt Harriet's Underground Railroad in the Sky, by Faith Ringgold (New York: Crown, 1992). A tribute to Harriet Tubman is told by two black children who magically travel back in time to the days of slavery. A great vehicle for discussing the issue with kids.

Being with You This Way, by W. Lisa-Nikola (New York: Lee & Low Books, 1995). Marvelous illustrations of kids playing together with an accompanying verse celebrating their physical differences.

For Children Ages Eight to Eleven

The Great Ancestor Hunt: The Fun of Finding Out Who You Are, by Lia Perl (New York: Clarion, 1990). Introduces ways kids can trace their family lines and respect their cultural background.

Meet Danitra Brown, by Nancy Grimes (New York: Scholastic, 1984). The friendship between two black girls is beautifully illustrated, and the issue of color is addressed in a most empowering way.

Molly's Pilgrim, by Barbara Cohen (New York: Lothrop, Lee & Shepard, 1983). A young immigrant girl is rejected for her cultural differences by classmates who finally learn that those differences are strengths.

My Dream of Martin Luther King, by Faith Ringgold (New York: Crown Publishers, 1995). A glorious interpretation of Martin Luther King's legacy and the civil rights movement that poignantly urges that intolerance, hatred, and prejudice be replaced by love, tolerance, and dreams.

Number the Stars, by Lois Lowry (New York: Dell, 1989). A compelling tale that takes place in Copenhagen in 1943, describing a ten-year-old girl's courage in saving her Jewish friend from the Nazis.

The Well: David's Story, by Mildred Taylor (New York: Dial, 1995). David's rural Mississippi family shares their well water with black and white neighbors in the early 1900s.

For Youth Ages Twelve and Older

Children of the River, by Linda Crew (New York: Dell, 1989). A thirteen-year-old girl flees Cambodia with her aunt's family to escape the Khmer Rouge, leaving behind her family and the boy she loves; she struggles to fit in at the American high school. *For advanced readers.*

The Chosen, by Chaim Potok (New York: Knopf, 1992). Set in Brooklyn in the 1940s, a poignant friendship evolves between two adolescent Jewish boys. Though each is raised as Jewish, the religious views of their families are quite diverse and have a tremendous impact on their friendship.

Dear Mrs. Parks: A Dialogue with Today's Youth, by Rosa Parks (New York: Lee & Low Books, 1996). A collection of letters exchanged between Rosa Parks and children all over the country; in each, Parks urges them to become a force for positive change in society.

The Hate Crime, by Phyllis Karas (New York: Avon Flare Books, 1995). High school sophomore Zack never thought being Jewish was any big deal until someone painted anti-Semitic graffiti on the Temple Israel.

The Invisible Thread: An Autobiography, by Yoshiko Uchida (New York: Morrow/Aron, 1995). A powerful memoir of a Japanese American girl who was held with her family along with 130,000 other Japanese American citizens in U.S. internment camps during World War II.

Night, by Elie Wiesel (New York: Bantam Books, 1982). A wrenching story based on the author's experiences in a concentration camp during World War II, in which he witnesses the death of his family. It is unforgettable and sends a clear message of how immoral intolerance can be.

Warriors Don't Cry, by Melba Pattillo Beals (New York: Simon & Schuster, 1995). The remarkable true story of Melba Pattillo, one of the nine teenagers chosen to integrate Little Rock's Central High School, and the racism they endured.

Videos for Viewing with Children

An American Tail (MCA Home Video, 1986). An animated feature for younger kids about an immigrant Jewish family of mice at the turn of the century. The little mouse gets separated from his family and wanders through New York, meeting a series of multiethnic characters.

Fiddler on the Roof (Fox, 1971). One of the all-time great Broadway musicals with an underlying theme for anyone whose ancestors came to the United States to find something better for their families and tried to maintain traditions while adapting to changing circumstances.

Follow the Drinking Gourd (Rabbit Ears Productions, 1993). This thirty-minute animated tale of the story of the Underground Railroad and an eleven-year-old slave is a powerful introduction to slavery and racial injustice.

Miracle of Midnight (Walt Disney Home Video, 2000). An uplifting true story of how one Danish family risked their lives in a remarkable effort to save thousands of Jewish countrymen from the horror of concentration camps.

Perfect Harmony (Walt Disney Home Video, 1991). At an exclusive southern boys school in the 1950s, two boys of different races vie for a spot in the lead choir. Bigotry, hate crimes, and intolerance are all represented.

The Sneetches (Playhouse Video, 1960). The classic Seuss story about two groups—each thinking it's the best. This is a delightful way to introduce the concept of prejudice to very young children.

Videos for Viewing with Teenagers

The Autobiography of Miss Jane Pittman (Prism Home Video, 1974). Based on Ernest J. Gaine's novel, this is the life story of a fictional 110-year-old dignified former slave woman.

The Blue and the Gray (Columbia Tristar Home Pictures, 1990). This sweeping Civil War saga depicts how intolerance pits family against family in one of this country's most tragic wars.

The Buddy Holly Story (Columbia Tristar Home Pictures, 1978). This story follows one of the first rock-and-roll legends, Buddy Holly, from youth to stardom and then early death in a tragic plane crash; it also portrays the resistance he faced against his music. A very different catalyst for discussing tolerance.

The Defiant Ones (MGM, 1958). This movie is still powerful because the theme is timeless. It deals with two convicts—one black and one white—who are shackled together. The two must overcome their hostility to work together when they escape from a chain gang.

Ghosts of Mississippi (Columbia, 1996). The story of slain civil rights leader Medgar Evers and the attempts of a white assistant district attorney to convict his killer during racially charged times.

Glory (Columbia, 1989). A historical epic chronicling the first black volunteer infantry unit and their white commander in the Civil War. Great for discussing tolerance, empathy, and conscience.

The Long Walk Home (Artisan Entertainment, 1989). It's the 1950s in Montgomery, Alabama, and an affluent white wife tries to understand why her struggling black maid would protest racial intolerance by supporting a bus boycott led by Martin Luther King Jr.

Home of the Brave (Republic Pictures Home Video, 1949). A 1949 classic involving a black engineer who volunteers for a dangerous reconnaissance mission with four white soldiers during World War II. Explain that the armed services were segregated and that the intolerance he faced was common.

Remember the Titans (Walt Disney Pictures, 2000). A true story of a Virginia high school ordered to be integrated in 1971. The new black coach must get the once all-white football team to learn to work together and respect each other as human beings. He succeeds, and they become state champs.

Organizations and Websites Promoting Tolerance

American Friends Service Committee, 1505 Cherry Street, Philadelphia, PA 19102. Telephone: (215) 241-7000. Advocates for social justice and racial harmony.

Anti-Defamation League (ADL), 823 United Nations Plaza, New York, NY 10017. Telephone: (212) 490-2525. Website: http://www.adl.org.

Association of MultiEthnic Americans (AMEA), 1060 Tennessee Street, San Francisco, CA 94107. Telephone: (415) 548-9300. Website: http://www.ameasite.org. A national organization offering a list of local member organizations.

Center for Healing Racism, P.O. Box 53290, Washington, DC 20009. Telephone: (800) 500-9040. Provides newsletter, resource list, and listing of interracial support groups.

Center for the Study of Biracial Children [http://www.csbc.cncfamily.com].

"The KidsCom Page" [http://www.kidscom.com/orake/wall.html]. Encourages the appreciation of cultural diversity; offers the chance for twelve- to fifteen-year-olds to chat live with kids around the globe.

National Association for the Advancement of Colored People (NAACP), Washington bureau, 1025 Vermont Avenue NW, Suite 1120, Washington, DC 20005. Telephone: (202) 638-2269. Website: http://www.naacp.org/.

Simon Wiesenthal Center, 9760 W. Pico Boulevard, Los Angeles, CA 90035. Telephone: (310) 553-9036. Website: http://www.wiesenthal.com/. The center has launched a public service campaign designed to raise consciousness about hate on the Internet and offers resources about tolerance.

"Teaching Tolerance" [http://www.splcenter.org/teachingtolerance.html]. The Southern Poverty Law Center, 400 Washington Avenue, Montgomery, AL 36104. Telephone: (334) 264-0286. A national education project that fosters respect and understanding in the classroom and beyond.

THE 7TH ESSENTIAL VIRTUE: FAIRNESS

For Parents and Teachers

Gang Free, by Valerie Wiener (Minneapolis, Minn.: Fairview Press, 1995). If you are concerned about your child's selection of peers or gang involvement, this is a must-read.

Good Friends Are Hard to Find, by Fred Frankel (Pasadena, Calif.: Perspective Publishing, 1996). This book lays out a step-by-step guide to help five- to twelve-year-olds make friends, take turns, solve relationship problems fairly, share, and deal with unfair peer treatment.

The Kid's Guide to Social Action, by Barbara Lewis (Minneapolis, Minn.: Free Spirit, 1997). A rich compilation of ways kids can make a difference in the world. See also Barbara Lewis's other books: *The Kid's Guide to Service Projects, Kids with Courage,* and *What Do You Stand For?*

What to Do . . . When Kids Are Mean to Your Child, by Elin McCoy (Pleasantville, N.Y.: Reader's Digest, 1997). Helps kids get along and deal with unfair peer treatment, such as teasing and bullying.

Why Doesn't Anybody Like Me? A Guide to Raising Socially Confident Kids, by Hara Estroff Marano (New York: Morrow, 1998). Helpful hints on boosting social competence in kids. Includes strategies to help kids handle relationship problems, get along, take turns, and deal with bullying.

For Children Ages Three to Seven

Alexander Who Used to Be Rich Last Sunday, by Judith Viorst (New York: Atheneum, 1978). Alexander thinks it's unfair that his brothers have more money than he does, but he nevertheless chooses to spend his.

Cap It Off with a Smile: A Guide for Making and Keeping Friends, by Robin Inwald (Kew Gardens, N.Y.: Hilson Press, 1994). Simple ideas to help kids learn the first steps to fairness.

Fat, Fat Rose Marie, by Lisa Passen (New York: Henry Holt, 1991). A little girl must stand up to the class bully who keeps picking on her overweight friend and treating her most unfairly.

How to Lose All Your Friends, by Nancy Carlson (New York: Viking, 1994). The kinds of things to do if you don't want to have friends, such as bullying, not sharing, and being a poor sport.

It's Mine! by Leo Lionni (New York: Knopf, 1985). Three selfish, frisky frogs fight over everything until a big storm blows in and a toad helps the frogs find the value in sharing.

Me First, by Helen Lester (Boston: Houghton Mifflin, 1992). The story of a greedy pig who always has to be first at everything and how he finally learns the lesson about taking turns.

The Rainbow Fish, by Marcus Pfister (North-South Books, 1992). A wonderful, eye-dazzling tale of a beautiful but self-centered fish who discovers that sharing leads to friendship.

School Isn't Fair! by Patricia Baehr (New York: Four Winds Press, 1989). Little Edward describes all the unfair things that happen to him at school. Use it to talk about unfairness with kids.

For Children Ages Eight to Eleven

The Gnats of Knotty Pine, by Bill Peet (Boston: Houghton Mifflin, 1984). Members of the animal community work together for a common cause against injustice and take social action against the hunters.

The Kids Can Help Book, by Suzanne Logan (New York: Perigee Books, 1992). A wonderful compilation of ways kids can volunteer and make a difference in the world.

Roll of Thunder, Hear My Cry, by Mildred Taylor (New York: Dial, 1976). A black family in Mississippi during the Depression refuses to give in to the unfair treatment and social injustice exhibited by white neighbors. The film based on the book is also highly recommended.

Teammates, by Peter Golenbock (Orlando, Fla.: Harcourt Brace, 1990). Portrays the racial prejudice and unjust treatment experienced by a black player in major league baseball and the difficulty of getting along as a team.

The Well: David's Story, by Mildred Taylor (New York: Dial, 1995). In the early 1900s, David's rural Mississippi family shares its well water with black and white neighbors.

For Youth Ages Twelve and Older

Black Like Me, by John Howard Griffin (New York: Signet, 1996). A true story about a white man in the 1950s who darkens his skin so he can "become" a black man living in the Deep South. The racism and unfairness he encounters are just wrenching.

Farewell to Manzanar, by Jeanne Wakatsuki Houston and James D. Houston (New York: Bantam Books, 1973). The touching true story of a Japanese American family who were uprooted from their home and sent to live at the Manzanar internment camp because of their Japanese ancestry.

Manchild in the Promised Land, by Claude Brown (New York: Simon & Schuster, 1999). It is a thinly fictionalized account of Brown's childhood as a hardened, streetwise criminal trying to survive the toughest streets of Harlem and *making it.* It is affirmative, inspiring, and rich with values.

Nothing but the Truth, by Avi (New York: Orchard Books, 1991). A ninth grader's suspension for refusing to sing "The Star-Spangled Banner" during homeroom becomes a national news story. Fascinating discussion possibilities about citizenship, fairness, and justice.

The Outsiders, by S. E. Hinton (New York: Puffin, 1995). This remains a favorite of boys and does present great discussion possibilities. It addresses a vicious gang of kids whose idea of a good time is to beat up the greasers until one night things go too far. There is also a movie version.

To Kill a Mockingbird, by Harper Lee (New York: Warner Books, 1960). A deeply moving novel about prejudice and injustice as seen through the eyes of a little girl, the daughter of a lawyer who defends a black man against an unfair rape charge in a southern town in the 1930s.

The Witch of Blackbird Pond, by Elizabeth George Speare (New York: Dell, 1972). Sixteen-year-old Kit in a Puritan community balks at its narrow-mindedness. She later befriends a lonely old woman who is unjustly accused of being a witch, and eventually Kit is unjustly accused as well.

Videos for Viewing with Children

The Dog Who Stopped the War (HBO Video, 1984). This French-Canadian film is one of the best antiwar films for kids. The story centers on a group of children who decide to play "war games." The fun quickly dissipates as conflicts rise and relationships break apart. For older kids: subtitled.

Freedom Song (Warner, 2000). Set in 1961 in Mississippi, it's a wonderful vehicle for acquainting children with the civil rights movement and the unsung small-town citizens who risked their lives to stand up for justice and bring change at the grassroots level. For slightly older children.

Lone Star Kid (Public Media Video, 1992). Twelve-year-old Brian discovers that a victim of an auto crash dies because medical assistance was too far away. The boy decides to do something so the tragedy can never be repeated: he runs for mayor, gets himself elected, and makes sure a clinic is built. A gem—and a true story!

Pride of the Yankees (Key Video, 1942). One of the best baseball films ever made portrays Lou Gehrig and his teammate Babe Ruth and their long-standing feud that finally ended the day Gehrig retired.

The Rescuers (Walt Disney Home Video, 1997). Two mice work for the Rescue Aid Society and rescue children in trouble throughout the world.

The Sound of Music (CBS/Fox Video, 1965). A young woman becomes a governess to seven unruly kids. When Nazi Germany unites with Austria, she's forced to attempt a daring escape with her new family. A way to gently expose kids to injustice and affirm how people can make a difference.

Videos for Viewing with Teenagers

Amistad (Universal Studios Home Video, 1997). Africans in 1839 sold into slavery were transported to the United States on a Spanish ship and claimed as property by both the Spanish crew and their American captors. It's a stirring display of injustice. *Rated R for violence and nudity.*

The Hurricane (Universal, 1999). Wrongfully accused of murder, boxer Rubin "Hurricane" Carter channels his frustration by writing his own story from his cell. After reading the story, an alienated youth mounts a campaign to get him released from prison. Powerful, but for older kids.

Inherit the Wind (Fox, 1960). The story of the famous Scopes "Monkey Trial" in 1925 Tennessee. William Jennings Bryan argues that Darwin's theory of evolution should not be taught to high school students. Renowned trial lawyer Clarence Darrow argues that it should. Thought-provoking.

Judgment at Nuremberg (MGM Home Entertainment, 1961). One of the most fascinating explorations of moral choices ever filmed: the actual Nuremberg trials that tried high-level Nazi officials for their atrocious war crimes during World War II.

The Nasty Girl (Home Box Office, 1990). A true story of a young German girl who expected her community to have resisted the Nazis but finds that many had aided Hitler and that some are in prominent positions. Despite attempts to stop her, she spends ten years working to document the truth.

The Ox-Bow Incident (Fox/Lorber Home Video, 1943). Two drifters ride into a small town in 1885, and a rumor spreads that they killed a popular rancher. A vigilante group decides to take the law into its own hands and hang them, only to discover later that the drifters were innocent. Based on a true story.

Spartacus (MCA Home Video, 1989). A rebellious gladiator slave leads a revolt against imperial Rome. Discussions can touch on the brutal treatment of the slaves and on Spartacus's courage, justice, fortitude, and never-ending quest to follow his conscience.

To Kill a Mockingbird (Universal Studios Home Video, 1962). A faithful adaptation of the unforgettable novel of a childhood in a sleepy southern town and the crisis of injustice that rocked it. Virtues addressed include empathy, fairness, tolerance, respect, conscience, and self-control.

Websites for Kids

"Human Rights Web" [http://www.hrw.org/]. Extensive information about human rights and links to human rights organizations.

"Legal Pad Junior for Teens" [http://www.legalpadjr.com/teens.htm]. Online legal information, chats, and a club room for teens.

"Servenet" [http://www.servenet.org]. Here's a place young people can learn about the importance of helping others and find opportunities to do so.

"Who Cares: A Journal of Service and Action" [http://www.whocares.org]. An online journal that offers ways to solve society's problems through volunteering and activism.

"Youth Venture" [http://www.youthventur.org]. A site for twelve- to eighteen-year-olds to encourage them to mobilize and develop service organizations to change the world.

Notes

Introduction

p. 1. U.S. youth homicide and suicide rates: American Academy of Pediatrics, "New AAP Policy Addresses Violence and Children" [http://www.aap.org/advocacy/archives/janviol.htm], Jan. 5, 1999.

p. 2. Homicide rates of U.S. and Canadian adolescents: A. Blumstein, "Youth Violence, Guns, and the Illicit Drug Industry," Working Paper Series (Pittsburgh: H. John Heinz III School of Public Policy and Management, Carnegie Mellon University, 1994); R. A. Silverman and L. Kennedy, *Deadly Deeds: Murder in Canada* (Scarborough, Ontario: Nelson, 1993).

p. 2. Suffocation: A. Murr and K. Springer, "Death at a Very Early Age," *Newsweek*, Aug. 28, 2000, p. 32.

p. 2. Six-year-old with semiautomatic: K. Naughton and E. Thomas, "Did She Have to Die?" *Newsweek*, Mar. 13, 2000, pp. 24–33.

p. 2. Youth stealing, lying, and cheating: Result of a survey of more than twenty thousand middle and high school respondents compiled by the Josephson Institute of Ethics and the CHARACTER COUNTS! Coalition, "1998 Report Card on the Ethics of American Youth" [http://www.josephsoninstitute.org/98-Survey/violence/98survey.htm], Oct. 19, 1998.

p. 2. American Academy of Pediatrics, "Underage Drinking" [http://www.aap.org/advocacy/chm98und.htm], 2000.

p. 2. Marijuana use: National Institute on Drug Abuse, *Peer Pressure: It's OK to Say No.* DHHS Publication No. (AADM) 83-1271 (Rockville, Md.: National Institute on Drug Abuse, 1983), cited in C. Schaefer and T. F. Di Geronimo, *How to Talk to Teens About Really Important Things: Specific Questions and Answers and Useful Things to Say* (San Francisco: Jossey-Bass, 1999), p. 68.

p. 2. "Study: Many Teens Try Pot, but Fewer Use Drugs Often," *Desert Sun*, Sept. 1, 2000. Although illegal drug use continues to drop among adolescents, kids are still experimenting with marijuana in numbers not seen since the late 1970s.

p. 2. L. Tanner, "Study Suggests More U.S. Kids Have Problems with Behavior," *Desert Sun*, June 6, 2000, p. A5.

p. 2. Teen suicide and depression: J. Cloud, "What Can the Schools Do?" *Time*, May 3, 1999, pp. 38–40.

p. 2. Gun availability: Josephson Institute and CHARACTER COUNTS! Coalition, "1998 Report Card."

The 1st Essential Virtue: Empathy

p. 13. D. Goodman, "Boy Who Killed at Age 11 Will Leave Jail at Age 21," *Desert Sun*, Jan. 14, 2000, p. A2; "Abraham Sentenced to Juvenile Facility." [http://abcnews.go.com/sections/us/dailynews/abraham000113.html], Jan. 13, 2000.

p. 13. J. Cloud, "For They Know Not What They Do?" *Time*, Aug. 24, 1998, pp. 64–66.

p. 15. J. Gottman, *The Heart of Parenting* (New York: Simon & Schuster, 1997).

p. 15. Study results: Institute of Social Research, University of Michigan, cited in S. C. Reuben, *Children of Character* (Santa Monica, Calif.: Canter & Associates, 1997), p. 42.

p. 15. *USA Today* poll, "Children's Time Spent with Family," cited in W. Pollack, *Real Boys* (New York: Henry Holt, 1998), p. 29.

p. 15. Longitudinal study on children's empathy: R. Koestner, C. Franz, and J. Weinberger, "The Family Origins of Empathic Concern: A 26-Year Longitudinal Study," *Journal of Personality and Social Psychology*, 1990, *58*, 709–717.

p. 15. Study on boys' empathy levels: S. Bernadette-Shapiro, D. Ehrensaft, and J. L. Shapiro, "Father Participation in Childcare and the Development of Empathy in Sons: An Empirical Study," *Family Therapy*, 1996, *23*(2), 77–93, cited in K. Pruett, *Fatherneed: Why Father Care Is as Essential as Mother Care for Your Child* (New York: Free Press, 2000), p. 48.

p. 16. Children's daily time with fathers: H. B. Biller, "The Father Factor and the Two-Parent Advantage: Reducing the Paternal Deficit," cited in M. Medved and D. Medved, *Saving Childhood* (New York: HarperPerennial, 1998), p. 189.

p. 16. Black children living in single-parent families: cited in Pollack, *Real Boys*, p. 124.

p. 16. L. K. Friedrich and A. H. Stein, "Aggression and Prosocial Television Programs and the Natural Behavior of Preschool Children," *Monographs of the Society for Research in Child Development*, 1973, *38*, 1–64; W. A. Collins and S. K. Getz, "Children's Social Responses Following Modeled Reactions to Provocation: Prosocial Effects of a Television Drama," *Journal of Personality*, 1976, *44*, 488–500. Prosocial television programs: M. Levine, *See No Evil* (San Francisco: Jossey-Bass, 1998), p. 39.

p. 16. J. H. Bryan, "Model Affect and Children's Imitative Behavior," *Child Development*, 1971, *42*, 2061–2065; J. L. Singer and D. G. Singer, *Executive Summary on Barney and Friends* (New Haven, Conn.: Family Television Research and Consultation Center, Yale University, 1995).

p. 16. American Academy of Pediatrics, "Joint Statement on the Impact of Entertainment Violence on Children," Congressional Public Health Summit [http://www.aap.org/advocacy/releases/jstmtevc.htm], July 26, 2000.

p. 17. L. R. Brody and J. A. Hall, "Gender and Emotion," in M. Lewis and J. Haviland, (eds.), *Handbook of Emotions* (New York: Guilford Press, 1993).

p. 17. Pollack, *Real Boys,* pp. 346–347.

p. 17. B. Perry, "Incubated in Terror: Neurodevelopmental Factors in the Cycle of Violence," in J. D. Osofsky (ed.), *Children in a Violent Society* (New York: Guilford Press, 1997), pp. 124–149.

p. 17. Perry's work: cited in S. Begley, "Why the Young Kill," *Newsweek,* May 3, 1999.

p. 18. M. Barnett, "K-State Professor Says Children Need to Learn Empathy," Kansas State University [http://www.mediarelations.ksu.edu/WEB/News/NewsReleases/empathy.html], Aug. 14, 1997.

p. 18. K. Srinivasan, "Child Abuse May Be Declining," Associated Press/ABC News Internet Ventures [http://abcnews.go.com/sections/living/DailyNews/childabuse990401.html], 1999.

p. 18. Child abuse: Children's Defense Fund, "Key Facts About Children and Families in Crisis," in *The State of America's Children, 1996–1997* (New York: Children's Defense Fund, 2000).

p. 18. National Exchange Club Foundation, "Frequently Asked Questions" [http://www.preventchildabuse.com/abuse.htm], Dec. 7, 2000.

p. 23. D. Kindlon and M. Thompson, *Raising Cain: Protecting the Emotional Life of Boys* (New York: Ballantine, 1999), p. 17.

p. 24. Gottman, *The Heart of Parenting.*

p. 29. Six basic emotions: P. Ekman, "Facial Expressions of Emotion," *American Psychologist,* 1993, *48,* 384–392.

p. 32. M. Schulman and E. Mekler, *Bringing Up a Moral Child* (Reading, Mass.: Addison-Wesley, 1985), p. 55.

p. 32. S. Nowicki and M. P. Duke, *Helping the Child Who Doesn't Fit In* (Atlanta: Peachtree, 1992).

p. 33. S. A. Denham, *Emotional Development in Young Children* (New York: Guilford Press, 1998, pp. 34–39.

p. 35. "Boy of Action," *People,* June 25, 1995, p. 121.

p. 36. E. Stotland, E. E. Mathews Jr., S. E. Sherman, R. O. Hansson, and B. Z. Richardson, *Empathy, Fantasy, and Helping* (Thousand Oaks, Calif.: Sage, 1978); described in Schulman and Mekler, *Bringing Up a Moral Child,* p. 50.

p. 37. M. Hoffman, "Development of Prosocial Motivation: Empathy and Guilt," in N. Eisenberg (ed.), *The Development of Prosocial Behavior* (Orlando, Fla.: Academic Press, 1983).

The 2nd Essential Virtue: Conscience

p. 46. B. T. Kelley, D. Huizinga, T. P. Thornberry, and R. Loeber, *Epidemiology of Serious Violence* (Washington, D.C.: Office of Juvenile Justice and Delinquency Prevention, U.S. Department of Justice, 1997).

p. 46. Youth homicide and suicide rates: American Academy of Pediatrics, "New AAP Policy."

p. 46. J. Garbarino, *Lost Boys* (New York: Free Press, 1999), p. 8.

p. 47. Bullying: National School Safety Center, cited in S. Fried and P. Fried, *Bullies and Victims: Helping Your Child Through the Schoolyard Battlefield* (New York: Evans, 1996), p. xii.

p. 47. Teen dating violence: Centers for Disease Control and Prevention, cited in "Teen-Dating Violence Targeted in Campaigns Across the Nation," *Desert Sun,* Feb. 28, 2000.

p. 47. J. Kellerman, *Savage Spawn: Reflections on Violent Children* (New York: Ballantine, 1999), p. 18.

p. 47. B. M. Stilwell, M. Galvin, and S. Kopta, "Conceptualization of Conscience in Normal Children and Adolescents," *Journal of American Academy of Child and Adolescent Psychiatry,* 1991, *30,* 16–21.

p. 47. School intimidation: National Education Association, cited in Fried and Fried, *Bullies and Victims,* p. xii.

p. 48. Bullies: American Psychological Association, cited in S. Peterson, "Bullies Shove Their Way into the Nation's Schools," *USA Today,* Sept. 7, 1999, p. D1.

p. 48. Shoplifting: National Organization to Prevent Shoplifting, cited in T. Lickona, *Educating for Character* (New York: Bantam Books, 1991), p. 14.

p. 48. Shoplifting survey: Josephson Institute and CHARACTER COUNTS! Coalition, "1998 Report Card."

p. 48. FBI statistics: cited in H. Snyder, "Juvenile Arrest Rates for All Crimes, 1981–1997."

p. 49. A. Goldstein, "Paging All Parents," *Time,* July 3, 2000, p. 47.

p. 49. U. Bronfenbrenner, P. McClelland, E. Wethington, P. Moen, and S. Ceci, *The State of Americans: This Generation and the Next* (New York: Free Press, 1996).

p. 49. Josephson Institute of Ethics, *The Ethics of America's Youth: A Warning and a Call to Action* (Marina del Rey, Calif.: Josephson Institute of Ethics, 1990), cited in Lickona, *Educating for Character,* p. 14.

p. 49. C. Kleiner and M. Lord, "The Cheating Game," *U.S. News & World Report,* Nov. 22, 1999, pp. 55–61.

p. 49. Student character: Josephson Institute and CHARACTER COUNTS! Coalition, "1998 Report Card."

p. 50. D. Q. Haney, "Report: U.S. Teen-Agers Changing Sex Practices," *Desert Sun,* July 11, 2000, p. A3.

p. 50. Alan Guttmacher Institute, *Teenage Reproductive Health in the United States, Facts in Brief* (New York: Alan Guttmacher Institute, 1994).

p. 50. Teen pregnancy: Alan Guttmacher Institute, *Sex and America's Teenagers* (New York: Alan Guttmacher Institute, 1994), pp. 19–20.

p. 51. Students being drunk in school: Josephson Institute and CHARACTER COUNTS! Coalition, "1998 Report Card."

p. 51. American Academy of Pediatrics, "Underage Drinking" [http;//www.aap.org/advocacy/chm98und.htm], 2000.

p. 51. National Clearinghouse for Alcohol and Drug Information, *Just the Facts,* Publication No. RP0884 (Rockville, Md.: National Clearinghouse for Alcohol and Drug Information, n.d.).

p. 51. Marijuana use: National Institute on Drug Abuse, *Peer Pressure.*

p. 51. M. Villalva, "Study: Teen Drug Use Higher in Rural Areas Than in Cities," *USA Today,* Jan. 26, 2000, p. A1.

p. 52. Lax enforcement of moral standards: *Newsweek* poll, cited in Medved and Medved, *Saving Childhood,* p. 172.

p. 52. P. Applebome, "Children Score Low in Adults' Esteem, a Study Finds," *New York Times,* June 26, 1997, p. A12, cited in Medved and Medved, *Saving Childhood,* p. 171. The study, titled "Kids These Days: What Americans Really Think About the Next Generation," was conducted by the nonpartisan group Public Agenda for the Advertising Council and Ronald McDonald House charities in June 1997.

p. 52. Peer pressure: cited in A. Goldstein, "Paging All Parents."

p. 52. American Academy of Pediatrics, "Alcohol: Your Child and Drugs" [http://www.aap.org/family/alcohol.htm], 2000.

p. 52. R. Coles, *The Moral Intelligence of Children* (New York: Random House, 1997), p. 58.

p. 57. M. Berkowitz and J. H. Grych, "Fostering Goodness: Teaching Parents to Facilitate Children's Moral Development," *Journal of Moral Education,* 1998, *27,* 371–391.

p. 58. T. Lickona, "Raising Children with Character: What Parents and Elementary Schools Can Do," lecture given at Grosse Pointe Farms, Mich., Apr. 22, 1997.

p. 60. "A Fearless Fifth Grader," *Newsweek,* July 4, 1988, p. 48.

p. 71. A. L. Scoresby, *Bringing Up Moral Children in an Immoral World* (Salt Lake City, Utah: Deseret, 1998), p. 54.

p. 75. T. Lickona, *Raising Good Children* (New York: Bantam Books, 1983), p. 12.

p. 75. N. Eisenberg, *The Caring Child* (Cambridge, Mass.: Harvard University Press, 1992), p. 96.

p. 76. L. Kohlberg, "Stages of Moral Development as a Basis for Moral Education," in C. Beck and E. Sullivan (eds.), *Moral Education* (Toronto: University of Toronto Press, 1971).

p. 77. W. Damon, *The Social World of the Child* (San Francisco: Jossey-Bass, 1997).

p. 77. Lickona, *Raising Good Children,* pp. 127–128.

The 3rd Essential Virtue: Self-Control

p. 81. G. Czudner, *Small Criminals Among Us* (Far Hills, N.J.: New Horizon Press, 1999), p. viii.

p. 81. K. Meadows, "Colleagues, Family Honor Teacher Allegedly Gunned Down by Student," *Desert Sun,* May 31, 2000, A4.

p. 82. K. Meadows, "Murderous Intentions" [http://abcnews.go.com/sections/us/DailyNews/fla_shooting000531.html], May 31, 2000.

p. 83. Mothers in the labor force: U.S. Bureau of Labor Statistics, cited in Children's Defense Fund, "Child Care and Early Education Basics" [http://www.childrensdefense.org/childcare/cc_facts.html], Apr. 2000.

p. 83. Single fathers: U.S. Census Bureau, cited in Pruett, *Fatherneed,* p. 2.

p. 83. Average time spent on the job: P. R. Breggin, *Reclaiming Our Children* (Cambridge, Mass.: Perseus Books, 1999), p. 48.

p. 84. E. Galinsky, *Ask the Children* (New York: Morrow, 1999); E. Galinsky, "Do Working Parents Make the Grade?" *Newsweek,* Aug. 30, 1999, pp. 52–56.

p. 84. J. Zimmerman, "Balancing Work and Children Means Keeping Hearts Linked," *Desert Sun,* Mar. 21, 1999, p. E4.

p. 84. Children in day care: Children's Defense Fund, "Child Care and Early Education Basics."

p. 84. Parents' time with children: P. Welsh, "The New Silent Generation: What Our Day Care Kids Don't Learn," *Washington Post,* Nov. 8, 1992, p. CO1.

p. 84. Cloud, "What Can the Schools Do?"

p. 84. H. Snyder and M. Sickmund, *Juvenile Offenders and Victims: 1999 National Report* (Washington, D.C.: Office of Juvenile Justice and Delinquency Programs, U.S. Department of Justice, 1999).

p. 85. D. Niehoff, *The Biology of Violence: How Understanding the Brain, Behavior, and Environment Can Break the Vicious Circle of Aggression* (New York: Free Press, 1999).

p. 85. Perry, "Incubated in Terror."

p. 85. Perry's work: cited in R. Karr-Morse and M. S. Wiley, *Ghosts from the Nursery: Tracing the Roots of Violence* (New York: Atlantic Monthly Press, 1997), pp. 159–169, 198–199.

p. 85. N. Regush, "The Young and the Reckless: What Goes On in the Minds of Kids Who Kill?" [http://abcnews.go.com/sections/us/DailyNews/tn980709_killers.html], July 9, 1998.

p. 85. Children's Defense Fund, "Key Facts."

p. 86. Ritalin consumption: International Narcotics Control Board, cited in Breggin, *Reclaiming Our Children*, p. 144.

p. 86. Ritalin use: A. Kipnis, *Angry Young Men: How Parents, Teachers, and Counselors Can Help "Bad Boys" Become Good Men* (San Francisco: Jossey-Bass, 1999), p. 63.

p. 86. Use of stimulants: International Narcotics Control Board, cited in Breggin, *Reclaiming Our Children*, p. 144.

p. 86. Medication for toddlers: Study published in the *Journal of American Medical Association*, cited in C. Kalb, "Drugged-Out Toddlers," *Newsweek*, Mar. 6, 2000, p. 53.

p. 86. American Medical Association, *The Physician's Guide to Media Violence* (Chicago: American Medical Association, 1997).

p. 86. American Academy of Pediatrics, "Media Violence," *Pediatrics*, 1995, *95*, 949–951.

p. 87. D. Shrifrin, "Three-Year Study Documents Nature of Television Violence," *AAP News* [http://www.aap.org/advocacy/shifrin898.htm], Aug. 1998.

p. 87. Viewing of violent acts on television: R. Taffel, *Nurturing Good Children Now* (New York: Golden Books, 1999), p. 18.

p. 87. Shrifrin, "Three-Year Study."

p. 87. U.S. Surgeon General's Scientific Advisory Committee on Television and Social Behavior, *Television and Growing Up: The Impact of Televised Violence: Report to the Surgeon General, U.S. Public Health* Service (Washington, D.C.: U.S. Government Printing Office, 1972); U.S. Department of Health and Human Services; Public Health Service; Alcohol, Drug Abuse, and Mental Health Administration; and National Institute of Mental Health, *Television and Behavior: Ten Years of Scientific Progress and Implications for the Eighties*, U.S. Department of Health and Human Services Publication No. ADM 82-1195, Vol. 1 (Washington, D.C.: U.S. Government Printing Office, 1982).

p. 87. American Academy of Pediatrics, "Joint Statement."

p. 87. American Psychological Association, "Summary Report of the American Psychological Association Commission on Violence and Youth," in *Violence and Youth: Psychology's Response*, Vol. 1 (Washington, D.C.: American Psychological Association, 1993), cited in Garbarino, *Lost Boys*, p. 198.

p. 87. Center for Media Education, cited in Taffel, *Nurturing Good Children Now*, pp. 17–18.

p. 87. Video games: J. Quittner, "Are Video Games Really So Bad?" *Time*, May 10, 1999.

p. 87. Preference for violent games: J. Leo, "When Life Imitates Video," *U.S. News Online* [http://www.usnews.com/usnews/issue/990503/3john.htm], May 3, 1999.

p. 88. K. Thomas, "Study Ties Aggression to Violence in Games," *USA Today*, May 10, 2000, p. D3.

p. 88. D. Grossman and P. Siddle, "Combat," in L. Kurtz (ed.), *The Encyclopedia of Violence, Peace, and Conflict* (Orlando, Fla.: Academic Press, 1999).

p. 88. American Academy of Pediatrics, "Joint Statement."

p. 89. D. Goleman, *Emotional Intelligence* (New York: Bantam Books, 1995).

p. 89. D. Goleman, "Foreword," in M. J. Elias, S. E. Tobias, and B. S. Friedlander, *Emotionally Intelligent Parenting* (New York: Harmony Books, 1999), p. xv.

p. 89. Tanner, "Study Suggests."

p. 95. Coles, *The Moral Intelligence of Children.*

p. 96. D. Reiss, J. Neiderhiser, E. M. Hetherington, and R. Plomin, *The Relationship Code* (Cambridge, Mass.: Harvard University Press, 2000); Reiss quote cited in S. Begley, "The Nature of Nurturing," *Newsweek,* Mar. 27, 2000, p. 64.

p. 99. "A Class of One," interview with Ruby Bridges and Charles Burks [http://www.pbs.org/newshour/bb/race_relations/jan-june97/bridges_2–18.html], Feb. 18, 1997.

p. 99. R. Coles, *The Story of Ruby Bridges* (New York: Scholastic, 1995), p. 12.

p. 105. M. Elias, "Ads Targeting Kids," *Desert Sun,* Mar. 21, 2000, p. D5.

p. 106. J. E. Grusec, "Socializing Concern for Others in the Home," *Developmental Psychology,* 1991, *27,* 338–342.

p. 106. A. Kohn, *Punished by Rewards* (Boston: Houghton Mifflin, 1999), pp. 106–107.

p. 108. Youth homicide and suicide rates: American Academy of Pediatrics, "New AAP Policy."

p. 108. "Overall U.S. Murder Rate down, but Youth Gun Killings up," [http://www.cnn.com/US/9901/02/murder.rate/], Jan. 2, 1999.

p. 108. Youth homicide in rural America: G. Fields and P. Overberg, "Juvenile Homicide Arrest Rate on Rise in Rural USA," *USA Today,* Mar. 26, 1998, p. A11, cited in Garbarino, *Lost Boys,* p. 8.

p. 108. Youth violence rates: Kelley and others, *Epidemiology of Serious Violence.*

p. 108. Homicide rates of U.S. and Canadian adolescents: Blumstein, "Youth Violence"; Silverman and Kennedy, *Deadly Deeds.*

p. 108. U.S. adolescent male homicide rate: World Health Organization, *World Health Statistics Annual, 1993: Causes of Death by Sex and Age* (Geneva: World Health Organization, 1995), tab. D-1.

p. 108. Carnegie Corporation study: cited in Kipnis, *Angry Young Men,* p. 16.

p. 108. Students hitting out of anger: Josephson Institute and CHARACTER COUNTS! Coalition, "1998 Report Card."

p. 108. Guns in school: Josephson Institute and CHARACTER COUNTS! Coalition, "1998 Report Card."

p. 108. Tanner, "Study Suggests."

p. 109. Y. Shoda, W. Mischel, and P. K. Peake, "Predicting Adolescent Cognitive and Self-Regulatory Competencies from Preschool Delay of Gratification," *Developmental Psychology,* 1999, *26,* 978–986.

p. 111. J. Dacey and L. Fiore, *Your Anxious Child: How Parents and Teachers Can Relieve Anxiety in Children* (San Francisco: Jossey-Bass, 2000), p. 51.

p. 112. Schulman and Mekler, *Bringing Up a Moral Child,* p. 20.

p. 113. M. L. Bloomquist, *Skills Training for Children with Behavior Disorders* (New York: Guilford Press, 1996).

The 4th Essential Virtue: Respect

p. 121. Survey: A. Siegler, "What a Nice Kid," *Child Magazine,* 1997, cited in Taffel, *Nurturing Good Children Now,* p. 58.

p. 121. Lickona, *Educating for Character,* p. 15.

p. 121. Study: Applebome, "Children Score Low."

p. 122. R. Tanner, "States Debate Proposals for Courtesy in Schools," *Desert Sun,* May 29, 2000, p. A5.

p. 122. D. L. Rosenhan, "The Natural Socialization of Altruistic Autonomy," in. J. Macaulay and L. Berkowitz, (eds.), *Altruism and Helping Behavior* (Orlando, Fla.: Academic Press, 1970), pp. 262–263.

p. 122. Eighteen to one statistic: National Parent-Teacher Organization, cited in S. Marston, *The Magic of Encouragement* (New York: Morrow, 1990), p. 100.

p. 122. Parental verbal abuse: R. Sobel, "Wounding with Words," *U.S. News & World Report*, Aug. 28, 2000, p. 53; M. Elias, "Teens Take Brunt of Parents' Verbal Abuse," *USA Today*, Aug. 16, 2000, p. D7.

p. 123. Poll of 1,005 adults conducted by KRC Research & Consulting with assistance from U.S. News pollsters, cited in J. Marks, "The American Uncivil Wars," *U.S. News Online* [http://www.usnews.com/usnews/issue/civil.htm], Apr. 22, 1996.

p. 123. "Who Wins Aggressive-Driving Derby?" *USA Today*, July 28–30, 2000, p. A1.

p. 124. M. Meyer, "Flying Wildly out of Control," *Newsweek*, Nov. 29, 1999, p. 42.

p. 124. C. Valles, "Airline Staffs Cry Out for Friendlier Skies," *Desert Sun*, July 7, 2000, p. A12.

p. 124. S. Smith, "Is the Choice Sportsmanship or Death?" *Knight Ridder/Tribune Information Services* [http://www.youthdevelopment.org], July 23, 2000.

p. 125. Rosenhan, "Natural Socialization of Altruistic Autonomy"; S. P. Oliner and P. M. Oliner, *The Altruistic Personality: Rescuers of Jews in Nazi Europe* (New York: Free Press, 1988), pp. 134–135.

p. 126. M. Starr, "Rocker's Wild Pitch," *Newsweek*, June 19, 2000, p. 58.

p. 126. A. Quindlen, "Ignore Them off the Field," *Newsweek*, Jan. 13, 2000, p. 68.

p. 126. "That Just Ain't Cricket," *Newsweek*, July 10, 2000, p. 54.

p. 127. J. Leland, "Why America's Hooked on Wrestling," *Newsweek*, Feb. 7, 2000, pp. 47–52.

p. 127. Screamin' Norman, *World Wide Wrestling*, TNT, Nov. 19, 1999.

p. 127. Lickona, *Educating for Character*, p. 16.

p. 127. N. Hellmich, "Today's Schools Cursed by an Increase in Swearing," *USA Today*, May 20, 1997, p. D4.

p. 128. Report on vulgarity: *ABC Nightly News*, June 2, 2000.

p. 128. K. Jurgensen, "Vulgar Content on TV Rises, Despite Industry Vows, V-Chip," *USA Today*, Apr. 12, 2000, p. A28.

p. 128. J. Evans, "Foul Language and Sex Content, 1996, All Films," *Preview Family Movie and TV Review*, Apr. 25, 1997.

p. 128. D. Bauden, "Eminem Stands Up," *Desert Sun*, Sept. 8, 2000, p. D1.

p. 134. Marston, *The Magic of Encouragement*, p. 84.

p. 135. Story of Kanésha Sonée Johnson adapted from "The Giraffe Project: [http//www.giraffe.org/giraffe/] and J. Cohn, *Raising Compassionate, Courageous Children in a Violent World* (Atlanta: Longstreet Press, 1996), pp. 183–185.

p. 147. Signing: L. Lantieri and J. Patti, *Waging Peace in Our Schools* (Boston: Beacon Press, 1996), p. 34.

p. 149. "I" messages: T. Gordon, *P.E.T.: Parent Effectiveness Training* (New York: New American Library, 1975).

p. 150. L. Baldridge, *More Than Manners!* (New York: Rawson Associates, 1997).

The 5th Essential Virtue: Kindness

p. 159. Eisenberg, *The Caring Child*, p. 88.

p. 159. W. Mitchell and C. P. Conn, *The Power of Positive Parenting* (New York: Wynwood Press, 1989), p. 159.

p. 159. Spending less time with kids: J. Cloud, "Just a Routine School Shooting," *Time*, May 31, 1999, cited in Breggin, *Reclaiming Our Children*, p. 64.

p. 160. Parents' critical comments: National Parent-Teacher Organization, cited in Marston, *The Magic of Encouragement*, p. 100.

p. 160. Violent acts on television: G. Gerbner, M. Morgan, and N. Signorielli, *Television Violence Profile No. 16: The Turning Point* (Philadelphia: Cultural Environment Movement, 1994), cited by Levine, *See No Evil*, p. 39.

p. 160. Bullying rate: K. Peterson, "Bullies Shove Their Way into the Nation's Schools," *USA Today*, Sept. 7, 1999.

p. 160. Adolescent bullying: M. Elias, "Bullying Fuels Teen's Hatred, Study Finds," *USA Today*, Aug. 24, 1999, p. A1.

p. 161. National School Safety Center, cited in A. Mulrine, "Once Bullied, Now Bullies—with Guns," *U.S. News & World Report*, May 3, 1999, p. 24.

p. 161. Negative peer influence: J. R. Harris, *The Nurture Assumption* (New York: Free Press, 1998).

p. 161. Effect of repeated viewing of violence: R. S. Drabman and M. H. Thomas, "Does Media Violence Increase Children's Toleration of Real-Life Aggression?" *Developmental Psychology*, 1974, *10*, 418–421.

p. 161. R. E. Goranson, "Media Violence and Aggressive Behavior: A Review of Experimental Research," in L. Berkowitz (ed.), *Advances in Experimental Social Psychology*, Vol. 5 (Orlando, Fla.: Academic Press, 1970), cited in Levine, *See No Evil*, p. 43.

p. 162. J. L. Singer, D. G. Singer, and W. S. Rapacznyski, "Family Patterns and Television Viewing as Predictors of Children's Beliefs and Aggression," *Journal of Communication*, 1984, *34*(2), 73–89.

p. 165. Development of kindness: Hoffman, "Development of Prosocial Motivation."

p. 166. Instilling kindness: P. Mussen and N. Eisenberg, *Roots of Caring, Sharing, and Helping* (New York: Freeman, 1983).

p. 166. Hoffman, "Development of Prosocial Motivation."

p. 167. "Packing Promise," *People*, Oct. 19, 1999, p. 72.

p. 167. P. Wingert, "Children's Crusade," *Newsweek*, Oct. 4, 1999, p. 76.

p. 168. Eisenberg, *The Caring Child*.

p. 169. E. Midlarksy and J. H. Bryan, "Affect Expressions and Children's Imitative Altruism," *Journal of Experimental Research in Personality*, 1972, *6*, 195–203.

p. 171. S. Simon, *I Am Lovable and Capable* (Allen, Tex.: Argus Communications, 1973).

p. 172. Simon, *I Am Lovable and Capable*.

p. 173. Parental critical comments: B. Deporter, *Quantum Learning* (New York: Dell, 1992), p. 24.

p. 173. Eighteen to one statistic: National Parent-Teacher Organization, cited in S. Marston, *The Magic of Encouragement* (New York: Morrow, 1990), p. 100.

p. 174. Eisenberg, *The Caring Child*.

p. 175. J. Windell, *Six Steps to an Emotionally Intelligent Teenager* (New York: Wiley, 1999), p. 102.

p. 176. M. Hoffman, "Parent Discipline and the Child's Consideration for Others," *Child Development*, 1963, *34*, 573–588.

p. 179. C. Moorman and D. Dishon, *Our Classroom: We Can Learn Together* (Portage, Mich.: Personal Power Press, 1983), p. 190.

p. 180. National Threat Assessment Center of the Secret Service, cited in T. Henry, "Secret Service: School Shooters Defy 'Profiling,'" *USA Today*, Apr. 7, 2000, p. A1.

p. 180. National Association of School Psychologists, cited in P. Rohland, "Bothered by Bullies?" Central Penn. Parent; family.com [http://family.go.com/Features/family_1998_01/penn/penn18bully.html], 1998.

p. 180. Fear of using school bathrooms: Mulrine, "Once Bullied."

p. 180. School bullies and victims: C. Goodnow, "Bullying Is a Complex, Dangerous Game in Which Everyone's a Player," *Seattle Post-Intelligencer* [http://www.seattle-pi.com/lifestyle/bull1at.shtml], Sept. 1, 1999.

p. 180. National Education Association, cited in Fried and Fried, *Bullies and Victims*, p. xii.

p. 182. F. Frankel, *Good Friends Are Hard to Find* (Los Angeles: Perspective Publishing, 1996), pp. 159–167.

p. 185. E. Staub, *The Development of Prosocial Behavior in Children* (Morristown, N.J.: General Learning Press, 1975).

p. 186. Oliner and Oliner, *The Altruistic Personality*, pp. 164–168.

p. 188. S. Silverstein, *The Giving Tree* (New York: HarperCollins, 1964).

p. 189. Oliner and Oliner, *The Altruistic Personality*, pp. 164–168.

The 6th Essential Virtue: Tolerance

p. 191. Definition of tolerance: T. Lickona, personal communication, Oct. 4, 2000.

p. 191. K. Abel, "Parent Alert: Hate Crimes and Our Kids" [http:familyeducation.com], Mar. 30, 2000.

p. 191. K. Klein, "Student Accused of Posting Threats on Web Sentenced," *Desert Sun*, Apr. 18, 2000, p. A1.

p. 192. "Ramblings of Hatred Found in Diary of Teen Accused of Planning Attack," *Desert Sun*, Mar. 4, 2000, p. A10.

p. 192. Perpetrators of hate crimes: L. Duvall, *Respecting Our Differences: A Guide to Getting Along in a Changing World* (Minneapolis: Free Spirit Press, 1994), p. 154.

p. 193. Two aspects of tolerance: T. Lickona, personal communication, Oct. 23, 2000.

p. 194. C. Figley, cited in J. Daw, "Kids Killing Kids," *Family Therapy News*, Aug.-Sept. 1998 [http://www.aamft.org/resources/kidskillingkids.htm], accessed Apr. 26, 1999.

p. 194. J. Comer, cited in Elias, Tobias, and Friedlander, *Emotionally Intelligent Parenting*, p. 2.

p. 195. W. Damon, cited in W. Herbert and J. Marks, "From Way Cool to Out of Control," *U.S. News & World Report*, May 3, 1999, p. 21.

p. 195. T. J. Leydon, cited in K. J. Shay, "Hate Speech," *OneWorld News Service* [http://www.one.world.org/news/reports98/thomas_leyden.html], June 27, 1998.

p. 195. T. J. Leydon, cited in Shay.

p. 195. J. Willwerth, "Confessions of a Skinhead," *Time*, Aug. 19, 1996.

p. 195. Poll of 409 American teenagers thirteen to seventeen years old conducted for *Time*/CNN on Apr. 27–29, 1999, by Yankelovich Partners, Inc., and published in D. Okrent, "Raising Kids Online: What Can Parents Do?" *Time*, May 10, 1999, pp. 38–43.

p. 195. Racist video games: C. Taylor, "Digital Dungeons," *Time*, May 3, 1999, pp. 48–49.

p. 196. D. E. Levin, *Remote Control Childhood? Combating the Hazards of Media Culture* (Washington, D.C.: National Association for the Education of Young Children, 1998), p. 9.

p. 196. Minorities on TV: R. Eisler, *Tomorrow's Children* (Boulder, Colo.: Westview Press, 2000), p. 207.

p. 197. Levine, *See No Evil*, p. 16.

p. 197. Stockton school shooting: D. Morgin and C. Ingram, "Gunman Attended School He Turned into a War Zone," *Los Angeles Times*, Jan. 18, 1998, p. A1.

p. 202. P. Aftab, *The Parent's Guide to Protecting Your Child in Cyberspace* (New York: McGraw-Hall, 2000), p. 66.

p. 206. C. W. Ford, *We Can All Get Along: Fifty Steps You Can Take to Help End Racism* (New York: Dell, 1994), p. 78.

p. 209. Story of S. Reed Smith adapted from M. T. Brill, *Extraordinary Young People* (New York: Children's Press, 1996), pp. 152–155.

p. 212. G. Allport, *The Nature of Prejudice* (Reading, Mass.: Addison-Wesley, 1979; originally published 1954).

p. 212. G. Allport, cited in S. Bullard, *Teaching Tolerance* (New York: Doubleday, 1996), p. 44.

p. 212. B. Mathias and M. A. French, *Forty Ways to Raise a Nonracist Child* (New York: HarperPerennial, 1996), p. 47.

p. 213. Mathias and French, *Forty Ways to Raise a Nonracist Child*, p. 19.

p. 214. J. Arnow, *Teaching Peace* (New York: Perigee, 1995), p. 56.

p. 215. M. A. Wright, *I'm Chocolate, You're Vanilla: Raising Healthy Black and Biracial Children in a Race-Conscious World* (San Francisco: Jossey-Bass, 1998), p. 6

p. 216. B. D. Tatum, *"Why Are All the Black Kids Sitting Together in the Cafeteria?" and Other Conversations About Race* (New York: Basic Books, 1998), pp. 3–4.

p. 218. J. Elliott discrimination lesson: W. Peters, *A Class Divided: Then and Now* (New Haven, Conn.: Yale University Press, 1971).

p. 220. Stages of race awareness: Wright, *I'm Chocolate, You're Vanilla*, pp. 266–267.

p. 223. Bullard, *Teaching Tolerance*, pp. 180–181.

p. 223. Ford, *We Can All Get Along*, p. 79.

The 7th Essential Virtue: Fairness

p. 229. Web posting: Academic Advising, "Why Don't I Get What I Desire Most?" [*http://dogpile.askme.com/op/View*], June 15, 2000.

p. 229. D. Howlett, "Teen May Face Trial in Sports Injury," *USA Today*, May 5, 2000, p. A3.

p. 231. J. Bowlby, "Separation Anxiety: Review of the Literature," *Attachment and Loss*, Vol. 2: *Separation: Anxiety and Anger* (New York: Basic Books, 1973), pp. 375–398.

p. 231. Child abuse: S. Bloom and M. Reichert, *Bearing Witness: Violence and Collective Responsibility* (New York: Haworth Press, 1998), cited in Breggin, *Reclaiming Our Children*, p. 51; Children's Defense Fund, "Key Facts."

p. 232. B. Kantrowitz and D. McGinn, "When Teachers Are Cheaters," *Newsweek*, June 19, 2000, pp. 48–49.

p. 232. Questioning teacher ethics: E. Thomas and P. Wingert, "Bitter Lessons," *Newsweek*, June 19, 2000, pp. 50–52.

p. 232. Parental social justice and children's morality: D. Rosenhan, "Learning Theory and Prosocial Behavior," *Journal of Social Issues*, 1972, *28*, 151–164, cited in N. Eisenberg and P. Mussen, *The Roots of Prosocial Behavior in Children*, 2nd ed. (New York: Cambridge University Press, 1995), p. 76.

p. 233. T. Griesinger and G. Westerfield, "Schools' Obsession with Performance Measures Spurs Cheating," *Journal of Educational Psychology,* 1998, *90*(1), 84–93.

p. 233. P. Wingert, "Plight of the Preschoolers," *Newsweek,* May 15, 2000, p. 76.

p. 234. TV viewing by children: Medved and Medved, *Saving Childhood,* p. 19.

p. 234. Game sales: K. T. Greenfield, "Mattel: Some (Re)assembly Required," *Time,* Oct. 25, 1999, pp. 57–58.

p. 234. University of Michigan study: F. Donlan, "Too Busy to Play," *Desert Sun,* Aug. 14, 2000, p. D1.

p. 244. Learning through modeling: Eisenberg and Mussen, *Roots of Prosocial Behavior,* pp. 68–72.

p. 246. R. Dreikurs, *Children: The Challenge* (New York: Hawthorn Books, 1964).

p. 250. Stages of fairness and justice: W. Damon, *The Social World of the Child,* pp. 282–330.

p. 250. Stages of fairness: adapted from Lickona, *Raising Good Children.*

p. 251. T. B. Brazelton, cited in "Doctor Urges Parents to Teach Kids to Share," *Desert Sun,* June 7, 2000.

p. 251. Frankel, *Good Friends Are Hard to Find,* pp. 104–106.

p. 252. W. Damon, *The Moral Child* (New York: Free Press, 1988), p. 36.

p. 256. Rules: adapted from Frankel, *Good Friends Are Hard to Find,* pp. 59–68.

p. 259. "Trevor's Endeavors" [http://www.philanthroserve.org/Trevor/TrevorHistory.htm], July 11, 2000.

p. 264. H. Gardner, *Frames of Mind: The Theory of Multiple Intelligences* (New York: Basic Books, 1983).

p. 264. M. Borba, *Parents Do Make a Difference* (San Francisco: Jossey-Bass, 1999), pp. 210–211.

Book Discussion Guide

1. Why did you or your group choose to read *Building Moral Intelligence*? What preconceptions about morality did you have before you began reading? Which of your views were challenged or changed by your reading?

2. Do you think raising moral kids today is easier, no different, or more difficult than when your parents raised you? Why?

3. Many people feel there is a "crisis of character" in today's children. Do you? What factors may be preventing children from fully developing their moral intelligence capacities?

4. A recent nationwide survey found that 93 percent of responding adults believed parents have failed to teach children honesty, respect, and responsibility. How would you have responded? Why?

5. The book describes seven virtues essential for achieving moral intelligence. Which virtue do you feel is most essential for ethical living? Why? Which do you consider most difficult to nurture? Which virtue do you

emphasize most in your family? Least? Which would you like to empha-size more? What could you do to help your child acquire the virtue?

6. A major theme of the book is that morality is learned and that parents do make an enormous difference in influencing their children's moral growth. How much influence do you think parents actually have? How did your parents influence your moral development? At what age do you think parents start losing their moral influence? Do you think that the ability to influence kids comes back? If so, at what age? What influences children's moral development most: peers, pop cul-ture, parents, or something else?

7. *Building Moral Intelligence* emphasizes that one of the best ways our kids learn moral behaviors is by watching us. How would your child describe your moral behavior? Which virtues best exemplify your character? Which virtue or character trait would you like to strength-en in yourself, and how would you do so?

8. What kind of person do you want your child to become? How will you help your child become that person?

9. The book emphasizes that children are born with the potential for empathy, but unless it is properly nurtured it will remain dormant. What outside factors are hindering the development of this first essential virtue? What are you doing to enhance empathy in your child? What could you do to enhance this critical virtue even more?

10. To what extent are violent pop music lyrics and images on television, video games, the Internet, movies, and the news contributing to the increase in aggression among children? What are your family policies about viewing violence? Are they effective? What other factors may be contributing to the rise in peer cruelty and violence? How are you helping your child learn self-control?

11. How important is it to you to have a tolerant child? When you were growing up, how did members of your family demonstrate tolerance toward one another? Can you think of specific instances in which they

demonstrated intolerance? What prejudices were passed on to you by your parents? Do you feel you are passing any of these on to your child? If so, which ones? What can you do to stop your prejudice from filtering down to your child?

12. How was discipline handled in your family as you were growing up? How did it affect your moral views? What is the most common method you use to discipline your child? How effective is it in enhancing her moral growth? What improvements would you like to make?

13. What are some of the sayings, proverbs, or experiences you recall from your childhood that helped you define your values? How are you passing on your moral beliefs to your child? What is the single most important moral belief you would like to instill in your child? What have you done with your child recently to reinforce that conviction?

14. How committed are you to enhancing your child's moral intelligence? From everything you read, is there one strategy you would like to try with your child or family? Why did you choose it? Describe what you will do and when you will begin.

15. What would you like your greatest legacy to be for your child? What will you do to ensure that your child attains that legacy?

16. If you were telling a friend whether or not to read this book, what would you say about it?

About the Author

Michele Borba, Ed.D., has worked with more than half a million parents and teachers over the course of more than two decades. A dynamic and highly sought-after speaker, she has presented hundreds of keynote addresses and workshops throughout North America, Europe, Asia, and the South Pacific on enhancing children's character development, self-esteem, achievement, and behavior. Her down-to-earth speaking style, inspirational stories, and practical strategies appeal to audiences worldwide.

Dr. Borba is the author of eighteen books for parents and educators, including *Parents* Do *Make a Difference,* selected by *Child Magazine* as one of the outstanding parenting books of 1999, and *Esteem Builders,* used by more than a million and a half students worldwide, as well as several audiocassette programs, including *The Five Building Blocks of Self-Esteem* and *Strengthening At-Risk Students' Achievement and Behavior.* Her latest video is *Working with Underachievers.*

Dr. Borba has appeared frequently as a guest expert on television and National Public Radio talk shows, including *The View, ABC Home Show,*

The Parent Table, The Jenny Jones Show, To Your Health, Turning Point, and *Success Radio.* She has been interviewed in numerous publications, including *Newsweek, Parents, Redbook, First for Women, Family Life, Working Mother,* the *Chicago Tribune,* the *Los Angeles Times,* and the *New York Daily News,* and currently serves as the "moral intelligence parent pro" for Oprah Winfrey's *Moms Online.* Her numerous awards include the National Educator Award, presented by the National Council of Self-Esteem; Santa Clara University's Outstanding Alumna Award; and the award for Outstanding Contribution to the Educational Profession, presented by the Bureau of Education and Research.

Dr. Borba was formerly a classroom and college teacher and has had a wide range of teaching experience, including work in regular education as well as work with children with learning disabilities; children with physical, behavioral, and emotional disabilities; and gifted children. She and her husband were partners in a private practice for troubled children and adolescents in Campbell, California. She received her doctorate in educational psychology and counseling from the University of San Francisco, her M.A. in learning disabilities, and her B.A. from the University of Santa Clara; she earned a life teaching credential from San Jose State University. She currently lives in Palm Springs, California, with her husband and three teenage sons.

To contact Dr. Borba regarding her work or her media availability or to schedule a keynote or workshop for your organization:

Dr. Michele Borba

Web: http://www.moralintelligence.com

Index

164–165; impact of, 169–170; and influence of unkind peers, 161; lack of modeling for, 159; practicing, 186–188; signs of, 163; teaching meaning and value of, 166–170; three steps to building, 165–189; and zero tolerance for unkindness, 171–183. *See also* Unkindness

King, M. L., Jr., 218
Klebold, D., 192
Kocher, C., 14
Kohlberg, L., 3, 75–77
Kohn, A., 106
Ku Klux Klan, 195, 196

L

Labels, negative, 242
Lake, R., 129
Lake Worth, Florida, 81
Lakeview School (Robbinsdale, Minnesota), 138
Language, obscene, 127–130
Lansing, Michigan, 64
Lehman, D., 192
Levin, D., 196
Levine, M., 16, 161–162, 197
Lewis, D., 85
Lewis, R., 126
Leyden, T. J., 195
Lickona, T., 58, 75, 77, 121, 127, 193, 250
Linguistic learners, 264–265
Listening, 136; and empathy, 22–26
Literature, multicultural, 214
Liverpool, England, 13
Logical-mathematical learners, 265
Los Angeles Unified School District, 48
Lost Boys (Garbarino), 46
Love, unconditional, 136

M

Magic of Encouragement, The (Marston), 134
Manners: list of, 152–153; and respect, 149–155
Manners, good, 149–155
Manzanar internment camp, 258
Marshmallow Test, 109–110

Marston, S., 134
Maryland, 232
Mathias, B., 212, 213
Meanness, reasons for, in children, 177. *See also* Unkindness
Media: barrage of cruel images in, 16–17; disrespectful behavior flaunted by, 128–130; and glorification of out-of-control behavior, 86–88; and intolerance, 195–197; and unkindness, 160–161
Mekler, E., 32, 112–114
Michigan, 13, 45, 64, 179
Midlarsky, E., 169
Minneapolis, Minnesota, 65
Minnesota, 21, 65, 138
Mischel, W., 109–110
Modeling: of essential fairness behaviors, 242–246; and family ground rules for sharing, 244; and kindness, 159, 166–167; new courtesy skills, 151–154; and self-control, 92–100; teaching meaning of respect through, 133–141; and tolerance, 201–210
Molly's Pilgrim (Cohen), 65
Moorman, C., 179
Moral beliefs, sharing, 57
Moral core, 7–8
Moral development: creating context for, 55–61; stages of, 76–77
Moral erosion, decade of, 46
Moral growth. *See* Moral development
Moral intelligence: building, 9–10; conscience as cornerstone of, 51–53; definition of, 4–6; seven essential virtues of, 6–8; virtues that enhance, 68
Moral Intelligence of Children, The (Coles), 3, 95
Moral reasoning, 50, 58
More Than Manners! (Baldridge), 150
MTV Video Music Award, 128
Musical learners, 265

N

National Association of School Psychologists, 48, 180
National Association of Sports Officials, 124

National Education Association, 47–48, 180
National Institute of Mental Health, 87
National Parent-Teachers Organization, 173
National School Safety Center, 47, 160–161
National Threat Assessment Center (United States Secret Service), 180
Naturalists, 265
Nature of Prejudice, The (Allport), 212
Neglect, 17
Netherlands, 50
New Orleans, Louisiana, 99–100
New York Giants football club, 126
New York Times, 121
New York University, 85
Newsweek magazine, 52, 126
Nickelodeon channel (television), 52
Niehoff, D., 85
Nintendo (video game), 14
Nowicki, S., 32

O

Obscenity, 127–130
Oklahoma City bombing, 35
Oliner, P, 186, 189
Oliner, S., 186, 189
Olympic Games, 1968, 225
On My Honor (Bauer), 65
Orlando, Florida, 97
Others: empathy for point of view of, 36–44; enhancing sensitivity to feelings of, 26–30

P

Palm Springs, California, 57, 221
Parental practices: for development of strong conscience, 56–59; and essential fairness behaviors to model for children, 242–246; for raising tolerant children, 202–206, 212; that nurture respect and love, 134–138
Parents: and absence of supportive fathers, 15–16; emotional unavailability of, 15; influence of, on altruistic behavior, 189; moral behavior of, 59–61; overworked, stressed-out, 83–84
Parents Do *Make a Difference* (Borba), 264
Parent's Guide to Protecting Your Children in Cyberspace (Aftab), 202

Parents Television Council, 128
Peers: influence of unkind, 161; rise in cruelty of, 47–48
Pennsylvania, 13
Peoplemaking (Satir), 38
Perry, B., 17, 85
Personal identity, four ways to help develop, 206–210
Peter Pan (video), 221
Piaget, J., 3
Pinocchio (video), 53, 65
Point of view: empathy for other, 36–44; ways to gain new, 43
Pokemon, 127
Pollack, W., 17
Pontiac, Michigan, 13
Portland, Oregon, 201
Power assertion, 73
Praise: comparative, 242; encouraging internal, 103; and self-reliance, 106–107; and sensitivity, 31
Prejudice, zero tolerance for, 218–226
Preview Family Movie and TV Review, 128
Punishment by Rewards (Kohn), 106

R

Race awareness, stages of, 220
Rainbow Fish, The (Pfister), 65
Raising Cain: Protecting the Emotional Life of Boys (Kindlon and Thompson), 23
Raising Good Children (Lickona), 75, 77, 193, 250
Ralph Sheppard Elementary School, Vancouver, British Columbia, 178
Raphael, S. J., 129
Reade, C., 1
Real Boys (Pollack), 17
Real World (television series), 129
Reasoning, moral, 58
Reinforcement, 70, 102–106
Reiss, D., 95–96
Relationship Code, The (Reiss), 95–96
Remote Control Childhood (Levin), 196
Reparation, 77–78, 79
Respect: for authority, 141–149; crisis of, 121–130, 156; definition of, 7, 8; discussion of, with children, 141; evaluation

314   *Index*

of, 130–132; and good manners, 149–155; modeling and teaching of, 133–141; overview of, 130; parenting practices that nurture, 134–138; and respectful disagreement, 148–149; signs of, 131; teaching meaning of, 138–141; three steps to building, 132

Riceville, Iowa, 218, 219

Richmond, California, 81

Ritalin, 85, 85–86

Rochester, New York, 61

Rocker, J., 126

Role models: breakdown in, 231–232; decrease in, 124–125

Role-playing: for developing empathy, 38–40; and rotation of meeting roles, 248–249; and virtue, 66–67

Rosenhan, D., 232

Rudy (video), 65

Rules: and common courtesy, 247–248; instilling respectful, 140–141; seven, for playing fairly, 256; setting decision-making, 247–248

S

Santa Clara, California, 38; Santa Clara University, 133

Satir, V., 38

Saving Private Ryan (film), 162

Scacco, M., 51

Schoolwork, comparisons of, 241–242

Schulman, M., 32, 112–114

Scoresby, A. L., 71

See No Evil (Levine), 16, 161–162, 197

Self-concepts, positive, 137

Self-control, 7, 8; and anger control strategies, 107–118; commitment to, 97; crisis of poor, 82–88, 118; developmental stages of, 113; discussing, with children, 89–90; and encouragement of self-motivation, 100–107; evaluation of, 90–91; family practices that nurture, 95–98; and family self-control motto, 97–98; modeling of, 92–100; overview of, 89–90; prioritizing, 92–100; signs of, 90; and spending, 105; teaching meaning and value of, 96–97; three steps to building, 91–118

Self-esteem, 172–173

Self-Esteem: A Classroom Affair, Vol. 4, 117

Self-reliance, 13; and praise, 106–107; and self-control, 89

Self-talk, use of, 111

Sensitivity, six ways to nurture, in children, 31–32

Sensitizing, 41

Sexual promiscuity, rise in, 50

Sharing: and boundaries, 251; effect of, on others, 251; encouragement of, 251–252; three ways to foster, 251–252

Shinsetsu, 160

Simon, S., 171–172

Simon Wiesenthal Center, Los Angeles, 195

Six Steps to an Emotionally Intelligent Teenager (Windell), 175

Skills Training for Children with Behavior Disorders (Bloomquist), 113

Smashnova, A., 126

Snyder, M., 167

Social justice problems: and choosing project based on child's interests and talents, 260–263; and matching child's interests and strengths, 264–265; seven tips for, 260–263

Spatial learners, 265

Sportsmanship, 255

Springer, J., 129

St. Louis, Missouri, 92

Standards, explaining, 59

Stanford University, 109, 195; Center on Adolescence, 195

Staub, E., 185

Stealing, rise in, 48–49

Stereotypes, countering, 218–226

Stevenson, A., 126

Stilwell, B., 47

Stockton Unified School District (California), 197

Stop and freeze tactic, 114

Stotland, E., 36, 38

Straus, M. A., 122

Stress, repeated, 17

Substance abuse, 2; rise in, 51

Suicide rates, 1–2, 108

Survivor (television series), 129
Suspicion, price of, 124–125

T

Tarango, J., 126
Tatum, B. D., 216–217
Teaching Peace (Arnow), 214
Teaching Tolerance (Bullard), 223
Teen dating violence, 47
"The Real Slim Shady" (Eminem), 128
Thompson, M., 23
Thompson, R., 13
Time magazine, 52, 195
Tolerance: and countering stereotypes and prejudice, 218–226; crisis in development of, 192–197, 226–227; definition of, 7, 8; description of, 197–199; discussing, with children, 210–218; evaluation of, 199–200; and instilling appreciation for diversity, 210–218; modeling, 201–210; signs of, 199; three steps to building, 200–226
Trauma, early: and development of empathy, 17; and self-control, 85

U

Unfairness: and breakdown in role models, 231–232; crisis of, 230–234; and early attachment problems, 231; and emphasis on competition, 233; and reduction of unstructured play, 233–234
United States, 1–2, 46, 50, 86, 108
United States Census Bureau, 83
United States Department of Health and Human Services, 18
United States Secret Service, 180
United States Surgeon General's Office, 87
University of Maryland, 226
University of Massachusetts, 185
University of Michigan, 234; Institute for Social Research, 51
University of New Hampshire, 122
University of Washington, 15, 24, 36
Unkindness: desensitization to, 161–162; and four ways to reduce child's unkind behavior, 174–178; helping children to counter, 180–182; and influence of unkind peers, 161; in media, 160–161; stamping out, in schools and families, 178–180; zero tolerance for, 171–183
Unstructured play, reduction in, 233–234
Urges, impulsive: and acting right, 116, 118; stop and freeze tactic for, 114; and thinking, 115; three–part formula for control of, 112–117
U.S. News & World Report, 49, 123
USA Today, 123, 127, 230

V

Velveteen Rabbit, The (Williams), 65
Venables, J., 13
Vietnam War, 88
Violence, 19, 108, 110, 180; rise of, 46–47; and teen dating violence, 47
Virtues: fun ways to cultivate, 69–71; reinforcing, 67, 70; and role-playing, 66–67; teaching, that promote development of strong conscience, 63–68; that enhance moral intelligence, 68
Vocabulary, feeling, 110
Vulgarity, 2

W

We Can All Get Along (Ford), 206, 223
Who's Who Among American High School Students, 49
"Why Are All the Black Kids Sitting Together in the Cafeteria?" and Other Conversations About Race (Tatum), 216–217
Why Johnny Can't Tell Right from Wrong (Kilpatrick), 3
William Franz Elementary School, 99
Wimbledon tennis tournament, 126
Windell, J., 175
Wooten, T., 126
World War II, 88
World Wrestling Federation (WWF), 127
Wright, M., 215, 220

Y

Yale Child Study Center, 194
Your Anxious Child (Dacey and Fiore), 111